"This unique, thoughtful volume articulates the major global challenges posed by one of the most overlooked, but critically important issues of our time. The work optimistically presents practical solutions in a hopeful, positive manner. It establishes a compelling case to invest scarce resources to address failing infrastructure and water resources, and will do for water what *Silent Spring* did for chemical regulation."

— **Mark D. Charles** | Environmental Management Chief,
City of Rockville

"A compelling read for those working to create business advantage through innovation and resilience. The CEOs in this book understand the pivotal role that water plays in creating long-term business value. This type of insight and corporate leadership is needed to prosper in the emerging marketplace of a natural resource-constrained world."

— **Carol Singer Neuvelt** | Executive Director, The National
Association for Environmental Management

"Donna Vincent Roa's passion for communicating the true value of water is impressive and incredibly important. The future of our industry— and society itself—depends on both public and stakeholder understanding of the many ways water availability and services contribute to prosperity."

— **Kevin Westerling** | Chief Editor, Water Online

"Our nation and this world face many challenges. At the top of the list is providing a safe, reliable, affordable supply of water that respects the environment. This book helps crystalize the necessary connections among the environment and economy, water and energy, and the present and the future. Anyone who recognizes the challenges will appreciate the forward thinking and wide range of solutions."

— **Honey Rand, PhD, APR, Fellow PRSA** | President, Environmental
PR Group and Author: *Water Wars: A Story of People, Politics and Power*

"Acknowledgement of the value of water has come a long way in the last two years, in large part because we are now driving a meaningful public dialogue using effective terminology and tapping into the hearts and minds of the public. Having recently moved to Texas, where water is now one of the top three public and political issues, I've realized that people who live with water scarcity increasingly understand the connection between water and the economy. In short, they realize that Water Works! I am proud of the industry leaders captured here who have cast a great vision for the "utility of the future" by applying innovation, advancing water resource recovery infrastructure, and attracting a new generations of professionals into the water sector."

— **Matt Bond** | Black & Veatch, and 2011-2012 President,
Water Environment Federation

"I'll admit, when I started reading, I thought "another book about water? What could anyone say?" Well, if you read one book about water this year—read this one. The CEO essays are not just for the water "experts;" they are just as relevant for the average citizen, the politician, and definitely for the communicators. They present historical, environmental and economic perspectives, and clear, practical solutions. This book will help anyone working in the water sector worldwide to advocate improved water sector governance."

— **Patricia Hotchkiss Bakir** | Independent Water Sector Consultant,
Amman, Jordan

"Innovative technology solutions are vital to water's cause. This seminal book showcases the fact that new technologies coupled with progressive management thinking and updated business models are needed to advance the value of water conversation. The essayists' ardent focus on making water a central priority and investing in its future is something we all need to hear...over and over again."

— **Karen D. Sorber** | Executive Chair/CEO, Micronic Technologies

"Donna Vincent Roa brings with this compiling of essays from CEOs a unique look inside the world of water. Perspectives on virtual water, social, economical, and technical challenges and how this brings water consumption to the forefront of everyone's life is well described and blended with insights on adaptation and commercialization of new methods which will improve water availability. All of this is well documented with real comments from real CEOs from water technology companies, providers, and utilities. A must read for academia and professionals who aim to change the way we deal with water in the future."

— **Henrik Skov Laursen** | Director, GRUNDFOS Silicon Valley

"This book offers a realistic view of technology and development, and explores in detail how executives, government officials, engineers, communicators, and technologists in the water sector can meet current and future demands and realize positive systemic change. Essayists probe ethical questions, and forward the practical discussion of water as a right, alongside implications for and constraints on industry and utilities. Sustainability is a robust theme throughout the book, which writers consider in light of the natural environment, the complex relationship between water and energy, finance, security, and other human needs."

— **David P. Davis, PMP, CQE** | Division Manager, Strategic Planning and Program Performance, New West Technologies, LLC

"Dr. Roa has plumbed the depths of the top thought leaders in the water space by compiling their wisdom and vision in the form of hard-hitting essays. These essays, written by CEOs of water companies and utilities, provide readers a clear roadmap for how water will be valued and what that means for the provision and treatment of water and the reconciliation of competing demands. It is rare to find such thought leadership in any market sector bound in one book, but Dr. Roa has pulled it off. If you want to know the future of water, this is the book for you."

— **Gordon M. Davidson** | Senior Advisor to The Horinko Group

"Donna Vincent Roa has accomplished an incredible feat in tackling this issue—possibly the most important issue of our time—and placing it front and center with an impressive group of CEOs joining in on the effort. A must read for anyone whose life or livelihood is touched by water issues."

— **Michelle Villalobos** (vee – ya – low - bos) | Speaker, "Professional Brandstormer" & Founder of The Women's Success Summit

"Thought provoking information and ideas provided by a diverse group of knowledgeable water community leaders call us to do our part in clarifying and promoting the 'true value of water.' The authors challenge us to be good stewards of our water resources—and to find innovative ways to assure that an adequate quantity and quality of water remains available for its many life-sustaining uses, and that we use that water wisely. It is time to begin acknowledging the 'water' footprint of our decisions."

— **Dr. Timothy A. Wolfe, P.E., BCEE** | Vice President, MWH Global, Honorary Member, and George W. Fuller Awardee – AWWA

"Powerful in its simplicity and straightforwardness, this collection of essays is must-reading for utility executives looking to manage the utility of tomorrow, as opposed to the 'good enough' utility operations of the past. Tomorrow's problems will never be solved using yesterday's solutions, and the concepts presented here define the forward thinking that will guide our industry into the future."

— **Rob McElroy, P.E.** | General Manager, Daphne Utilities, Daphne, Alabama

Water...

CONNECTS US

GROWS JOBS & OPPORTUNITY

KEEPS US SAFE & HEALTHY

SUSTAINS OUR ENVIRONMENT

Water Works!

The Value of Water: A Compendium of Essays by Smart CEOs

Donna Vincent Roa, PhD, ABC
and The Value of Water Coalition

THE VALUE OF WATER: A COMPENDIUM OF ESSAYS BY SMART CEOS

Bulk Sales and Speaker Bookings: Corporations and associations interested in discounts for bulk quantity purchases or an event speaker, please contact Donna Vincent Roa at donna@vincentroagroup.com or 1-818-397-9867. You can also sign up for notifications about the book at www.valueofwaterbook.com.

Cover Design: Daryl C. Orosco
Editorial and Project Team: Rachel LaVigna; Chere Poole; Christopher Wm. Baines, Sr.; Satyajit Nandi; Nandita Biswas; Guli "Lily" Du; and Alex Roa
Value of Water Coalition—Book Project Committee: Linda Kelly, Water Environment Federation; Lorraine L. Koss, U.S. Water Alliance; and Marybeth Leongini, National Association of Water Companies
Publicity and Press Interviews: Environics Communications, Inc. at 1-202-296-2002 or water@ecius.net

ISBN-10: 0990733106
ISBN-13: 978-0-9907331-0-2

Dedication

To Barry Liner, director of the Water Environment Federation's Water Science & Engineering Center, who provided the referral that opened the door to making this project happen, and to Victor Roa, my husband, who believes in the power of my ideas and patiently watched our favorite TV shows alone during the production of this book.

About the Project

THOUGHT LEADERSHIP ON WATER AND ITS VALUE

Water, with its high-profile risk, poses a threat to business continuity, reputation, product margins, and growth while at the same time creating value and opportunities. Businesses compete for access to water and must continually adapt to its availability, quality, and access. CEOs, C-suite executives, and other leaders are at the helm of this evolving business dynamic and have the narratives that can change our understanding of the value of water from a business perspective.

Donna Vincent Roa, in collaboration with the Value of Water Coalition, created *The Value of Water: A Compendium of Essays by Smart CEOs* to feature industry leaders' perspectives about the value of water and its relationship to brand, reputation, business continuity, innovation, economic success, technology, public health, and more.

This book documents CEOs' insights on the value of water, probes complex issues, informs the conversation about water's future for business, explores how the value of water leadership has resulted in improved business performance, shows that "business as usual" exploitation of water needs to change, and shares industry best practices and calls to action.

We hope that these essays inform your perspectives about water, convince you that we all need to be stewards of this precious resource, and ultimately, change your water consciousness and awareness about the value of water.

Originator & Executive Producer

DONNA VINCENT ROA, PHD, ABC

An IABC-accredited business communicator and water and sustainability communication executive, Dr. Roa is the managing partner and CEO of Vincent Roa Group, a full-portfolio business communication firm that specializes in communication about the earth and its people™ (e.g., water, science, environment, sustainability, public health and technology). The firm serves CEOs and utility executives who need to re-engineer their communication portfolios, maximize resources, and improve bottom line results. A blogger for Water Online and Speaking Up About Water, Dr. Roa served on the inaugural WEFTEC Innovation Showcase and Pavilion executive committee, is a former Rockville, Maryland environment commissioner, a past president of the largest U.S. IABC chapter, and one of ten social scientists to carry out research in major world capitals for the U.S. Treasury's first redesign of the $100 bill.

Roa was a senior communication consultant for the start-up of Sanitation and Water for All, and received the AWC-DC Matrix Award for her work in global communication focused on water and sanitation. She developed The Roa Conceptual Model on Water Communication™—an industry tool and color palette for standardizing visual communication about water.

A master strategist affiliated with the Water Sector Communication Practice at Environics Communications, she is a senior counselor to executives at water utilities; is a frequent speaker for corporations, associations, and conferences; and has a PhD in Communication.

She resides in Rockville, Maryland with her husband Victor, children Gretchen and Alex, and Max, their rescue dog.

Her passion for water is unbridled. To learn more, visit www.donnavincentroa.com or www.vincentroagroup.com

Collaborator

VALUE OF WATER COALITION

The Value of Water Coalition is a broad alliance of public and private sector leading water companies, utilities, national associations, and safe drinking water and clean water interests working together to shift public attitudes about and increase investments in America's water infrastructure. Through its Water Works! campaign, the coalition educates the public on the importance of clean, safe, and reliable water to and from every home, business, and community to help ensure quality water service and to grow jobs and economic opportunity for current and future generations. The coalition includes American Water, American Water Works Association, Association of Metropolitan Water Agencies, CH2M HILL, MWH Global, National Association of Clean Water Agencies, National Association of Water Companies, United Water, Veolia, Water Environment Federation, Xylem Inc., and the U.S. Water Alliance (Project Manager).

Value of Water Coalition
c/o U.S. Water Alliance
1250 24th Street N.W., #300
Washington, DC 20037
www.thevalueofwater.org

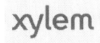

Acknowledgements

Thanks to the essayists who took the time out of their busy corporate and public service leadership days to pen an essay documenting their insights and perspectives on one of the most important issues of our day—the value of water.

We would also like to thank the essayists' representatives and colleagues who worked with the CEOs and the project team to shepherd the project deliverables through to completion, and the Value of Water Coalition Book Project Committee and other senior leaders in the coalition who referred us to the CEOs.

Table of Contents

FOREWORD

PAUL O'CALLAGHAN
FOUNDER & CHIEF EXECUTIVE OFFICER
O2 ENVIRONMENTAL AND BLUETECH RESEARCH

Necessity Is Ushering in a New Era of Water by Driving Innovation and Change

n absolute terms, there is no shortage of water. We are not running out of water. We are running out of locally available, renewable freshwater. As scarcity dictates value, the value of water is increasing.

Our current water system is built upon readily available sources of freshwater, just as the current energy system was built upon readily accessible sources of cheap energy. As we have seen with the recent boom in unconventional fossil fuels, we are not running out of energy in absolute terms either. We are simply running out of the easily accessible supplies.

Overall, this is good news: We are not fundamentally resource limited when it comes to either energy or water. What it will mean, however, is that the value of water will increase, which will change the way we think about, use, and manage water. We will be driven to innovate.

If necessity is the mother of invention, then by extension, a lack of necessity stifles innovation and invention. There is no point in innovation for the sake of innovation. It is not an end in itself; rather, it must solve a problem and deliver its own value.

The last major era of water systems innovation, which gave us safe potable drinking water and sanitation in the latter half of the 19th century, was driven by necessity—the necessity to prevent deaths from disease.

The importance of water disinfection and the provision of sanitation are comparable with the discovery of the vaccines and antibiotics as key factors that have increased human longevity. For proof, simply look at the high mortality rates in regions of the world that lack these necessities.

Having created a water system that by and large worked, we then rested on our laurels for almost 100 years. To paraphrase leading water thought leader Glen Daigger, who also provides an essay in this book, in these next 100 years, the world evolved from a world of 2 billion people, mostly rural, with a lack of modern technology, to a world of over 62 billion, in mostly urban settings experiencing energy and resource constraints.

Intelligent Design or Evolution?

To help understand our current water system, it is good to ask, "Is our current system an example of intelligent design or evolution?"

It is most certainly an example of evolution. It is important to note that our current water system was not designed with efficiency in mind;

in fact, it was not really designed at all. It just happened over time. Water supply was introduced into cities as a means to put out fires, which enabled the development of a potable supply and the water closet. Sewers were later constructed in the 1850s to take wastes "seaward" (hence the origin of word "sewer"). Noticing the environmental impact of raw sewage on receiving waterways, we started to build large treatment plants at the end of these waterways, and as cities expanded, we simply built longer pipes, bigger reservoirs, and more treatment plants, and so on and so forth until we arrived to where we are today—with an energy and capital-intensive, inefficient system.

In terms of water management systems, we have been swimming in the same direction for over 100 years. We built the water system that supports our society on the basis that renewable freshwater is freely available. Yet the world has changed enormously in the past 100 years. There was no way these developments could have been anticipated when we began building these systems.

American evolutionary biologist Steven Jay Gould tells an analogy of a green sea turtle that makes a 4,000 kilometer round trip each year from the coast of Brazil to lay its eggs in the Azorean islands, which are in the middle of the Atlantic Ocean. When the turtle initially started this journey hundreds of thousands of years ago, the Azorean islands were much closer to the coast of Brazil. Over time, the tectonic plates gradually moved Brazil and Azorean islands further apart, and each year, the green turtle continued to make this journey without noticing the gradual increase in distance. The changes in our water system took place over a much shorter period, just 100 years. Yet we have seen more change in that time span than in the previous thousand years. The question is whether we will keep trying to swim in the same direction or stand back, reevaluate, and develop a more fit-for-purpose system for the 21st century.

In the current system, as long as there was readily accessible freshwater, there was no need to change. The lack of innovation in the water sector is largely explained by the phrase, *"If it ain't broke, don't fix it."*

To date, we have enjoyed access to safe drinking water and sanitation in the western world. In many cities, states, and regions of the world, due to mounting global pressures including population increases, urbanization, climate change, rising energy costs, and the need for water to provide energy, we can no longer afford an inefficient and wasteful system. This is driving real change in how we manage water and is creating opportunities for technology development.

Is Water Undervalued?

It is often said that water is undervalued and underpriced, which is a roadblock to water innovation. If water were properly priced, so goes the logic, then innovation would flourish. It is worth remembering that the raison d'être of the water industry is not to provide a vehicle for water technology companies and venture capital investors to make profits. Rather, it is to provide water services in the most efficient manner possible. When a new technology can do this, it has a commercial advantage with the potential to make double-digit returns. However, the technologies and solutions need to reflect market realities, not the other way around. There is no onus on the water industry to alter its value and pricing systems to facilitate water technology companies and investors.

Breakthrough innovation does not need to be subsidized, and in fact, subsidies create a very rocky foundation on which to build a business. I think it more the case that the value of water is increasing, and I think this is creating new opportunities and providing a catalyst for change.

The Water–Energy Nexus

One of the main inputs to producing water is energy. In fact, energy represents the single largest controllable cost of providing water services. As we run out of easily accessible, renewable freshwater, we increase the energy footprint of water. This is due to the need to desalinate water, move water over ever-increasing distances, or use recycled water. Each of these options is more energy intensive than simply taking water from a nearby river or lake and providing basic treatment.

The ascendancy of unconventional fossil fuels and the resulting demise of the "cleantech" renewable energy revolution are working in tandem to compound water pressures. Although the cleantech energy revolution would never solve our water issues, its absence exacerbates them. The continued dependency on fossil fuels as a source of primary energy will exacerbate both water scarcity and water excess. Climate change may be off the political and media agenda, but it continues to do its work quietly in the background and sometimes loudly in the form of droughts and extreme weather events. Water management is now more than ever inextricably linked to the future of how we provide energy for the planet and feed the people on it.

"Value" is Connected to Service

Much of the "value" that we assign to water is not related to the water itself; it is related to the service that the water enables us to provide.

The same analogy applies in energy. We are dependent on oil, yet if I gave you a barrel of oil, you would have no use for it. What you need are the energy services it can provide, such as electricity for lighting your home, central heating to keep you warm, and gasoline to move your home to your place of work. We have taken the mantra that water is essential for human life, which it is, and we have extended this to mean that water is essential for everything we use water for, which it is not. This includes providing cooling in buildings and power plants, transporting human wastes (e.g., flushing toilets), removing dirt from clothes and even growing food.

We need these services, and they are valuable. Water, in so far as it is a means to providing these services, is valuable, and the scarcer this water becomes, the more valuable it becomes.

Water also has a binary value. As long as you have one more drop than you need, it has a certain value; once you are on the wrong side of that balance sheet, the value increases exponentially. You cannot run a power plant without water, you cannot run a sewer system without water, and you cannot grow food without water. At some point, you therefore are willing to evaluate any and all alternatives.

As an illustrative example, recently during a cold weather spell, the pipes in my home froze. Having soldiered on for three days with my wife and young children using bottled water to wash dishes and flush toilets, our family eventually moved in with my mother-in-law until the water was back on again. Faced with this as an ongoing issue, I would seriously consider installing a grey water recycling system, which can be done for little more than the cost of changing the windows.

Our appetite for change is directly proportional to the desirability of the alternatives. We have options for dealing with the municipal and urban water use situation. This is not an intractable problem. If you reduce leakage, use less and move to direct or indirect potable use, you start to make this urban and municipal water issue very manageable. The issue of agricultural water use is the more intractable issue and is the "elephant in the room." This will require some blue-sky thinking and solutions, such as the use of salt-tolerant crops, advances in biotechnology or intensive water reuse-based agriculture.

As the value of water increases, this provides the key ingredient of "necessity" to catalyze change, and a number of things will happen. First, we will embrace water reuse. Not a single new drop of water has been added to the water inventory over the millennia, and it continues to reinvent itself. Although water has no memory, the general public certainly does, and we do not like the thought that in the not too distant past, the particular drop of water we are drinking was recently used to flush our toilet or, worse still, someone else's.

However, such barriers are in the mind and all that is required to facilitate water reuse is a change in thinking, and that is already happening in places like Singapore and Orange County, California.

We will look to see how we can provide water services without using water. This creates new opportunities and will change the water industry.

Those at the forefront may be those that develop vacuum sewers, super critical carbon dioxide laundries, and salt-tolerant halophyte food crops.

Water Is a Local Issue

Increasingly, we will deal with water issues locally. We believe that water is a global issue, because it affects everyone on the planet. However, at its heart, it is a local issue. Current economics dictate that we cannot move water as we do oil. Therefore, we will see more focus on water solutions that deal with water issues locally.

As we are forced to change, we will reevaluate systems level efficiencies. American physicist and environmental scientist Amory Lovins uses the analogy of using a chainsaw to cut a pound of butter to illustrate this. We can either focus on how to make the chainsaw more efficient at converting gasoline into motive energy, or ask if there is a more efficient way of cutting a pound of butter? Perhaps a butter knife would be a better idea. Much of our efforts to optimize our current water system have been focused on how to "make the chainsaw more efficient," as opposed to standing back and asking if there a better way to achieve the result.

Providing Water Services Without Using Water

I believe that much of the innovation we are likely to see is how we can deliver water services with less water or alternative sources of water or without water completely.

In terms of where the opportunity lies, I believe four key areas represent the greatest opportunity for growth over the next decade: Energy and resource recovery, water reuse and alternative water, unconventional fossil fuels, and smart water.

There is cause for optimism. The current system is so inefficient and wasteful that everywhere you turn there are examples of where we can use a "butter knife" in place of a "chainsaw." We can do more with less by recovering resources and generating energy from wastes. Therein lies the potential for a BlueTech Revolution. It will be enabled as much by changes in management practices and new business models as it will be by new technology. It is a quiet revolution, and this "Brave Blue World" is already being ushered in city by city, with little fanfare or anyone heralding its arrival.

In the coming years, we will look back and marvel at the wasteful nature of the 19th century water system with a degree of wonder, and the relationship and perception of the value of water will have changed.

The essayists in this book showcase evidence of leadership that will propel us in a new direction and innovative thinking that will transform the sector. This book features champions who are making water a central priority, developing sustainable solutions, and investing in its future.

The author adapted this foreword from material in his forthcoming book, Brave Blue World™, *and is reproduced here with the kind permission of O₂ Environmental.*

Introduction

BEN GRUMBLES
PRESIDENT
U.S. WATER ALLIANCE

The Power of One

One water, one voice—that is the recipe for blending together the many views and visions described on the following pages. It is also the strategy for changing the public's perception of water from invisible to invaluable and moving our nation toward a more integrated and sustainable approach to our underfunded and underappreciated water infrastructure system.

The Value of Water (VoW) Coalition was formed to create that one voice to shift the U.S. trends in a positive direction for water sustainability. The coalition uses the collective voices of its members to create a common, empowering message to unify differing sectors: Water is valuable, infrastructure is vulnerable, and opportunity is achievable when we work together to raise awareness and support. By building public awareness and support, the coalition seeks to enable local leaders to make the investments needed to ensure America's water future.

With a balanced mix of private water companies, national water associations, and consulting firms, the VoW Coalition has joined talents and financial resources to amplify the messages beyond the sum of the voices. Members include American Water, American Water Works Association, Association of Metropolitan Water Agencies, CH2M HILL, MWH Global, National Association of Clean Water Agencies, National Association of Water Companies, United Water, Veolia, Water Environment Federation, Xylem Inc., and the U.S. Water Alliance (Project Manager).

There's no doubt a coalition of forces is needed to meet the challenge. One water main breaks every two minutes in the United States. It is estimated the nation must invest $1.3 trillion in repairs and upgrades over the next 25 years.

Valuing water means taking into account not only the cost of getting it clean and getting it to the right place at the right time, but also the cost of not having it where you want it in the way you want it. Extreme weather will be teaching us all some extremely hard lessons if we do not invest upfront in improved planning and resiliency.

To improve public awareness of the value and vulnerability of existing infrastructure systems, the coalition is implementing a multifaceted communication strategy. Initial tactics have included employing social media, and a website (www.thevalueofwater.org), to generate and promote relevant articles and events. Communication opportunities are also pursued through an earned media approach.

The coalition recognizes that all water is local and beyond local too, particularly when factoring in downstream, regional, economic and security impacts. With that in mind, a second strategy is to mobilize its massive utility network through the associations and local colleagues to sing the same tune and reach out to that fluid group called the general public.

The following are examples of helping local leaders do more: Conducting research and opinion surveys, providing a toolkit for communicating effectively with ratepayers, creating national forums for general managers and private water chief executive officers to tell their compelling stories, and spreading the news of key facts and trends.

Special events by the VoW Coalition draw attention from the public and policy makers (e.g., the Congressional event on the steps of the U.S. Capitol in September 2014) to water and jobs as documented in a report—*The Economic and Labor Impact of the Water Sector*—by the Water Environment Research Foundation and Water Research Foundation.

The report found that 30 large water and wastewater agencies alone would be investing $254 billion into the economy in the next decade. This will result in $52 billion in annual economic output and support 289,000 jobs annually.

A third strategy is reaching out to those sectors that are stakeholders in water, whether they know it or not (i.e., business, manufacturing, labor, agriculture, etc.). Water Works! is the theme that can draw all these sectors together and is reflected in the campaign's four key message points—water connects us, grows our economy, keeps us safe and healthy, and sustains our environment.

The U.S. Water Alliance acts as project manager for the Value of Coalition. This was a natural role for us as a nonprofit, educational organization with broad constituencies and the mission to *Unite People and Policy for "One Water" Sustainability*. The alliance's goal is to drive an integrated, innovative, approach. We strive to band together broad segments of the water sector, public and private, East and West, urban and rural, quantity and quality, surface and ground, and inland and coastal to increase integration, efficiency and effectiveness.

The first principle of the alliance's strategy is valuing water. In 2010, one of its beginning National Dialogues was to answer the question "What's Water Worth?" Over a day and a half, scores of diverse thought leaders and decision makers from the water sector, plus the energy, agriculture, environment, health care, transportation, and finance sectors discussed and debated the deep question.

The answer to some is simple, yet accurate: "More than we're willing to pay." To all, though, the responses laid out a roadmap for a greater understanding of water's services to communities and ecosystems.

As our country flows toward a national water management crisis, it is important for private sector and public sector leaders to stand up, speak out, and join together. A united national message that raises awareness to get local results will help prevent what Robert Glennon describes as a crisis becoming a catastrophe.

Water works for all, if given the chance. That means seeing, believing, and valuing water's great potential.

PAUL FREEDMAN
PRESIDENT AND CHIEF EXECUTIVE OFFICER
LIMNOTECH

Business Values Water and Is Investing to Protect It

grew up during the 1950s and 1960s in Cleveland Ohio, where residential water was cheap and plentiful. The financial value of water was not a topic of conversation at the dinner table. I grew up only appreciating the value of water for its recreational use and ecological importance. These values were visibly stolen by gross pollution of that era. Cleveland was the poster child of the environmental movement, located on the shores of Lake Erie, once declared dead by the media, and on the banks of the Cuyahoga River, infamous as the "burning river." In my mind, and for many, the value of water was immeasurable. There was no economic consideration that could be valued, and certainly not something that we expected to pay for.

However, my view of the value of water quickly evolved with the realities revealed working for clients in my environmental career and business at LimnoTech. Early in my career, I focused on water pollution from municipal and industrial sources. Therein was an appreciation of the value of water due to the costs for pollution control and remediation and an understanding of the enormous financial needs for aging and inadequate infrastructure.

However, few had a true appreciation of the value of water to business, because it was generally a cheap and plentiful commodity. As the turn of the century approached, issues of pollution and scarcity grew from local issues into widespread global problems. The availability of adequate water was becoming an issue relevant in most every country, every state or province, and every aspect of our society including businesses and the economy. As Ben Franklin is often quoted, "When the well runs dry, we shall know the value of water"... and the well was running dry in all too many places, for all too many needs. Understanding of the value of water was becoming more apparent.

At the turn of the century, the issue of water scarcity was emerging in the general public's awareness but mostly for humanitarian and environmental concerns. The human impacts ranged from the tragic 1.5 million deaths of children annually to the more subtle impacts on society as women and girls in poor water-stressed areas walked miles and hours every day to obtain water for their families. Countless small streams and rivers had run dry or were stressed due to low flows; even a number of the world's major rivers were known to run dry. Rivers such as the Colorado and Rio Grande in North America, the Murray River in Australia, and the Indus, Ganges, and Yellow Rivers in Asia all have at times run dry. These conditions captured headlines, but the widespread understanding of the value and economic importance of water still only slowly emerged.

Today, however, the value of water has captured the attention of individuals and companies as its scarcity begins to impact the availability and price of goods, the profits of companies, and the vitality of economies. Over one third of the global land mass is currently under significant water stress and predictions are that by 2025, over two thirds of the world population could experience water shortages. The consequences are becoming more apparent to the general public and the value apparent to business as their operations are affected or threatened.

A paradigm shift in our understanding of the value of water first began to emerge in the early 1990s with the creation of the concept of virtual or imbedded water. Tony Allen, a British geographer, was studying the economies of the arid Mideast and reflected on how their economies could flourish, even in the face of severe water scarcity. What he determined was that to be productive these economies needed to be smart and import water, not in tankers but imbedded in products, thereby taking advantage of plentiful water in other areas of the globe and saving their scarce local water for strategic and public needs. From this research, Professor Allen created the concept of "virtual" water and began to examine world economic trade in the context of trade in virtual water. The global economy and international trade could now be represented as a flow of not only goods and dollars, but also virtual water, with this "value" flowing from region to region and country to country. With this simple concept, we all became interconnected with the global issues of water. Water scarcity and pollution were no longer just a local environmental or humanitarian concern, but of significant global economic importance.

Leveraging this concept, Arjen Hoekstra and his colleagues at University of Twente in the Netherlands advanced the idea for a water footprint. The water footprint of a product was the amount of water required to produce a product from cradle to grave, throughout its supply chain, production, and use. This new concept and its application was an eye opener for individuals and companies of how much water was required to produce products we used or sold and, hence, the intrinsic importance and value of water.

For example, 2,500 liters of water was required to produce a single T-shirt, 140 liters for a cup of coffee, and 10 liters for a sheet of paper.

Citizens were astonished by the numbers, previously only appreciating the water they used from their faucets. More so, companies took notice. Water may not have been a large enough cost to appear on their financial statements, but it was intrinsic and essential to their operations. It may have had little cost, but the revenue and profits at risk due to a disruption in supply were potentially enormous. Herein, they began to appreciate the "value" of water in terms of how it posed a significant risk to their operations and profits.

These financial risks to business were not just hypothetical; countless examples of real impacts were being documented every year. The food and beverage industries were naturally the first to appreciate the risks and important value of water, as they are most connected to its use. As examples, beverage companies like SAB Miller have had to curtail beer production due to water shortages in South Africa. Coca Cola and PepsiCo had to close plants or curtail operations in India due to water shortages, and this year, coffee futures have more than doubled because of water drought in Brazil. Even in the United States, generally viewed as water rich, the bottled water and beverage companies have had challenges locating and maintaining operations, while the impacts of recent droughts have resulted in as much as $100 billion dollars in agricultural-related losses.

The financial risks from water scarcity were not limited to the food and beverage industries. The textile and apparel industry has often been affected by huge fluctuations in the price of cotton caused by regional droughts, said to cause as much as one- to 10-dollar impacts on the cost of products like blue jeans. Many mining operations are also particularly vulnerable, such as gold mining, as illustrated in 2010 when Barrick Gold had to shut down one of its mines for weeks due to inadequate water supply. The energy industry, dependent on water for cooling and production, also sees impacts routinely and at times catastrophically. In one costly example, Electricity de France experienced a $500 billion loss in 2003 during a heat wave and drought when they could not get adequate water for cooling many of their nuclear plants. They had to shut down and/or curtail operations at 17 plants. The list goes on, and few industries are spared risks, if not actual impacts.

Textile and apparel are of course heavily dependent on water to grow cotton, which typically grow in arid, but intensely irrigated regions like Southern California, Texas, Pakistan, Egypt, and Uzbekistan. The electronic chip industry uses enormous amounts of ultrapure water to clean and rinse manufactured chips. Intel and Texas Instruments alone use over 11 billion gallons every year, and according to JP Morgan, a shutdown at any single plant could result in $100–200 million in lost revenues per quarter. Even the automotive industry is at risk, not just from the supply chain of the electronic wizardry they now include, but also for the energy they depend on, the manufacture of steel and aluminum, textiles in their interiors, and countless uses of water for cooling and cleansing in production.

The 2012 drought in Mexico put GM on notice. Mexico represents six percent of their global products, and CDP estimates that just a month disruption would result in a $27 million loss in net income. The list of industries at risk is comprehensive. The economic importance of water, or rather the absence of water, is now being appreciated by businesses worldwide, in all sectors, as they assess and manage their financial risks due to water supply disruption.

The concept of value at risk means different things to different people. To corporations and investors, it means loss in revenue or profits, stranded assets. To investors, it relates to loss in stock valuation. My colleagues at Equarius Risk Analytics are researching these issues developing new metrics that monetize these risks and impacts from water, and they can be significant. For example, in one case study over two years for Duke Energy, we found that the impacts from down-rating events due to water issues had as much as two to three times the impacts on the quarterly share price volatility as fluctuations in the price for coal.

On the positive side, conducting research on water and corporate risk in cooperation with MSCI (formerly Morgan Stanley Capital

International), we found a positive correlation of reduced share price volatility with best practices in water management, as measured by the MSCI Environmental, Social and Governance (ESG) index. Reduced share price volatility is very important not just to corporate managers, but also to investment bankers (owners of big blocks of shares) who by regulation have to maintain a minimum of cash reserves. Consequently, water is also becoming a financial issue of "material" importance to the investment community.

The economic risks of water supply disruption can be very large. Many corporations have huge investments in physical plants or reserves that they can hardly afford to allow to sit idle, but may if adequate water is not available. For example, MSCI estimates that the electric utility industry has $21 billion in assets vulnerable, the gold mining industry has $221 billion in reserves at risk, and the steel industry has $17 billion in sales at risk. In a Carbon Disclosure Project (CDP) survey of 593 global corporations, 70% identified water as a substantial business risk, half having already experienced impacts in the last five years, and two thirds expect to within the next five years.

The business community has begun to mobilize investment and expertise in addressing the growing global water crisis and protecting its value. Businesses like Coca Cola, PepsiCo, Dow, GE, SAB Miller, Goldman Sachs, Bloomberg, Dow, and others have invested many millions of dollars, partnered with institutes and NGOs to develop databases, assessment tools and information needed to assess problems and devise strategies for solutions. More so, companies like these are investing millions and even billions in specific activities to improve their water use practices and to help solve water problems for business, people and nature.

Financial Times reports that Coca Cola, a global leader in water stewardship, and its bottlers have spent over $2 billion dollars in the last 10 years on water issues, working to ensure the value of their assets and market, reducing their water uses and impacts, and also helping communities with water supplies, and replenishing water to the environment. Companies are now understanding the value of water to their businesses and investing to protect it.

Steven Solomon, in his book *Water: The Epic Struggle for Wealth, Power and Civilization*, recounts how water has been a central lynchpin for almost all ancient and modern cities, and their economies and society. Today many are threatened by scarcity. He asserts that water has replaced oil as the major threat to our economies. Fortunately, today we are seeing an alignment of interests in water from governments, NGOs, and companies and a shared value, albeit for different interests, but nonetheless shared value.

As companies see the economic importance of water, we are now seeing substantial collaboration on efforts to protect its availability for people, nature and business. There may not be agreement on the monetary value of water, but it is exciting to see a universal consensus on its critical value.

HEINER MARKHOFF
PRESIDENT AND CEO
GE POWER & WATER, WATER & PROCESS
TECHNOLOGIES

The True Value of Water: Addressing the Water-Energy Nexus

Historically, interactions between water and energy have been considered on a regional or technology-by-technology basis. At the national and international levels, water and energy systems have been developed, managed and regulated independently. More recently, the world is waking up to the fact that water and energy are not only connected, but also tightly intertwined. It is about time.

Severe drought affects more than a third of the United States, constraining operations of some power plants and other energy production processes. Time and again, hurricanes and other natural disasters powerfully demonstrate that vital water infrastructure can be seriously impaired when it loses power. In addition, the recent boom in domestic unconventional oil and gas development—spurred by hydraulic fracturing and horizontal drilling—has added complexity to the national dialogue about the symbiotic relationship between water and energy resources.

These are stark reminders of how precious our water and energy resources are, and these highlight the pressing need to prioritize sustainable management of both. Meanwhile, several trends are further escalating the urgency to address the water-energy nexus in integrated and proactive ways. Climate change is affecting precipitation and temperature patterns across the United States. Population growth and regional migration trends indicate that population in arid areas such as the Southwest is likely to continue to increase. New technologies in water and energy domains are starting to shift water and energy demands.

The intensified need for limited water supplies puts increasing pressure on water-intensive energy producers to seek alternative approaches, especially in areas where energy is competing with other major water users (agriculture, manufacturing, drinking water for cities, etc.) and where water uses may be restricted to maintain healthy ecosystems. Uncertainties related to the growth and evolution of global energy production (e.g., via growth in unconventional sources of oil and gas, or biofuels) can create significant risks to water resources and other users.

Separate and together, all of these factors present not only considerable challenges, but also distinct opportunities for the future of water and energy. We cannot escape the strong link between the two resources; they are not independent variables. We all need water and energy, and we all need to take part in the efforts to secure them for generations to come.

Water reuse, policies and partnerships, and innovative technology solutions are vital to the cause.

Water Reuse

In the United States, water reuse—defined by using water more than once before passing it back to the natural water cycle—is one of the most beneficial and cost-effective strategies for water conservation. According to the results of a recent GE-sponsored survey, most Americans support the recycling of water and are more likely to patronize businesses using technology that enables it. The findings were contrary to the popular, long-held belief that the "ick" factor plays a role in consumer decision making.

The benefits to business from water recycling extend further than a lowered utility bill. According to the survey, 57% of Americans reported being more likely to patronize a business that prioritized water reuse, and 42% reported they would patronize the company reusing water even if their product or service cost more—up to 12.4% more. Consumers are clearly willing to invest in water that is sustainably sourced in the interest of protecting future generations.

However, there's also clearly a need for all parties to work together. The vast majority of Americans want utilities, large industries, and agriculture to take the lead in water reuse and hold the most favorable impressions of those that use recycled water. Government needs to step up too and help protect water resources: 77% of survey respondents agreed water scarcity is a national issue, and 84% agreed protection of water resources is a national issue.

Policies and Partnerships

Historically, energy and water decisions have been made independent of each other. Water planners assume they have the energy needed, and energy planners assume they have the water needed. Both are likely use different strategic planning: Private companies acting under market forces dictate the location of energy infrastructure, while water infrastructure is often located using public interest criteria. A disconnect in planning objectives prevents the beneficial siting and combing of the technologies. Likewise, water policy in the United States is mostly structured from the bottom-up with decisions driven by local water authorities, because water supply management is generally the responsibility of the states. Energy policy, however, is structured top-down, with federal agencies setting standards and requirements.

Cross-sector communication, engagement, and collaboration are imperative. New policies are needed to build the confidence of leaders in both the water and the power sectors, motivating everyone to go beyond compliance. To shepherd in this new era of stewardship, industry and government must work closely together. Companies are turning to inventive ideas and tools to help them assess and respond to increasing water risk globally. Programs such as the Aqueduct Alliance, a consortium of private and public sectors, nonprofit organizations, and academia, bring influential entities together to provide "unprecedented levels of water risk information for business and government." Initiatives like WaterMatch—an innovative new, free online website dedicated to promoting beneficial reuse of municipal effluent for global industrial use— are a step forward in responsible water management, and in partnerships between industries and municipalities.

Governments must also take strong action to promote more water reuse and recycling. There are four well-documented, major types of policies currently in play around the world to increase this initiative:

- **Education and outreach** efforts support recognition awards and certificate programs, information dissemination and reporting of water consumption, discharge and recycling data
- **Removing barriers** by revising plumbing codes and alleviating stringent permitting and inspection requirements for recycled water, allows companies and communities to meet obligations that were otherwise difficult to attain
- **Incentives** such as direct subsidies reduce government payments for the reintroduction of recovered water and provide regulatory

relief for recycled water users through structured pricing mechanisms

- **Mandates and regulations**—through the requirement of water recovery systems and recycled water for certain large volume activities (e.g., irrigation)—continue to reinforce these initiatives along with the strong need for government participation

Through more creative, public partnerships among industries, communities, municipalities, and government, we can protect and enhance performance and competitiveness, as well as the needs and interest of key stakeholders—the most important environment. Future success depends on our ability to work together. New levels of efficiency must continually be enforced through education, conservation, governance and incentive. Understanding the risks—and the opportunities—will place businesses and governments in a more competitive position to lead and succeed in a carbon and water-constrained economy, and ultimately secure a future of water sustainability.

Innovative Technologies

Advanced technology also plays a key role. The energy content of municipal wastewater is two to four times greater than the energy required to treat it. However, current technologies and practices do not exploit this to the full extent. As a result, energy demand for wastewater treatment remains significant: In the United States, it represents three percent of the total electricity demand, and it is anticipated that this demand will continue to grow globally as emerging countries improve their levels of sanitation and developed nations pursue higher levels of treatment for reuse and discharge to the environment.

Sustainable wastewater treatment promises to help address the multiple and multifaceted challenges of energy shortage, resource depletion and environmental pollution. Advances in technologies strive to help achieve balanced investment and economic output, stable treatment performance, high effluent quality to meet water reclamation and reuse requirements, less resource consumption, minimized environmental footprints, and energy-neutral operations.

Energy for Water

It is time to shift how we view wastewater treatment and move to longer-term, strategic infrastructure solutions. Wastewater treatment plants are not waste disposal facilities, but water resource recovery facilities that produce clean water and have the potential to reduce the nation's dependence on fossil fuels through the production and use of renewable energy and implementation of energy conservation.

According to the Environmental Protection Agency, community drinking water and publicly owned wastewater systems use 75 billion kWh of energy per year—as much as the pulp and paper and petroleum industries combined, or enough electricity to power 6.75 million homes. Energy is the second highest budget item for municipal drinking water and wastewater facilities, after labor costs, with utilities spending about $4 billion annually. Energy consumption by drinking water and wastewater facilities can comprise 30% to 40% of a municipality's total energy bill.

Water utilities are highly regulated entities whose primary goals are to meet regulatory requirements for protecting public health and the environment to provide services for reasonable and fair rates. The energy efficiency of these utilities generally has not been a primary goal or considered as an element of rate determinations. Nevertheless, as populations grow and environmental requirements become more stringent, demand for electricity at drinking water and wastewater plants is expected to grow by approximately 20%. Moreover, as electricity rates increase, energy conservation and efficiency are issues of increasing importance. By some estimates, potential energy savings by drinking water and wastewater utilities are in the range of 15% to 30% per year.

More needs to be done to achieve the aspirational goal of energy-neutrality, both by reducing consumption and recovering the energy contained in the wastewater.

Membrane-Aerated Biofilm Reactor (MABR) for Energy-Neutral Wastewater

GE's latest innovation ushers in the next generation of technology for energy-neutral wastewater treatment. A new, patent-pending flowsheet in development by GE follows two parallel paths: (1) minimizing the energy required for the removal of solids, organics, and nutrients, and (2) maximizing the conversion of organics to usable energy. Based on a membrane-aerated biofilm reactor (MABR) process that uses innovative gas transfer hollow fiber membranes, the flowsheet is:

1. Electricity neutral; the electricity produced meets the electricity demand for treatment
2. Capable of nitrogen removal
3. Not reliant on co-digestion (e.g., of food wastes) to increase energy production
4. Cost-competitive with conventional treatment
5. Applicable for new plants and retrofitting existing plants

Still in development, MABR can treat municipal wastewater producing the same effluent quality while reducing energy consumption by four times. This presents significant potential for addressing and evolving the water-energy nexus of municipal wastewater treatment.

The Future of Energy and Water

As water and energy demand and supply continue to shift, managing the two resources in tandem will help regions worldwide maintain reliable and sustainable supplies of both. This is especially of critical importance as the global economy continues its deep exploration of new energy and renewable energy sources. However, to sustain energy production and a dependable water supply, we must all gain even more detailed understanding of the interdependencies of water and energy systems, balance the needs of all users and continue developing technologies to reduce water use and promote water recycling. These are the key drivers of the future of the water-energy nexus; these are what will allow us to realize the true value of water for generations to come.

BERTRAND CAMUS
CHIEF EXECUTIVE OFFICER
UNITED WATER AND
SUEZ ENVIRONNEMENT NORTH AMERICA

Why Water Needs an Economic Cycle

A few months ago, one of our crews, working within view of Manhattan's skyline, unearthed a section of water main stamped with the date when it was originally laid. It reads 1897. That was the year in which William McKinley succeeded Grover Cleveland as president of the United States, the year that prospectors flocked west to the Klondike, and the year that Boston ran its first marathon, with just 15 competitors. For almost 120 years, that pipe carried clean, freshwater to people's homes. Like most of us today (about seven in 10 people, according to a 2012 study of U.S. households), successive generations would have scarcely given a second thought to how that water got there when they turned the tap on. Why would they when, compared to the cost of living—or even a cup of coffee—that water seems to cost next to nothing?

Maybe a sense that water *should* cost nothing is why there is often protest whenever water rates rise. As playwright Oscar Wilde said, "Nowadays people know the price of everything and the value of nothing." Water is essential for life. No one can live without it. Yet with ever more stringent standards and regulations, there is significant cost attached to treating and delivering it to our taps—and that cost is rising all the time. Although you cannot put a price on water itself, you can—and must—properly value its management as an increasingly scarce resource. Failure to do will guarantee that it is squandered—and ultimately impact our ability to meet basic human needs.

The problem lies in the assumption that water will be "there" without recognizing the need to invest in the water infrastructure to treat and deliver it. Buried beneath our streets, water infrastructure is mostly out of sight and out of mind. For decades, cities across the United States have deferred investment to update water systems to the point where, every two minutes, a water main now breaks in a city somewhere. The price tag to put things right over the next 25 years is estimated at more than $1.3 trillion. Who, in today's world, has that kind of money? Government does not. Federal support for water infrastructure renewal is at a trickle. And cities—many of which face budget and credit crises of their own—all have schools, roads, fire, and police departments competing for the same scarce funds. That leaves private investors with the remaining lifeline.

The majority of water systems in the United States—about 85%—are municipally owned, funded, and operated. Private sector utilities have varying degrees of involvement in the rest. Tax breaks have made issuing bonds an attractive way for cities to raise money (though little of that is usually invested in water infrastructure). Over the years, bonds have become more costly to service as municipal credit ratings have fallen. Some cities are trying to kicking that can down the road by issuing bonds that mature in 100 years (backed by infrastructure assets designed to last much less than that), making it an issue that will continue to plague future generations.

A Circular Economy for Water

Investment and reinvestment is part of what we see a larger *circular economy*. Much like the actual water cycle—in which rain runs through rivers and aquifers, is used by people, animals, and plants; makes it way to the oceans; then evaporates to once again become rainclouds—the circular economy of *water* refers to a closed cycle in which wastewater also serves as an input, not a discarded and undesirable by-product.

We are used to—and readily accept—recycled materials in many products that touch our daily lives. The time has come to accept water in that routine. A circular economy for water requires three things:

- Reduce water consumption and waste
- Reclaim previously used water
- Recycle water so that it can replenish water sources, such as aquifers, or be reused

The need for such change is clear. A 2010 report by McKinsey & Company for the Ellen MacArthur Foundation concluded that it is untenable for the human race to continue its use-and-discard approach to manufacturing, consumption and waste management. "As the global middle class more than doubles in size to nearly five billion by 2030, consumption and material intensity will rise accordingly, driving up input costs and price volatility at a time when access to new resource reserves is becoming more challenging and expensive," the report says. "Perhaps most troubling is that this sudden surge in demand may have adverse effects on the environment that further constrain supply. Symptoms of these constraints are currently most visible in the food and water supply."

As a water company, we have the ability—and responsibility—to provide solutions. A circular economy of water is already part of our operations and those of our customers and partners. Since 2009, we improved our energy efficiency by 28.5%, reduced greenhouse gas emissions by 16.5%, and reduced water leaks and other unaccounted water losses by 2.4%.

In 2013, we expanded our annual—and public—sustainable development report to include 40 specific, measurable indicators (previously we had 12). These additions allow us to make meaningful changes over a broader area. Some of the new indicators are specific to United Water, but many of them draw upon the experience of our parent, SUEZ ENVIRONNEMENT, which developed its indicators with the consensus of stakeholders and with the scrutiny of objective third-party advisers globally. Each looks at a specific challenge in the United States water segment, including aging infrastructure and water loss, energy efficiency and renewable energy, climate change and water resource protection. These performance indicators help us ensure that we are improving profitability and efficiency, while protecting the environment. They are not zero-sum concepts. For example, technology to reduce the number of leaks in the water distribution networks and more accurate water metering means we will use less of it and reduce energy and other inputs in treating and distributing the water that we actually need.

The ability to reduce water consumption is in everyone's hands. Of 50 state water managers, 40 expect water shortages under average conditions in some portion of their states over the next decade, according to the U.S. Environmental Protection Agency. Overall, the annual U.S. water footprint—that is, the amount of water required per person overall, including for agricultural and cattle (two of the biggest uses), is 751,000 gallons per person—is more than twice the global average and about 25% more water than is needed to fill an Olympic-sized pool; that is per person.

At the household level, we can all use 30% less water by installing water-efficient fixtures and appliances. The average household spends as much as $500 per year on water and sewer charges. Just that change would save them about $170 per year. At the community level, consumers can support businesses that invest in 21st century research and development that support that aim. We developed a comprehensive computer water supply model, known as OASIS, that helps keep to the Hackensack River Reservoir System—four area reservoirs (Lake DeForest, Woodcliff Lake, Lake Tappan and Oradell Reservoir) with a storage capacity of 13.9 billion gallons and a watershed of 112 square miles— more adaptive and resilient in an uncertain and changing future, for example, by simulating the impact climate change may have on water resources.

Although demand is rising to reuse and reclaim water, more must be done to treat it properly. In addition to primary contaminants (inorganic chemicals, disinfectants, and organic chemicals) that continue to be flushed into the global water system, new pharmaceuticals are now entering the water ecosystem, increasing the burden of the water industry's efforts to safeguard consumers. Meanwhile, human development and migration place greater burdens on distribution systems than ever before, as we see, in the Southwest.

In response to these challenges, we have increased our collaboration with water companies around the world through the R+i Alliance, the research consortium of SUEZ ENVIRONNEMENT. This collaboration has led to the deployment of water treatment equipment (specifically, high-rate clarifiers and ultrafiltration barriers) that improves drinking water quality, reduces the need for facility expansion, and preserves surrounding wetlands.

United Water in 2012 also became a member of the WateReuse Foundation, an educational, nonprofit public benefit corporation that serves as a centralized organization for the water and wastewater community to advance the science of water reuse, recycling, reclamation, and desalination.

With the support of SUEZ ENVIRONNEMENT, United Water also has been a worldwide leader in water recycling and reclamation. For the past 20 years, United Water has operated and maintained the Edward C. Little Water Recycling Plant and four satellite plants for West Basin Municipal Water District in El Segundo, California. The continued success of the plant—the only public recycling facility in the world that produces five different types of usable water out of wastewater—has recycled more than 150 billion gallons of water since 1995 and is key to the success of drought-prone Southern California's Water Reliability 2020 program.

The Edward C. Little Water Recycling Facility produces over 40 million gallons of water every day for industrial and other uses. The plant produces approximately 12 million gallons a day of highly purified water for use as barrier water that protects local groundwater from seawater intrusion and also augments local groundwater supplies.

Commitment and Investment

Moving from our linear economy—in which resources are used once and discarded—to a sustainable, circular one requires commitment and investment. Long-term private sector and private equity partnerships are an essential part of that.

Private equity investment in U.S. roads, bridges and airports is not new—it is new when it comes to investment in water infrastructure. The first private equity investment in a U.S. municipal water system became final in December 2012. KKR in partnership with United Water won a 40-year water and wastewater contract from the city of Bayonne, New Jersey that included an upfront $150 million payment used by the municipality to eliminate debt, plus a commitment to invest a further $157 million to repair, maintain and upgrade the city's water system. All the while, system ownership and control and rate rises remain in city hands. Immediate system improvements have been made in Bayonne, such as the installation of wireless meters that pinpoint at-risk pipes before they break.

Although private equity investment in the water systems is a new frontier, it is by no means a speculative endeavor. Yet it requires proper pricing and appreciation of water's value at all points of its cycle. In future decades, the need for clean and safe water will only grow and so will present-day water problems if the money to address them is not found.

No one organization can write a blank check. Private equity in partnership with water companies equipped with innovative technology and system management skills offer an alternative source of investment that the nation needs.

GLEN T. DAIGGER, PHD, PE, BCEE, NAE
SENIOR VICE PRESIDENT AND CHIEF TECHNOLOGY
OFFICER, CH2M HILL, AND PRESIDENT,
INTERNATIONAL WATER ASSOCIATION

What Is Water Worth?

hy do people not understand the value of water? Do they not understand that it is the most essential element for human life, next to air?
The need for air (oxygen) is more insistent because one can only live
a very few minutes without it, but water is next as one can only survive
three to four days without it. This compares to weeks without food, and
despite what younger folks think, a lifetime without a smartphone.

Do they not understand that water is essential for human health?
Have they not read the results of the *British Medical Journal* survey of
health officials that determined that modern water and sanitation was
the greatest contribution to public health of the past 150 years?[1]

As smart as Bill Gates is, it took the Gates Foundation some time to
realize that medicine is not the first and most effective step to improving
health outcomes in developing countries, rather implementing an effective, if basic, water and sanitation system is. They are now acting on this

---

[1] *Medical milestones.* (2007). British Medical Journal, 334: S1–S20.

knowledge, with the expected (highly positive) results. Such a system is also a key step to eliminating poverty in developing countries as it allows people to be more productive. Healthy people are more productive and healthy children can function more effectively in school. Moreover, less time must be spent in acquiring the (poor quality water) needed by the family, thereby freeing up time (typically for women and girls) that can be used more effectively. It is clear that the economic value created by even a basic but effective water and sanitation system far exceeds the cost. In developed countries, we already have such an effective system in place and are receiving the health and economic benefits. Since the benefits exceed the costs, why do not we value them?

What would the economy be without water? Water is a key component of many products and is essential in the production of nearly all products and their subcomponents. We are now fully aware of the concept of virtual water—that water is needed to produce essentially everything that we need and use. Water is also used to transport the goods that we consume as much of it is transported over rivers and the oceans. Water transport is one of the most economical and energy-efficient means of transporting the goods that we use. The value of water to the economy is clearly significant, but poorly quantified—an area of future efforts.

Water also has aesthetic value to people—we are drawn to it. Water features are iconic elements of iconic places. Think about San Francisco, and one immediately thinks of San Francisco Bay. Sydney has Sydney Harbor, and San Antonio has the River Walk. Fountains and other water features attract people. People boat, canoe, river raft, fish, and swim. Waterfront views have economic value, as people are willing to pay more for it. Many people have a spiritual relationship with water. Perhaps this is because we are mostly water (around 70%).

So why are people not willing to pay for water, which is nearly as essential as air? But wait, people do not pay for air, at least directly. We pay for air through the costs of protecting it that are embedded in the products and services we buy and through the adverse impacts when air quality is not properly protected. But this is also the case for water. In contrast to water, air moves freely and is available. Thus, as long as we manage air pollution to control air quality, it is available as needed. Could this be because air is light, widely available, and moves freely? Water, on the other hand, is heavy, variable in its availability, and does not move as freely. Hence, it is necessary to collect it and store it (so that it is available when we need and want it), and it is more susceptible to contamination. This is the reason that water must be paid for separately, not for the water itself but for the service of having it provided to us in the quantities and the quality where and when we want it. This is what we want people to pay for.

Perhaps the issue is how the water profession and the water industry communicate with people. In this, perhaps we can take a lesson from the science of psychology, specifically Abraham Maslow's Hierarchy of Needs.[2] This theory categorizes human needs in an ascending order, as presented in Table 1. This hierarchy is relevant as it affects human behavior in a number of ways.

Table 1. Maslow's Hierarchy of Human Needs	
Need	**Attributes**
Self-Actualization	Morality, Creativity, Spontaneity, Problem Solve, Lack of Prejudice, Acceptance of Facts
Esteem	Self-Esteem, Confidence, Achievement, Respect of Others, Respect by Others
Love/Belonging	Friendship, Family, Sexual Intimacy
Safety	Security of: Body, Employment, Resources, Morality, the Family, Health, Property
Physiological	Breathing, Food, Water, Sex, Sleep, Homeostasis, Excretion

First, individuals differ in their emotional state concerning where they are on this hierarchy. Some may be at the basic, physiological level, while others may be at the esteem or self-actualization levels. Second, irrespective of where an individual is on this hierarchy, what motivates them to action is the opportunity to reach the next level. Third, individuals feel threatened by actions, which may compromise their ability to

[2] Maslow, A. (1954). *Motivation and personality*. New York, NY: Harper.

remain at their current level. Note from Table 1 that water is at the basic, physiological level.

Although achieving this level may be material for the poor in developing countries, it is not for most people who believe that they have attained this level and are operating at a higher level on the hierarchy. Thus, they are not motivated to action by water, as they inherently take it for granted and may be threatened by suggestions that it may not be available to them.

How can this knowledge be operationalized from a communication context?

First, we need to understand where those we are communicating with are at on this hierarchy. Second, if we want to get their attention, we need to connect water to the next level up. Trying to communicate with them based on their current level, or especially lower levels, will be unsuccessful, as they already believe that they have secured the attributes at these levels that are relevant to them.

Third, and in contrast, we can communicate effectively with people if external actions cause them to question whether they truly are secure in those attributes. Floods or droughts, for example, provide opportunities to mobilize actions to improve water management. Although we need to use such events opportunistically, I question whether we should depend on them.

Let us review the most frequent communication that the water profession has with the public. It is the water (and sewage) bill. What we communicate is that if you pay your bill you will continue to receive water (and sewage) service, but if you do not, these services will be terminated. However, the threat of termination is a hollow one in an increasing number of locations as water and sanitation is now recognized internationally as a human right (via the recent declaration by the United Nations), and the termination of service is increasingly being prohibited.

The key point is that we are communicating with people at the basic, physiological level while many people are operating at a higher level on the hierarchy. No wonder the public does not react well to our communication efforts!

There are positive examples, however, of alternate approaches that achieve positive results. Perhaps the most widely recognized example is that of Singapore, which communicates consistently and in several ways with their customers. Their fundamental communication message is "Conserve, Value, Enjoy," which conveys the dual message of responsibilities by PUB, but also the customer to secure a sustainable water future (the lower levels of the hierarchy), and that water provides broader benefits to individuals and their collective society (higher levels of the hierarchy).

They cleverly tied water security to national security as they launched the NEWater (used water reclamation) and desalination initiatives, effectively using the NEWater Visitor Center as a key educational component. The Marina Barrage is a highly visible element of their water management infrastructure, which also creates economic and social benefits. Through their Active, Beautiful and Clean (ABC) program, they create obvious benefits for the public through effective water management, which also enhances the urban environment and creates recreational opportunities. Fortunately, Singapore is just one example of what some of the more progressive utilities are doing around the world.

There would be those who point out these efforts cost money. This is certainly true, but such investments must be balanced by the value they create. If they result in the public support that further results in more effective water management, which also provides added value to the community, then such investments can produce returns for both the utility and the communities that they serve which greatly exceed the investment.

One may conclude that historical communication strategies are a key reason that the public does not value water appropriately. We may also conclude that at least some utilities have learned how to communicate effectively with their customers, resulting in increased support that leads to more effective water management and greatly enhanced social and economic benefits to the communities they serve.

We might also conclude that understanding our customers and paying attention to some basic psychology might provide insights that can lead to improved communication that will ultimately help our customers truly understand the worth of water and support efforts to protect and provide it. These, at least, are my conclusions.

TERRY MAH, PHD
CEO AND PRESIDENT
VEOLIA NORTH AMERICA

Water Is Not For Fighting Over

t's doubtful whether Samuel Clemens ever said, "Whisky is for drinking and water is for fighting over." What we are certain of is that Clemens derived his pen name, Mark Twain, from his experience as a Mississippi River steamboat captain.

The leadsman on a riverboat would indicate the river's depth of two fathoms (12 feet) with the cry of "by the mark twain." Twain was an old-fashioned expression for two, and in this case, two marks of six feet indicated safe passage for steamboats of the day.

Many people repeatedly cite Twain's purported quote, never knowing the truth of the matter. With greater pressure and increasing importance on water resource management, it is important we think critically, review data and question conventionality.

Twain did in fact know a thing or two about water. His ability to understand the water he was interacting with—depth measurement and the flow and speed of currents, swirls, and eddies—indicated success or failure in commerce, safety or danger, even life or death. The role of water in society, and our awareness of how to interact with it, will also determine our fate, just as it did for Twain.

Today, we are even more reliant on our knowledge about water. We usually think of it in typical technical terms of pH, turbidity, dissolved oxygen, and contaminants. Given the importance of water, however, we must expand our knowledge to include concepts that encompass availability and scarcity, among others, that highlight water's central role in our collective physical and economic vitality.

The impacts we have been experiencing that are related to water highlight a need for increased awareness and change. Whether these impacts are naturally occurring, for example, droughts and floods, or the result of our direct behavior, such as increasing pollution or competition for use, their realities present great challenges to our vitality as a society. Success or failure depends upon our ability to understand the real value of water and the vital role it plays in all aspects of our lives.

New Realities Need New Approaches. Many different groups recognize the value of water and work to protect and preserve this valuable resource to ensure adequate access and efficient use for generations to come. Governments, cities, industries, NGOs and citizens have come to the realization that there needs to be a balance between protection, preservation, and use in order to sustain communities and growth. New awareness and vernacular around the topics are needed to allow meaningful and effective collaboration of all stakeholders to raise the awareness and recognition of the true value of water to ensure a bright future.

Innovation from cooperation is emerging. Different organizations continue to learn how to complement one another's goals, funding, research, conservation and outreach, and managing greater challenges together. New and old models work when they rely on best practices or create news ones. From an operational perspective, traditional solutions like public–private partnerships or private-sector operation of other companies' assets enable risk absorption and greater performance via incentivized payments and success metrics. Similarly, industrial efforts to reduce water consumption or discharge higher quality water, combined with the efforts of conservation groups, are leading to collaborative successes.

The Economic Challenge. Twain understood economic challenges. After much fame and fortune, the great writer experienced bankruptcy due to failed business ventures.

A Columbia University study showed the economic challenges faced by U.S. water infrastructure to ensure our basic need for safe water utilities. Over a 10-year period, water utility debt increased by 33% and water rates increased by 23%, on average. At one-third of the nation's utilities, both debt and rates increased more than 100%. This begs for increased awareness and support of citizens for the needed infrastructure improvements and increased operational efficiency of the utilities serving society.

The world's growing, thirsty population is triggering new, more, and not-always-understood demands that more closely link water and economics. The complexity and speed of these challenges is stunning.

Growth will aggravate these trends through additional resource and infrastructure pressures. Indeed, "safe water" scarcity and competition for its use will escalate. Most people take water for granted, as well as its connection to economics. In 2008, leaders at the World Economic Forum set out a call to action to better understand how water's link to economic growth and to highlight water security challenges "if a business as usual approach to water management is maintained." In 2012, water security emerged as a top five systemic global risk in the group's annual survey of global thought leaders. From public health, food security, energy production, water scarcity, pollution and disruption of global supply chains to the sheer science and cost of water treatment, the management and use of water is now recognized as having the ability to cause tsunami-like waves throughout society.

Principles With Embedded Solutions. Water's value can mean very different things. It can be a very specific number that monetizes the direct and indirect risks associated with the cost of a glass of water, or it can be viewed as the carrier of life, enabling essentially every activity in the natural world and of people, from agriculture to microchip manufacturing. Yet public awareness about water's value lags.

From national leaders to individual citizens, all of us need to understand and appreciate water's social and environmental "value." Most people will never have to calculate the cost to produce water or to make a return-on-investment business case linked to water. Yet if we understand the fundamental role of water not only in our lives, but also to the economy and the very stability of society, we will be more careful and considerate of conservation and stewardship that can lead us to a sustainable water supply for generations to come.

It is incumbent upon leaders to ensure thoughtful, responsible, and sustainable action. Some of the statistics may appear bleak, but many solutions already exist that can guide us forward. To progress, we need a framework of principles that most, if not all, interested parties can abide by. From those principles, more solutions will emerge.

Gauge and Recognize the True Value of Water. Water is cheap relative to its actual value. Disconnects between price and value limit awareness and hinder innovation and the behavioral changes needed to sustain and benefit people and the preservation of water as a valuable resource. The value of water needs to be recognized as the financial or societal impact it can have beyond the direct price paid to procure it. Because these costs are very low, it is difficult to make the business case for more sustainable solutions or behaviors because the return on investment is very low or requires a lengthy payback period. When you add in many of the indirect costs on a unit basis—treatment, regulatory permitting, ecosystem health, impact to a company's or city's brand, and social license to operate—that same water becomes more valuable in terms of impact.

However, considering the cost of not having it results in a much more accurate assessment. All of a sudden, the case is clearer when one realizes how much of a financial or societal impact water, or lack thereof, can have on society.

One visible example is the oil sands sector in Canada. A multi-industry collaboration developed an approach that helps monetize water's true cost and value. Some oil sands producers have collaborated with local interest groups to understand the impact and value of natural water sources to the local population who value these as sacred natural resources. As a result, they have taken a more innovative and sustainable approach to ensure better water stewardship and conservation. The true value of water approach helps make the case for more sustainable practices.

Growth Must Be Responsibly Managed—No More Business As Usual. As in the case of the oil sands, water offers a multitude of complexities. Both industrial and societal growth must be responsibly managed. Today, 36% of the world's population and 22% of global GDP are in areas with unsustainable water use levels. Analysis by the International Food Policy Research Institute suggests that half of the world's population and 45% of global GDP will be exposed to severe water scarcity by 2050 if a business-as-usual model perpetuates. Growth, infrastructure demands, economic constraints, and climate change are intersecting with increased competition for resources, creating great pressures on cities and businesses. New and old models and ideas that represent the best thinking, best results, and best practices are required. A "blue model" of growth can improve productivity while using less water and finding ways to sustainably replenish sources. Cities and industries must adopt more efficient consumption, higher levels of reuse, and true innovation or risk the consequences.

Speed It Up. If problems are not at a business-as-usual pace, then our solutions cannot be either. Innovation and speed are required. We should learn from other industries. For example, NASA recently focused on a faster-better-cheaper approach to unmanned mission, achieving great successes in planetary exploration at a fraction of the time and expense previously required. This approach can address our down-to-earth but profoundly important water issues.

Measurement and Best Bractices. That which is measured gets done. Measurement of best practices enables public utilities, companies and societies to benchmark against one another. There are many examples of communities and industries that incorporate innovation in green infrastructure solutions, renewable energy partnerships to reduce water use in energy production, and carbon footprint reductions.

More Investment and Improved Operational Efficiency. The entire economy is fueled by water. Green investments can produce direct jobs and stimulate economic activity, but some lend the impression that increasing infrastructure investment will solve most of our water woes. Investments create jobs, both directly and indirectly, but we must also ensure our investments are well considered, well placed and targeted toward efficiency and preservation.

Explore the Circular Economy. The circular economy is not a household word, but it will be if we take the use, reuse, recovery, and restoration of natural resources seriously. In a circular economy, we seek to learn from nature, making waste a resource or raw material. We minimize or negate environmental impact. Energy use becomes much more efficient and based on renewables. Our pattern of "taking-making-disposing" is altered, relieving considerable pressure on our natural resources, especially energy and water.

In Honolulu, a wastewater reclamation facility uses highly sophisticated technologies to produce two distinct beneficial reuse water products. What was once wastewater becomes either a product for irrigation of parks, green spaces and golf courses or an ultrapure water for industry that meets much higher standards than drinking water requirement.

Innovation From Cooperation. As stated before, all stakeholders must strive for more collaboration to innovate together—NGOs and industry, and public entities with private corporations.

One example of a private-public collaboration model is the Peer Performance Solution approach that supports public utilities that still want a public workforce. Great innovation and efficiency has been gained from private-sector managers using methods and experience from their operations while embedded in a public workforce to help tackle essentially any challenge.

<u>Limit Ideology—Liberate Solutions</u>. Ideology often plays a role in many places, but more constructive, rather than destructive, dialogue is needed between all of the stakeholders. While protesting shows great passion, the time has come to realign that passion into constructive collaboration.

<u>Greater Public Awareness and Involvement Equals Greater Results</u>. Collectively, the water industry is working on awareness. However, it will take a continuous beat, not an occasional gong in the form of drought or water main breaks, to shape human behavior. Consciousness goes hand in hand with conservation and thoughtful programs, and so transparency and empowerment of people is required. Data about water rates, quality (at home and in local watersheds) and availability is abundant, but not centralized nor easily understood.

Consolidating and transforming the data captured by these traditional sources combined with crowd-sourced data will generate information that will enable education, storytelling, and greater knowledge about water and its true value.

With the phenomenon of social media and instant information, the potential to increase awareness has never been so great. This increased knowledge will transform behavior.

The value of water will always be best defined through economics and culture—economics because we should seek to obtain as many economic, social and environmental benefits as possible, and culture because we must decide what we, collectively, are willing to do to sustainably manage resources to meet needs. Antoine Frérot, chairman of Veolia, argues, "The new culture of water will be one of responsibility." Who plays a part? Frérot argues everyone.

Indeed, every solution noted above requires people working together. Water—the very nexus of growth—can and should be a catalyst for cooperation and prosperity.

In that context, then, I'd hope that if Mark Twain were alive today, he'd offer this: "Water isn't for fighting, water is for cooperating."

GREG MCINTYRE
GLOBAL WATER MARKET PRESIDENT
CH2M HILL

Providing Innovative Solutions to Protect the World's Water

Water is one natural resource we all share. It is used in every industry, and the demand for it is only increasing as global population soars, precipitation patterns change, and competition for water resources intensifies. In the United States and other first world countries, we expect access to safe and reliable water supplies. When we turn the faucet, we anticipate water to flow freely. We take for granted that we have plenty of water to irrigate crops, water our lawns, operate water parks, manufacture products, and more.

However, for developing countries and rural communities around the world, easy access to safe, clean water is more difficult to achieve. In many countries, women and children are responsible for walking hundreds of miles to fetch and carry water back to sustain their families. Despite the community outreach and desire to change the water crisis equation, nearly one billion people lack access safe drinking water and

2.5 billion people live without sanitation. These startling statistics are the primary factors for an influx in illness related to contaminated water.

Although water is readily available in the United States, aging infrastructure, population growth and economic development are depleting our water supplies. Recently, we have seen these water stressors become amplified by climate-related severe weather events such as Hurricane Katrina, Superstorm Sandy, tornadoes, wildfires, floods, and severe drought. In fact, the World Economic Forum's recent report on global risk names water crises, climate change mitigation, and extreme weather as three of the top 10 concerns cited by today's CEOs.

Water issues affect everyone. Therefore, industries, utilities and agriculture need to work with local communities to make resource management decisions that make sense with respect to economic, social, and ecological needs. We are all influenced by the water cycle and our challenges are intertwined. We must work together to find solutions that balance our needs. Water availability is intensely connected to weather and climate patterns; and from the United States and Canada to India and Australia, water scarcity is a common problem—with major consequences on our global economy and environment. Today, the Southeastern United States and the West Coast, especially California, battle severe drought conditions. These conditions have dire effects on the state's large agricultural economy and our nation's food supply.

Challenges look the same across the world—Australia's economy and lifestyle have been completely transformed by water restrictions and the availability of cheap, abundant sources of water. Countries in Asia and the Middle East are seeking solutions to address water resource management too.

As the availability of water resources shifts (too much water in one location, not enough in another) forward-thinking water utility managers are looking for holistic solutions to address their water system challenges and better prepare their assets for the future. From climate risk mitigation plans to creative financing, to smart water solutions and resource recovery, our water providers are proactively ensuring we have safe, abundant water supplies for decades to come.

For example, on the East coast, the New York City Department of Environmental Protection developed an award-winning NYC Wastewater Resiliency Plan. The plan is the nation's most detailed and comprehensive assessment of the risk climate change poses to a wastewater collection and treatment system. On the basis of quantified impacts of climate change and population growth on the city's sewer, drainage and wastewater systems, the study evaluated each asset to see how storm surge under future sea level rise scenarios would be affected. The study was one of the first to assess coastal flooding risks under future sea level conditions, and although it is hugely beneficial to New York City, it will also serve as a national model for other cities to consider as they plan their future storm response.

As the world and our environment change and the challenges our clients face evolve, it is up to us to continue thinking differently about the way we manage our assets and natural resources. In the United States for instance, water issues are further exacerbated by the high volume of our nation's water and sewer systems, pipelines, and facilities in need of repair or replacement. Nevertheless, replacements and repairs come with a price tag, and a big question our industry struggles with is how to pay for these projects.

For years, public sector decision makers have successfully partnered with private industry to plan, design, construct, and even operate water and wastewater infrastructure. We are seeing forward-looking governments and their consulting partners identifying innovative ways to team with local businesses to help finance infrastructure solutions, effectively extending the reach of government resources using public–private partnerships (P3s) to get projects off the ground.

Using a P3 approach to deliver creative, sustainable solutions can preserve and enhance a community's economic and environmental health. A recent example of collaborative delivery includes the new advanced water reclamation campus, Agua Nueva, which was delivered ahead of schedule using a design-build-operate (DBO) approach on be-half of Pima County, Arizona. The project was part of the county's Re-gional Optimization Master Plan to expand and upgrade infrastructure to meet new regulatory mandates and potential future requirements. The DBO delivery approach ensured Pima County received maximum value for its investment. Agua Nueva was carefully integrated into its surrounding Sonoran Desert environment, and the water reclamation facility saves energy and water, reduces waste, and increases the use of recovered materials—significantly reducing capital and operations costs. The award-winning project has received accolades from across the in-dustry, recently earning the Grand Prize for Design by the American Academy of Environmental Engineers & Scientists, as a prime example of the sustainable and environmental benefits that can result from such an infrastructure project.

In addition to seeking alternative financing options and delivery ap-proaches, cities are also tapping game-changing technologies to solve their water challenges. Take the city of Cincinnati, for example. The city's water challenges are not unique. Like many cities across the United States and the world, they are faced with aging infrastructure, combined sewer overflows, declining water usage, and operational deficiencies.

However, rather than solving these challenges in traditional ways, the city is leveraging machine-to-machine (M2M) cellular technologies to improve water quality, to protect the environment, and to get smart information about their water and wastewater systems to more effec-tively manage water supplies and maintain a sustainable economy for their city. Applying M2M solutions is enabling not only Cincinnati, but also other progressive utilities to cost-effectively collect, transmit, and use system and asset data, and turn it into actionable information to make critical decisions related to operations, maintenance, and capital investments.

With the growth of mobile technology, it makes sense to leverage this same technology to help utilities and cities operate and function more efficiently and protect our natural resources—especially one as valuable as water. Given that much of the west is facing severe drought, cities understand the connection between economic development, job creation and the cost of water. We lose nearly 1.7 trillion gallons of water from our water infrastructure each year. Investing in water infrastructure, changing the way we view and protect water, and advancing technologies and solutions that address our freshwater supplies, benefits everyone.

Heavy water users in the industrial and agricultural sectors are directly affected by the rising cost of water. They welcome technologies and solutions that will reduce cost and improve water quality for greater public health and resource management. At CH2M HILL, we thrive by working with clients to change these statistics and turn our world's complex challenges into opportunities. In other ways, we are helping clients change the water landscape in increasing sustainability by optimizing water systems to operate more efficiently and cost effectively, while also emphasizing potential water reuse along with innovative energy options.

Industry requires an abundant and reliable water supply, much like the agricultural sector. Roughly 75% of all industrial water withdrawals are used for energy production. In the United States, 49% of all water use is for power plants, as more than 200 billion gallons of water are needed just to generate electricity. One power plant in New York, the Empire Generating Power Plant, is changing that equation. This 535-megawatt power station uses non-disinfected municipal secondary effluent as its only process water supply. The facility conserves freshwater consumption by as much as seven million gallons per day.

Another example of innovative resource recovery is in the Midwest. The Milwaukee Metropolitan Sewerage District is developing a plan for energy independence to meet the utility's goal of achieving 100% net renewable energy with 80% of the energy being supplied by internal sources. These innovative and game-changing solutions that help our industry reimagine water use and better manage the resources we have.

Water reuse is also a sustainable option for both the private and the public sector. Whether we realize it or not, every drop and glass of water has a rich history. There are no new water supplies being created; rather, all water has been recycled or reused from the water cycle. In regions where water scarcity is a major concern or in applications that do not require highly treated water, water reuse provides a viable option. Singapore's NEWater project was a milestone in the advancement of potable water recycling technology. Singapore's national water agency—Singapore Public Utilities Board—developed NEWater, Singapore's own brand of high-grade reclaimed water, which currently provides 30% of the country's water supply.

Through extensive public outreach and the NEWater Visitor Centre, Singapore's NEWater overcame common challenges associated with water reuse projects, and it illustrates to the world how technology and public understanding can be successfully aligned. By promoting understanding of the full spectrum of water supply solutions needed to address shortages of freshwater, the Centre helps build support of water treatment technologies and their benefits, not only for Singapore, but also for other regions of our world facing similar challenges.

Given that water is weaved into nearly everything we touch and do—from the composition of our body to entertainment, sanitation, and sustenance, we cannot continue to take it for granted, using as much as we want, whenever we want. I am reminded daily by the project work we do with our clients, and how technology and innovative engineering solutions are making an impact on our water crises and challenges. It is truly a privilege and an honor to work in an industry that understands the true value of water, but there is always more we can do.

We are helping our clients find creative and innovative solutions to address some of the biggest and most complex water and energy challenges our world is facing, and it is time to start talking more with the public on how these solutions impact them and their relationship with water.

Droughts and extreme weather events are hot topics in the news to-day—clearly, water is on people's minds. While we have their attention, let us focus on sharing solutions and inviting them to reimagine our existing relationship with water and consider—from an individual standpoint—what each of us can do to help provide solutions for the future.

EILEEN J. O'NEILL, PHD
EXECUTIVE DIRECTOR
WATER ENVIRONMENT FEDERATION

Great Water Cities: Reflections on Leadership in Urban Water Management

Water has always been central to human development. It is essential for life and prosperity and plays a unique role in many cultures. Access to water to meet public, industrial, or transportation needs has influenced where people have settled and has shaped communities. Industrialized countries have made huge investments in urban water infrastructure and institutions. Improving the quality of life in developing countries will require major investments—of both financial resources and ingenuity—in water.

There are many challenges for today's water profession, sector and institutions. In the developed world, these include financial pressures and competing priorities, such as the need to meet increasingly stringent regulations and also the need to replace or upgrade aging infrastructure.

In other parts of the world, cities are grappling with questions of basic services. Climate change and population growth and shifts are adding both urgency and uncertainty. Despite these obvious difficulties, I would argue that this is a wonderful time to work in water. New thinking and practices are emerging that point to more sustainable approaches to urban water management. These can be relevant for both communities with legacy water infrastructure and for those seeking to meet new demands or the needs of previously unserved or underserved populations.

Diverse cities around the globe are not only leading the way by making water a central priority and showing how it can be managed in a way that is not just more sustainable, but also providing benefits ranging from livability to economic vitality and overall resilience. At the Water Environment Federation in Alexandria, Virginia, we have begun using the term "Great Water Cities" to describe these leaders and the examples they provide. We believe there are lessons that can be learned from these innovators that can help others get on the path to being a Great Water City, and to that end, are convening a series of conversations to foster dialogue and identify effective and enabling practices.

Smarter Urban Water Management

Water researchers and managers from various parts of the world are defining the principles of smarter or more sustainable urban water management and how these can be more widely adopted and integrated with conventional or legacy systems. Australian researchers have described the development of urban water management as being in a series of stages ranging from the basic provision of water supply, to the development of sewer and drainage systems, to the protection of surface water bodies. They also have described a vision for a future Water Sensitive

City.[1] In such cities, planning for water would be central to urban design; water management (potable water, wastewater, stormwater, and surface water) would be fully integrated and flexible, and the built environment would both support water conservation and mimic natural systems and processes. While the full execution of these principles at a city scale still is providing fodder for academic research, already there are real-life examples of cities that are applying them. The city-state of Singapore literally has reinvented its water future. Cities, such as Philadelphia, are investing in ambitious plans to use green infrastructure to manage stormwater and decrease combined sewer overflows. In Hamburg, Germany, a housing development where water will be recycled and energy and heat recovered onsite already is under construction.

Insights From Early Adopters

Discussions with water leaders have taught me that there are several common attributes of water management in a Great Water City:

Vision. Leaders are defining an exciting future water vision that the public can understand and support. For Singapore, the vision was to become water-independent by 2060. In the United States, cities such as Philadelphia, Cleveland, and Milwaukee are "branding" their green infrastructure programs and promoting the benefits they will provide, such as more effective water quality management and flood control. In addition, the use of these practices also improves the urban environment and can enhance property values.

Leadership. Moving from great visions into action requires leaders who are willing to be champions. Credit for the installation of the Marina Barrage in Singapore is given to the former Prime Minister Lee Kuan Yew, who articulated a vision nearly two decades ago for creating a res-

---

1 Brown, R., Keath, N., & Wong, T. (2008). Transitioning to water sensitive cities: *Historical, current and future transition states.* 11th International Conference on Urban Drainage. Madrid and London: International Association for Hydro-Environment Engineering and Research and the International Water Association.

ervoir by damming the mouth of the Marina Channel to keep saltwater out and control flooding. This reservoir now can supply 10% of Singapore's needs. In the United States, water utility leaders often cite the presence a dynamic political leader, typically a mayor who "gets" water, as being a critical factor in groundbreaking investments or programs. These elected officials frequently champion long-term investment, for which the greatest beneficiaries will be future rather than current voters.

Innovation. Early adopters harness innovation. On a national level, countries such as Israel and Singapore have turned a water challenge into an opportunity by embracing innovation. In the United States some regions, cities, and entities are taking a similar approach and investing in research and ingenuity. Individual agencies and utilities literally are transforming their operations from waste management entities to managers of valuable resources that generate useful products, such as energy, fertilizers, and recovered water. Although these activities may not be new—biogas was used in Victorian times to power street lamps in Britain, and Thames Water in the U.K. reports that it has been generating electricity from wastewater for more than 50 years—their scale and integration into the philosophy of our sector represent a sea change.

Adaptability. Leaders are looking for ideas from other sectors and other parts of the world and adapting these in a flexible way. We are also seeing the integration of decentralized approaches into centralized systems. Great Water Cities are combining what at one time seemed almost philosophically different approaches in ways that save energy and water.

Community Engagement. Leading organizations' engineers increasingly are engaging with their customers. As Sue Murphy, CEO of the Water Corporation of Western Australia, puts it, today's water managers need to "listen more" rather than leading with the solutions first. By using this approach and working diligently in the community, the Water Corporation has been able to build support for water reuse and make great strides in conservation. With respect to the latter, Ms. Murphy credits the public with setting more aggressive goals than her agency would have proposed.

Reflect and Take the Long View. Knowing the life of their systems, sector leaders feel the responsibility of the decisions being made today. Christian Günner, director of planning for Hamburg Water, recently reflected on his organization's practice of considering a system life of 77 years when making infrastructure decisions. Other utility leaders stress the need to develop flexible systems. Otherwise, given the pace of innovation, changing community needs, and uncertainty of climate change, we risk investing in costly "white elephants." Henk Ovink, former director of the Netherlands Office of Spatial Planning and Water Management, recently urged U.S. water professionals to take the time to think before replacing disaster-damaged infrastructure and resist the urge to recreate what had existed before.

Resilient Thinking. In the face of more extreme weather events—from droughts to floods—leading cities are incorporating resilience into their water management approaches. With respect to flooding risk, there is intense interest in drawing on the experience of the Netherlands, which has learned that "build higher dykes" is an unsustainable strategy. The vocabulary of its new approach—"living with water" and "room for the river" readily evokes its philosophy. In the United States, the ambitious and visionary Greater New Orleans Urban Water Plan draws on extensive consultations with Dutch urban planners and water managers and suggests a potential pathway forward for the city. As Cedric Grant, executive director of the Sewerage and Water Board of New Orleans noted recently, "We can't build our way out of this."

Investment. Investment in water infrastructure drives growth and creates jobs, but the cost of providing the improvements required in U.S. cities is enormous. In the Washington, DC area, for example, $2.6 billion is being invested in combined sewer overflow control, $950 million to achieve the nutrient reductions mandated to help restore the Chesapeake Bay, and $400 million to upgrade solids management systems. The cost of implementing the ambitious New Orleans urban water plan has been estimated at $6.3 billion. Hence, we will be looking for innovative financing approaches and partnerships from our Great Water Cities. In a recent step, DC Water issued $350 million in taxable, "certified" green century bonds. This is the first municipal century bond issued by a U.S. water or wastewater utility. The utility reports it is financing a portion of the construction costs of its combined sewer overflow infrastructure with a century bond to "better match the useful life of the tunnel systems—expected to perform for at least 100 years."

I feel justified in my optimism that the water profession will develop the sustainable solutions to meet urban water needs. There certainly will be a continuing need for ingenuity and creativity. On the basis of predictions, 70% of the world's population will be urban dwellers by 2050.[2] Urban growth is most rapid in the developing world, where cities gain an average of five million residents each month.[3] We must hope that there will be future Great Water Cities among these growing ranks.

[2] United Nations Human Settlements Programme (2010). *State of the world's cities 2010/11: Cities for all: Bridging the urban divide.* London: Earthscan.

[3] UN-Water Decade Programme on Advocacy and Communication. (2010). *Water and cities facts and figures.* Zaragoza, Spain: UN-Water Decade Programme on Advocacy and Communication.

DENNIS DOLL
CHAIRMAN, PRESIDENT AND CEO
MIDDLESEX WATER COMPANY

Have We Kicked the Water Can Far Enough Down the Road? It's Time to Embrace a New Reality

Whether at the national, state or local level, it is nearly impossible these days to avoid hearing the phrase in the media "kicking the can down the road" in reference to a variety of major challenges. This phrase is also uttered now more frequently in connection with the desperate condition of our water infrastructure in many places around the country.

It is generally understood that this phrase is a catchall with respect to a variety of important matters that leaders are either unable or unwilling to address currently. The expedient course of action is to take no action at all, by leaving the needed difficult choices for some time into the future, and potentially to be made by others. The water industry has for a very long time delivered safe, reliable and affordable service. However, with national headlines about water shortages across the country, coverage of dramatic water main breaks and stories about the financial impacts of water service on customers, water has reluctantly stepped into the spotlight and taken on heightened awareness and importance. There is a new water reality where the general public is just beginning to understand that we cannot assume that going forward we will have all the water we want, when we want it, where we want it, and at the relatively low cost we have enjoyed since domestic water service first became available.

Water has, for over a century, been a service that went largely "under the radar." Customers would rarely concern themselves with their water service unless it was not there, did not taste good, was discoloured, or otherwise posed a health issue. However, as customers have grown more sophisticated and begun to expect more from their water service providers, the industry has worked to deliver a customer experience that rivals services customers have grown to expect from other types of consumer services. In addition, we have worked as an industry to educate them about their service. Let's face it, if we had an unlimited supply of high-quality water wherever it is needed, and whenever it is wanted, and the cost of that unlimited access was inconsequential, there would not be any need to further educate anyone about the value of water. The harsh reality is that water is in increasingly short supply in many places around the country, and preserving and protecting that supply is becoming an ever-greater challenge and an ever-greater priority. However, while customers may demand greater customer service and convenient technological enhancements, they remain largely unaware of the underlying framework that actually delivers the service, the growing need for expensive and invasive upgrades and replacements, and the costs of compliance with increasingly stringent water quality standards.

I want to first get specific about defining what I see as the problem, and then be honest about what I believe needs to be done to solve the problem. First of all, water can be a very emotional issue. As the only public utility service ingested by human beings, and therefore necessary to sustain life itself, it sometimes takes on ethereal characteristics, something to be held in high reverence. The public views the water service as very different from other utility services such as electric and gas. As one who earns my living playing a role in providing high-quality water service to a large population, I fully understand the importance of safe reliable water service for domestic, commercial, fire protection, and economic stability purposes.

The United Nations has gone so far as to say: "The human right to water entitles everyone to sufficient, safe, acceptable, physically accessible and affordable water for personal and domestic uses" (UN CESC - General Comment 15, para. 2). Although this, on the surface, sounds quite noble, it is nothing other than lofty rhetoric. Sweeping general statements such as this are merely feel-good proclamations which, without accompanying plans, funds, and tools to actually address the need, only serve to create further confusion for the public, and further incite activist behavior that does nothing more than distract from the honest discussions required to address the problems at their core. Proclamations such as this set unrealistic expectations that providing clean and reliable supplies of water to all humans is simple and can be easily accomplished just because we say they deserve it.

So what do we do to solve the nation's water problems? I'm not so bold as to believe I know all the answers, but I'll offer my personal perspective on what I believe are important steps toward ultimate success.

Step 1—Take the Emotion Out of the Water Provider Dialogue. Here is a news flash—water service can be, and is, provided quite satisfactorily by both the public AND the private sector. We need to quell the utterly irresponsible rhetoric that water service should only ever be provided by public entities. The emotional reaction by some activist groups to the fact that private entities earn a return for their investors by deploying capital to water infrastructure is an impediment to progress. The private sector has much to offer in terms of technical and management expertise, technology, and access to capital. There are certainly examples of both public and private failures in delivering acceptable water service at affordable rates, but without honest dialogue about the causes of those failures, the unproductive finger-pointing and distraction from the real infrastructure issues stymies meaningful progress.

Both public and private entities are subject to the same federal and state laws and regulations regarding water quality, whether promulgated by the U.S. Environmental Protection Agency or the various state environmental and natural resource agencies. Government also has ultimate responsibility for service quality and rates, whether those regulations and standards are established at the municipal level by a local governing body or by a state public utility commission, a subdivision of state government. Inflammatory statements demonizing private participation in domestic water service are rarely grounded in fact, are seldom challenged and vetted by the media, and are counterproductive. I would surmise that most people just want quality water service they can rely on at affordable rates. I see evidence of this time and again when I come in contact with individuals who do not even know who provides them with their water service. I do not necessarily view that as a problem. It tells me service quality and the related rates are working just fine. So part of Step 1 is to acknowledge that the playing field is large enough for both public and private entities to play a vital role in addressing the challenges.

Step 2—Let Us Try to Look Beyond the Politics. Here is where the "kick the can" analogy really hits home. We are all kidding ourselves if we fail to acknowledge the fact that for many of our most troubled systems, political resistance to addressing decades of inattention to water infrastructure and lack of prudent asset management programs have resulted in water systems that are barely in compliance with state and federal drinking water quality regulations.

There are examples of this at the local, state, and national levels. With much of the water infrastructure largely underground and therefore not visible to the public, an "out of sight, out of mind" mentality has prevailed in many places, particularly at the local level. A public official receives accolades (and votes) when a plaque dedicating a new community library is erected. However, he or she attains nowhere near the amount of attention and praise from their constituents when a large water main is installed, a new water treatment technology is implemented, or an aging pipe is rehabilitated. In addition, there is never enough local revenue from taxes, user fees, and other funding sources to do all the things a community would like. So in connection with the "out of sight, out of mind" mentality, where is the political value for an incumbent to move expensive, unseen, and boring infrastructure projects to the top of the priority list? It is often politically expedient to accept the risks and let the successor deal with it.

I am by no means suggesting there are not well-run public water systems in our country. The water industry is fortunate to include many very highly skilled professionals. In addition, there are many progressive local governments who have responsibility for very large, very well capitalized, and maintained systems with reasonable customer rates. They serve many large cities and surrounding suburban populations. My concern is with those water systems whose owners are not forward thinking, who choose not to acknowledge the true condition of their infrastructure, who are not willing to expend scarce resources and political capital on critical infrastructure needs, and who are unwilling to adequately manage the risks associated with potential major infrastructure failure. I have observed many examples of highly skilled public entity water professionals who understand the critical needs surrounding infrastructure upgrade and replacement. They are often, however, put in a precarious personal situation with respect to their ability to influence the funding decisions for the required improvements they have identified based on their years of well-developed professional expertise. They are faced with having to navigate this difficult dynamic with their governing bodies while also keeping their jobs.

Step 3—Adopt Full-Cost Pricing, Universally. Do you really know why your water charges are what they are? Who sets them, and what do they reflect? I believe there is a fundamental need for all stakeholders (customers, regulators and political officials) to know that the rates charged to the consumer for water service fully reflect the cost of providing that service. I often see comparisons of public and private customer water rates side by side in a not-so-subtle attempt to disparage the privates or other public entities whose rates are higher. However, this comparison of customers' rates is largely meaningless based on the unique operational characteristics of each system, and they become more meaningless if the rates do not fully reflect the cost of actually providing the service.

In a number of public systems I have observed, customers rates have been held artificially low for prolonged periods because no one wants an increase in rates on "their watch" (back to the politics). In other examples, otherwise financially sound public water utilities are viewed as a source by officials to help balance the local operating budget, thereby helping to mitigate property tax increases (again, politics). Complicating matters further is the challenge around the design of the rate structure in a manner that equitably allocates the cost of providing service to the various classes of customers (i.e., residential, commercial, industrial, and public and private fire protection). This lack of transparency with respect to the rate-setting process serves to further cloud the scope of the operational and financial challenges, and creates further confusion among consumers.

In contrast, private water purveyors who are under the jurisdiction of a state public utility Commission all practice "full-cost pricing." Full-cost pricing is an essential element of the rate base rate-of-return methodology that is required in many states and is inherent in the rate setting process. It is intended to keep the process fair and transparent and help ensure the ultimate user of the service pays no more or no less than is required to deliver such service.

Step 4—Stop Rewarding Bad Behavior and Level the Playing Field. I have heard the pushback by federal and state government officials, activist groups, and some consumers that investor-owned water utilities should not share in the same opportunities as publicly owned systems to access government grants and low-cost loans for infrastructure improvements. There is no logic to this conclusion. It is completely without merit and is largely an emotional reaction. In the case of under-maintained water systems, whether public or private, and whether for political or other reasons, access to these sources of funding in some cases is, in effect, a reward for years of this behavior.

A government subsidy or a bailout in any form may provide the much needed capital for necessary infrastructure improvements, but does nothing to hold entities accountable for past operational or fiscal performance, and does nothing to ensure irresponsible behavior will not be initiated or repeated in the future. Furthermore, the notion that investor-owned utilities should not share in these funding opportunities because they earn a return for their owners is based solely on emotion and a lack of understanding of basic utility rate-setting methodologies. The perception is often that such subsidies only line the pockets of investors and that this occurs at the expense of the taxpayer or the utility customer. The reality is that the rate base rate-of-return methodology employed by state public utility commissions generally requires that government grants be recognized as "contributed capital" and therefore, reduces the base upon which customers' rates are determined. The owners derive no financial benefit whatsoever from such grants. The grants all inure to the benefit of customers in the form of lower rates, as they should. Furthermore, interest expense incurred by investor-owned utilities on either government-subsidized loans or traditional borrowings, are effectively recovered dollar for dollar in customers' rates and, therefore, produce no element of profit whatsoever for the owners. Like grants, government-subsidized low-interest loans serve to benefit customers in the form of lower customers' bills. (Remember full-cost pricing).

Step 5—Explore Ways and Holistic Approaches to Harvest the Power of Water, Wastewater, and Energy. Although many view water and wastewater services as fundamentally separate and distinct—and the generation of electricity as even more separate and different, there is more to this relationship than meets the eye. There is an inherent relationship among these utility services whereby environmental and economic value can be maximized by exploiting what has been characterized as the "water-energy nexus." It is not just about the relationship of water used for the production of electricity and electricity used for the production of water. The wastewater stream also contains an incredible amount of organic matter that is a prime candidate for generating electricity. Plainly put, as long as we continue to flush toilets, there will be a never-ending supply of "feedstock" for this purpose. Adding to this environmental and economic opportunity is legislation recently passed in several states that no longer allows large producers of organic material (food wastes generated from commercial operations) to deposit this material in landfills. Food wastes are an incredible accelerant to the production of electricity through anaerobic digestion at wastewater treatment and other facilities.

As we further break down the various regulatory, political, and business model silos that impede a more holistic approach to water, wastewater and energy, I believe further benefits can be realized by those systems that aggressively seek to maximize those opportunities for environmental and economic benefit. As we work to determine how to pay for our vast infrastructure needs, the economic opportunities presented by this holistic view can be one of a number of tools to generate value from what is largely viewed as a waste stream that requires cost to be incurred for disposal.

Step 6—Embrace the New Reality. It is generally understood that water is an incredibly precious natural resource that needs to be preserved and protected. Yet we often squander it irresponsibly and also fail to consider how desperate life can be when we do not have all the high-quality water we want and need, when we want it and where we want it. We are only occasionally reminded of this reality when we experience events such as droughts, main breaks, severe weather events, and other circumstances that result in service disruptions. We fail to acknowledge that water has intrinsic value far beyond what we pay for it in our utility bills.

In restating the obvious, there has been increasing attention in recent years on the desperate state of our nations' aging water infrastructure and the staggering amount of capital investment needed to sustain our water systems for the long term. There have been endless articles, conferences, workshops, hearings, and other forums where many have become very adept at "defining" the problem. What I do not see in any of these forums is a clear path, a "solution," as to how all the needed upgrades and replacements will be funded and who is going to pay. Whether in the form of government grants, government-subsidized low-interest loans, customers' utility bills, local property taxes, state surcharges on water system operations, and so on, in the end, it is all going to be paid for in some form by the consumer/taxpayer, whether at the local, state, or national level. The problem with all of these different mechanisms is that each has its own political and financial consequences. In the end, each presently provides varying levels of transparency to the consumer as to what they are paying for and why.

We have to get to that place where prudent capital investments can be made in systems methodically, year in and year out, regardless of current economic conditions, politics, or the ratemaking cycle. Improvements need to be executed in a strategic, disciplined, and risk-based approach. In many of these investment decisions, it seems to always come down to the following: Do we pay now or do we risk paying substantially more later?

My definition of the new reality, although simple, is likely not popular. I believe that in the not too distant future, safe, reliable water service can no longer be one of the smallest components of the overall household budget. The cost to the average consumer in the United States of their domestic water service will need to be greater than what it is today, maybe significantly greater. It will need to become the new normal that the water utility bill will need to rival other more costly household expenditures. As a nation, we seem to have relatively little concern about paying a dollar or more for a bottle of water, which, on a per-gallon basis, can be more costly than a gallon of gasoline. Yet when asked to pay only a nominal incremental increase in our water utility bill to fund critically needed infrastructure upgrades and replacements, cries of protest emerge. The psychological, emotional and economic challenges associated with establishing this new normal in the minds of consumers, businesses, government officials, and others are complex. No one ever wants rates for water service to increase, let alone increase them as dramatically as may be required to sustain our infrastructure for generations to come. On a positive note, I believe unwelcome, relatively large increases over time in rates for water service will serve to further spur creativity and innovation among water purveyors, as well as in the products and services industry, to continually drive further efficiencies and reductions in cost that support both public and private water utilities.

As costs increase in various aspects of our lives all the time, innovation facilitated by the free market always becomes a priority in efforts to reduce our costs and to improve our quality of life. To come full circle, I believe the days of "kicking the can down the road" with our water infrastructure are numbered. We need to take our leaders, our municipal officials, regulators, and the like to task to embrace acceptance of the critical need behind infrastructure investment and the need for customer rates to fully reflect those investments. We need to engage customers in the dialogue about what it really takes to get clean, safe drinking water from the source to their tap, and we need to help society come to grips with this new reality if we really are to address these challenges at their core.

ALAN J. KRAUSE
CHAIRMAN AND CHIEF EXECUTIVE OFFICER
MWH GLOBAL

Quenching Water's Thirst for Value

Samuel Taylor Coleridge wrote the poem "The Rime of the Ancient Mariner" about a sailor on the ocean who, though completely parched and surrounded by water, cannot drink a single drop. It is a metaphor that is frighteningly relevant when examining our earth's resources today. Although 75% of the earth's surface is covered by water, less than three percent of it is freshwater, and only one percent of the world's fresh surface water is readily accessible for direct human use.[1]

Yet water is not valued like other commodities globally. Natural resources, such as oil and gas, rely on the economic models of supply and

---

[1] National Geographic. *Freshwater crisis.* Retrieved from http://environment.nationalgeographic.com/environment/freshwater/freshwater-crisis/ and Financial Times. *A world without water.* Retrieved from www.ft.com/intl/cms/s/2/8e42bdc8-0838-11e4-9afc-00144feab7de.html#slide0

demand. At the time of this writing, oil is valued around $100 per barrel, while water is sold at fractions of that cost in major cities around the world. Figure 1 compares water rates in those cities.[2,3,4]

Source: *Infrastructure* magazine, New York City Water Board, Prairie Research Institute

Figure 1.

Although the world's economies are improving at different rates, there is a lack of funding to support new and aging water infrastructure. This lack of funding is due to the recession, but it is also a result of the low value placed on water by the general public. Even in the best of economies, market forces of supply and demand do not prevail for infrastructure. This is an international problem, and it is clearly an area that we recognize as an integral part of civilization and growth for a community. In addition, because the price of water has been low historically, it is difficult to gain support for price increases to recover the full cost of water.

Perhaps this is why we do not value our water infrastructure systems enough to invest in them. Oddly enough, we are willing to pay a high price for bottled water and other drinks that are water-based. One MWH engineer calculated that the cost of one liter of bottled water is nearly 1,750 times more expensive than water delivered to individual

[2] Cantrell, Clint. (2014, May). *Infrastructure.*
[3] New York City Water Board. (2014, July). Rate Schedule.
[4] Prairie Research Institute. *Illinois state water survey.*
www.isws.illinois.edu/wsp/faq/wsmore.asp?id=q4

residences through public systems, and this does not include the cost or time spent to purchase bottled water.[5]

In the United States, Americans buy an estimated 42.6 billion single-serving (1 liter or less) plastic water bottles each year. People in Western Europe consume almost half of all bottled water produced, amounting to more than 100 liters per person each year.[6] Using the current cost of bottled water, the average person spends $242 per year on bottled water.

The total cost of monthly water bills would be $60,000 if tap water were the same price as bottled water.[7] It is interesting that we buy bottles of water at a high rate for convenience—not necessity—while we will not prioritize what needs to be done to facilitate sustainable water systems. In addition, generally, most Americans are not aware of the invisible cost of water, or costs that are required to grow and process food and other household goods. It is estimated that it takes 732 gallons of water to produce an average American meal, and it takes nearly 5,000 gallons of water to produce one set of clothes as simple as jeans, a t-shirt and shoes (Figure 2).[8]

How did we get here? Historians trace sophisticated water and sewerage systems back to ancient times. However, the modern water systems date back to the 1800s in the United Kingdom. This is the same time that MWH was founded, and we are proud of our heritage, which dates back two centuries. However, we are concerned that if the general public does not act as good stewards and global citizens, the next 200 years will be more challenging.

---

[5] Cantrell, Clint. (2014, May). *Infrastructure.*

[6] Raj, T.V. Antony. (2013, November 11). *Price of bottled potable water around the world.* Retrieved from http://tvaraj.com/2013/11/11/price-of-bottled-potable-water-around-the-world/

[7] Statistic Brain. (2014, January 2). *Bottled water statistics.* Retrieved from http://www.statisticbrain.com/bottled-water-statistics/

[8] Water Footprint Network, Water Utility Authority. Combined calculation from statistics.

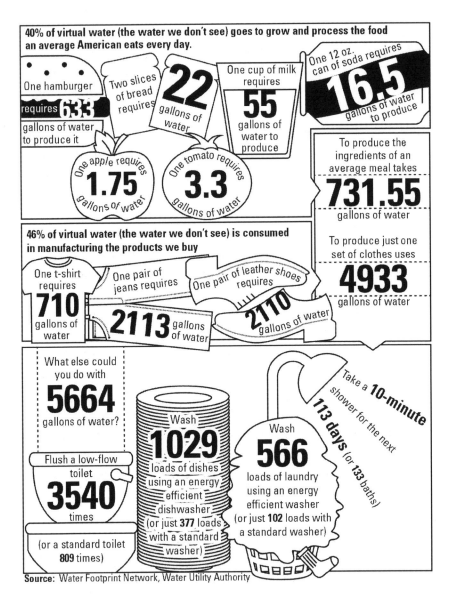

Figure 2.

It is important that everyone understands and respects the value of water and the opportunity to invest in its future. Although the solutions are different everywhere, there is one overarching opportunity, and that is education. We must help the general public learn the value of water to ensure people will pay a proper amount to receive it and, in turn, support the infrastructure needs to allow for sustainable systems.

The value of water education is the umbrella over which all water infrastructure repair and replacement options should fall. It is a long journey of education, but it will provide the full benefits of the importance in investing in water infrastructure. We must make water a business proposition, not an emotional one, and we cannot proceed without the full engagement of every stakeholder across the water delivery model.

Regardless of whether we represent professional associations, water utilities, companies in the private sector supply chain, businesses, or residential communities, we all have a crucial part in changing the perception about water's value. There are four key areas of focus:

In Deep Water. In North America, each day, it is estimated that there are 850 water main breaks resulting in a total annual repair cost of $3 billion.[9] Systems have aged to failure, and municipalities cannot make the needed investments to support the cost of infrastructure fixes. Policy makers and elected officials have a tendency to focus on other areas that will have a payback during their terms. In some cases, the problem is just too large, or is too much work, or the benefit is too far into the future. As a result, utilities and municipalities will be forced to repair infrastructure as it breaks, rather than improve it, as it is needed. This is a much more expensive option.

These challenges do not exist just in North America. Across the globe more progressive cities and corporations are taking a different approach by developing specialized asset management programs. These

---

[9] Retrieved from www.watermainbreakclock.com/

programs tailor investment needs with financial realities. Rather than focusing on the entire utility system, which can be costly and overwhelming with little early returns on investment, cities are strengthening each asset base individually and ultimately strengthening the whole system. For example, it is common for cities to invest money in water main breaks, but what about proactively investing in water meters? Cities are stretching their water meters to their full life potential, believing they are saving money on replacement costs; however, over time, the meters begin to provide less accurate readings. This, ultimately, affects their revenue stream. By implementing a progressive asset management program to understand the meter readings and recalibrate the meters to avoid losing revenue, cities are fully realizing the value of water consumed. This is just one example of how cities and municipalities can avoid falling into the "deep water."

Keeping Your Head Above Water. In the 20th century, the world's population tripled, and the use of renewable water resources has grown six-fold.[10] Every water utility and municipality should be considering water reuse programs, water recycling processes, water regeneration systems and eco-system development.

In 2013, the city of Anaheim, California began operating its new innovative and award-winning water-recycling program, demonstrating how urban developers can use low-impact development features in any location. The first-of-its-kind recycling center is capable of processing 100,000 gallons of water per day from raw sewage into water used for irrigation and toilet flushing in nearby commercial buildings. Located just 20 feet from Anaheim City Hall, the treatment facility expels neither noise nor odor.[11]

The project has been recognized as an Engineering Achievement of the Year by the state of California from the California Water Environ-

---

[10] World Water Council. *Water crisis.* Retrieved from
http://www.worldwatercouncil.org/library/archives/water-crisis/
[11] MWH. *Anaheim water recycling demonstration facility.* Retrieved from
www.mwhglobal.com/mwh-projects/anaheim-water-recycling-demonstration-facility

mental Association, and it has been honored with an Award of Merit by *Engineering News-Record California* as part of the Best Projects 2013 competition in the water/environment category.

It serves as an excellent example for what cities can be doing to proactively explore water supply opportunities, to educate the public about the value of water, and to keep their "heads above water."

<u>Test the Waters.</u> Ratepayers are generally more open to changes when they understand why their rates are changing. If the municipality or utility can be specific about the costs and identification of exactly what needs to be upgraded while introducing a realistic plan to update the water infrastructure, they will have a better opportunity to raise rates. The challenge with this scenario is its political viability and commitment.

The city of Santa Fe, New Mexico, successfully created a community effort surrounding the true cost of water. Following an acquisition of its water system from Public Service Company of New Mexico, the city realized its revenues were not sufficient to meet the requirements of the bonds issued to finance the acquisition. Meeting the demands of the bondholders required an immediate and drastic rate increase. Vowing to never let such a situation happen again, the city created a long-range financial plan with detailed projections of water demands, rates, and operating and capital costs. The city was able to finance its major water supply acquisition and maintain six successive years of eight percent rate increases. Cash reserves remain strong and the city of Santa Fe is able to fund millions of dollars of capital construction each year from its annual earnings without issuing any new debt.[12] This is an example of how cities and municipalities can "test the waters" with their customers and ratepayers and develop buy-in for long-term financial and serviceability goals.

---

[12] MWH. *New Mexico City water division financial strategy development.* Retrieved from http://www.mwhglobal.com/mwh-projects/financial-strategy-development

Singing in the Rain. Involving private investors in infrastructure development has been an innovative way to support infrastructure-funding gaps in non-water commodities. In this scenario, municipalities must identify the potential issues, develop a plan, and seek alternative financing and solutions from the private sector. By utilizing these public–private partnerships (PPPs) utilities can leverage the assets and capabilities of the private sector to make needed improvements.

The city of Fillmore, California recently completed a new recycled water scheme by proceeding with a PPP to enhance the antiquated wastewater treatment facilities that had been in place for decades. By implementing this approach, private capital and resources were utilized to build and operate new facilities. It is difficult to promise a one-size-fits-all solution that allows every utility to be "singing in the rain," but PPPs can offer distinct advantages for certain situations such as this one.

Ultimately, given where we are today, until organizations can change the public perception of the value of water, infrastructure will operate to failure. This means that more patches and repairs will be needed and more people will be inconvenienced. Also, the ultimate investment will be much more expensive. However, the optimistic side of me believes that with education and collaboration from many parties, we will be able to increase awareness of this issue. We need to be able to identify opportunities to fix, maintain, and build systems to manage growing needs through public and private funding so that we will not be surrounded by water without "any drop to drink."

SUE MURPHY

CHIEF EXECUTIVE OFFICER

WATER CORPORATION

Water Transformation Pays Off in Western Australia

One of the world regions hit hardest by climate change is the southwest corner of Australia, where rainfall has declined by 12% in the past 25 years, seriously depleting traditional water sources: dams and shallow groundwater reserves that have been shaky at the best of times. Runoff into the main supply dams of Perth, the capital city of Western Australia, fell by more than half while country scheme supply dams took losses of up to 80% or worse. It has been a bleak picture.

Although country dwellers and farm operators on this sprawling, dry land have always placed a high value on water, the city folks clinging to the coast have had it easier, thanks to large dams and groundwater bodies. However, as those foundations have been failing, the urban mindset has seen a big swing toward water conservation to protect their green lifestyle.

Water awareness has spread to the point where it is now an issue of top importance across the entire state of Western Australia, all 2.6 million square kilometers or about one million square miles of it.

This includes large swathes of agricultural and grazing land, from temperate zones in the South to tropical in the North, as well as mining and energy resource operations scattered all over, but concentrated in the remote and mostly tinder dry Northwest.

This has been driven by a vigorous and innovative water use awareness and efficiency campaign that has been at the core of a remarkable transformation of the state's water supply planning since the turn of the century when the big dry bit hard.

All this has been engineered by the state's major supplier of water and wastewater services—the Water Corporation—which is now recognized as a front-runner in worldwide efforts to address climate resilience and water efficiency.

Corporation planners realized they had a major problem on their hands when Perth found itself in the grip of an extraordinary drought in the winter of 2001, dubbed by my predecessor at the Water Corporation, Dr. Jim Gill, as "the winter from hell." However, this turned out to be the vanguard of what became the driest period on record for the city.

At the same time, the state, which is the engine room of the Australian economy, had been pushing ahead in its irresistible way developing huge new mining and energy ventures that have had repercussions in urban areas, feeding the residential sprawl with strong and sustained population growth, much of it from immigration.

The corporation planners needed to change the playing field to meet this unprecedented situation. An initial "security through diversity" approach represented the first break away from the "dams and groundwater" thinking that had existed since the first wells were dug in the fledgling British colony about 175 years before.

This produced a change of direction toward more diversified, climate-resilient water sources, and by late 2011, two major seawater desalination plants on the coast at Perth and further south were producing a fail-safe new water supply from the Indian Ocean.

The first plant, at Perth, was the first of its kind in Australia and the biggest seawater plant outside the Middle East. It was also the biggest of its kind to source power from renewable energy, in this case wind. To the Corporation's surprise and delight, it made the front page of the *Wall Street Journal*, which described the plant as a possible world model in the response to climate change.

The second plant, also sourcing its power from wind generation, was a more complex proposition, in engineering and environmental terms, and was announced as the desalination plant of the year in the Global Water Awards for 2012.

Together, the plants are now producing almost half of Perth's needs, which is a remarkable turn-around.

The security through diversity approach incorporated a package of diversifying sources while moving on a number of large source options in parallel, boosting water use efficiency through all communities and sectors, and pursuing much greater recycling of water.

The Water Corporation has been rolling out programs on all fronts and completely changed the water supply landscape in the process. Among them are the following: the retro-fitting of low water use fittings in thousands of homes, large scale installation of "smart" meters, the pressure reduction for supply schemes, a new and highly effective regime of rostering the use of garden sprinklers, and a program to manage the use of water by big business that has achieved huge water savings.

The effectiveness of all this, backed by strong support from the community and our industry partners, is evidenced by a substantial drop in average per capita water use in Perth of about 31% in the past 13 years, while total water use remained stable. We are ahead of schedule to meet our longer-term consumption targets.

Planning has evolved into a long-term program that we call "Water Forever—Whatever the Weather." This involves detailed plans for water and wastewater services in Perth and broad regional areas for the next 50 years to ensure that supplies and services are maintained without interruption or crisis.

Having led the nation in large-scale seawater desalination, we are now setting the pace in groundwater replenishment for which we conducted a three-year trial in Perth and will commence construction of a major scheme in late 2014.

This newest climate-independent jewel in our diversity crown will be the next major source for the city, with the capacity to produce about 20% of the city's drinking water needs by 2060. As it sources highly treated wastewater, it will also greatly boost progress toward our recycling targets.

Although we are, of course, immensely proud of all these achievements in so short a time, we cannot rest on our laurels, and we are acutely aware that we are now embarking on the long road to our enduring state of water security. We are doing it strategically and reforming our business at the same time.

Dealing with the drying climate has been a big draw on our resources and funds, but our achievements are now firmly embedded in the Western Australian community, and this allows us to turn more of our attention to fundamental matters that underpin our planning. This will cater for continuing state growth and ensure that all community sectors are able to pursue their objectives and dreams.

Hand in hand with water reliability is our pursuit of productivity and customer relationship reforms. We are realigning our business to drive efficiency and productivity so that the program of developments can continue sustainably. At the same time, we are intent on delivering real value and improved service to our customers in these times of increasing austerity. They have come on board the water train and done the right things to help us reposition our business, so now it is time to reap some rewards.

We are not alone in this. The Australian water services industry is now wholly focused on efficiency, productivity and cost reduction. In the west, thanks to the foresight and good planning of our corporation people, we are well advanced on these fronts.

However, our task is made more challenging by the sheer scale of our operating area, including everything from big cities to scores of remote communities, and the fact that our services touch just about everyone in this vast sprawl.

We are pursuing efficiency and productivity reform on a number of fronts. These include operational efficiency programs, a digital strategy for customer engagement, and increased partnerships with the private sector, which is now handling about 95 per cent of our capital expenditure program. Both of the seawater desalination projects were undertaken by international alliances, and a new alliance has been created for the groundwater replenishment project.

We set up partnerships with major resource companies to develop water services in the Northwest, and we have an alliance there delivering upgrades to two wastewater treatment plants that will enable much greater recycling.

We have developed different, but complementary strategies for our Perth metropolitan and regional operations, which have distinct profiles. Perth has large, complex treatment plants with highly integrated and sophisticated distribution and reticulation networks, while the regions have multiple small town stand-alone schemes, remote treatment facilities and pump stations, and vast distances between all Corporation installations.

Two recently established alliances handle all our metropolitan system operations and maintenance and, through integration and streamlining, have achieved significant improvements to our service and business efficiency which resulting in real ongoing benefits for our customers.

Our regional reform project, Building a Better Business, achieved efficiencies in administration, work scheduling and other areas.

In a "first" for the state water industry, we established a public-private partnership to construct a major water treatment plant on

Perth's outskirts. The partnership funded, designed, and built the plant, which was opened in early 2014.

Value for money was a major benefit of the partnership, and drivers for this lay in the issues of risk allocation, innovation, whole-of-life costing focus, and greater layers of competition.

In fact, value for money is one of our corporate mantras. "Valuing every dollar" is one of our new set of values that commits us to managing our time and spending effectively, knowing the dollar cost of our actions, and challenging the ineffective use of resources.

This applies in particular to our capital expenditure program. New efficiencies have produced substantial savings as we tackle our challenge to deliver the full program at a five percent discount.

I make a point of asking everyone in the Water Corporation to keep firmly in mind that every dollar we spend comes from our customers who are under increasing financial pressure and look to us to spend their money wisely.

Another of our values is to be customer focused. We are increasing our understanding of our customers and engaging more effectively with them by using new technology, such as digital, and taking advantage of the social media explosion. Online interaction is now the first choice for an increasing number of our customers.

In mid-2013, we launched a new website and an online account managing service, "My Water," and moved to two-monthly billing to help customers better manage their household finances.

Embracing opportunities like these and maximizing the resulting benefits are big challenges for us. Through a newly developed computer program, we are systematically and strategically communicating with some 24,000 key people and organizations, and this is a rapidly growing part of our operations.

Thorough communication with our customers and all of our varied stakeholders are an essential part of our business, and have allowed us to greatly improve our services as well as planning and project outcomes.

One striking example is our learning from the pioneering groundwater replenishment scheme of the Orange County Water District in California, particularly the extensive community engagement that was undertaken to gain public acceptance of wastewater recycling.

The OCWD scheme formed the foundation for the technology that we are using in our own.

Knowledge exchange such as this is a key to the success of our future efforts to meet a whole range of challenges facing the world water industry today. This includes the issues discussed above but extends to others such as pricing and competition for water and access to capital for much needed infrastructure development.

Perhaps now more than ever it is essential that effective communication and knowledge sharing occur to a greater degree across boundaries so we can plan responsibly and with vision to achieve the best outcomes for the industry, our stakeholders, and our customers. In doing this, we also need to maintain high levels of coordination and togetherness among all the players.

MARTIN A. KROPELNICKI

PRESIDENT AND CHIEF EXECUTIVE OFFICER

CALIFORNIA WATER SERVICES GROUP

California's Wake-Up Call

What is the real value of water? The answer to this question is the subject of much debate—debate that often becomes an emotional argument, rather than a reasonable and rational discussion, and for a good reason. Water is quite literally the lifeblood of our society. Hence, we argue about who should get it, the farmers or the cities, or the environment. We argue about who should control it, public versus private. We even argue when our water bill goes up a few dollars, never mind the fact that we all pay many times more for our cell phones or the 300+ channels of cable television to which we subscribe. As important as it is to our very existence, we Americans have come to expect and enjoy the quality of life that comes from having a reliable supply of clean water at our fingertips without fully appreciating the real value of water.

Taking all emotion out of it, the simple fact is there are real costs associated with delivering a reliable supply of high-quality water. Water may fall from the sky, but it does not magically appear at the tap. So for argument's sake, let us change our discussion from the *value of water* to the *real costs of not having enough water*. While this may seem strange, it is the real issue we are facing in California, and the negative economic effects are massive and having a ripple effect on the local, state, and federal economy.

First, let us size up California. When most people think about California, they think about San Francisco, Hollywood, Silicon Valley, and Disneyland. They may know that California is a large state and that we are the eighth largest economy in the world. What they may not know is that we have approximately 38.3 million residents in California, and that makes us the largest state in the union.

In California, the 2013 gross domestic product surpassed $2.0 trillion and represents approximately 13% of the U.S. gross domestic product. Agriculture is a major industry in California with an aggregate value of approximately $37 billion, which generates an estimated additional $100 billion in related economic activity. California is the largest grower of almonds in the world with a net export value in excess of $2.8 billion, and it is also the largest dairy state with an aggregate export value in excess of $1.4 billion. The dairy industry alone in California alone generates economic activity in excess of $45 billion and employs approximately 400,000 people. The bottom line is that California's agribusiness is more than twice the size of any other state.

However, California is not only about agriculture; the state has a wide geographic footprint containing a variety of leading industries employing millions of people. California is also home to refineries, wineries, and manufacturers of everything from computer chips to potato chips.

What makes California such an economic powerhouse? We have the weather. We have the beaches. We have the mountains. We even have the celebrities, if you consider that a draw. We also have room to grow, fertile land, and arguably some of the smartest people and best universities here in the Golden State.

However, what really makes it all possible is...you guessed it, water. First and foremost, California has been blessed with a natural water conveyance system that helps move water from the north to the south mostly with gravity. Most of the state's infrastructure was built in the 1950s and 1960s, and despite the massive growth in population, it has required little maintenance. Our population has increased 69% since the last major California drought in the mid-1970s. That bears repeating: The population in California during the 1950s was less than 11 million people. The population today exceeds 38 million. That is an increase of 245%. To think that the infrastructure built decades ago has been able to support this type of growth is simply incredible, and a tribute to the early planners for the state of California.

However, all good things come to an end. In August 2014, we experienced one of the worst droughts in California history. Most reservoirs are at record low levels, farmland lays fallow, and the economic consequences are starting to add up. A report published by University of California at Davis in July 2014 estimated current costs associated with the drought as follows:

Losses in crop revenue	$810 million
Increases in pumping costs	$454 million
Livestock and dairy losses	$203 million
Total direct losses	**$1.467 billion**

The drought will cost California more than $2 billion by the end of 2014 and result in over 17,000 job losses. That is 17,000 families directly affected financially, this year alone.

And the effects will be felt beyond California, increasing the prices of everything that the state produces, including food and other goods.

Now, let's get real. As an economist, I would argue that we need to be pragmatic and realize that the infrastructure we built in the 1950s and 1960s has gone above and beyond what it was originally designed to do. The water conveyance systems that the state relies on are in need of some serious investment, and it is not going to be cheap. I would also argue that this is not a problem that is isolated to one or two segments of our economy, but rather, it affects each and every one of us who live in the state. If we do not come together and invest in water, we will sacrifice billions of dollars of future economic growth that will ripple throughout the nation's economy.

However, when it comes to water, the pragmatism does not cut it. We need to get back to the emotion. We need to think about what water means to us, what it would be like to be without it. Because only then are we ready to do what needs to be done to ensure that our children and their children will continue to enjoy that luxury that we Americans have come to expect.

And what needs to be done? One, we need to fix California's infrastructure. Every day, I have the privilege of driving over the Golden Gate Bridge, and instead of enjoying the million dollar views, I think about the fact that 40% to 50% of the freshwater from the Sacramento River is flowing out to sea right underneath the bridge, instead of flowing to our farmers in the valley who are in desperate need of more water to grow the crops that feed us. That means fixing the Sacramento–San Joaquin Delta, building more water storage, and planning and budgeting for infrastructure maintenance.

Two, California needs to move from a fractured water management system to an integrated water management system for both groundwater and surface water. It is not your water or my water. It is our water. If we are not coordinated in our efforts, we won't be effective. Integrated water management is the way forward to ensure we maximize the value of our precious water supply.

Three, we need to get serious about water reuse and stormwater runoff. California has a tremendous opportunity to invest in water reuse. Small improvements in this area can yield big results and ease some of the demand on our drinking water systems. California needs to be a leader in water reuse and set the example for the other states to follow.

And four, we need to stay continuously focused on conservation. This simple fact is that water conservation is still the least-cost source of water, and although we have made great strides in this area, we have a long way to go. Saving water is everyone's business and helps ensure that our state has the precious fuel needed to sustain our growth and economic vitality.

So next time you are paying your cell phone bill, go get a glass of water from your tap and put it on the table in front of you, next to your cell phone. Ask yourself, "Which one is more expensive, and which one can I not live without?" Hopefully then you will begin to understand the real value of water.

DAVID ST. PIERRE
EXECUTIVE DIRECTOR
METROPOLITAN WATER RECLAMATION DISTRICT
OF GREATER CHICAGO

New Horizons for Water

On May 13, 1908, Theodore Roosevelt held the first Conservation Conference in the United States. He invited the Governors from each state to "consider the weightiest problem now before the nation." In his keynote address, he declares, "The occasion for the meeting lies in the fact that the natural resources of our country are in danger of exhaustion if we permit the old wasteful methods of exploiting them longer to continue." He points out the reckless path the country is taking in plundering the natural resources of the nation through unsustainable consumption. He asks, "What will happen when our forests are gone, when the coal, the iron, the oil, and the gas are exhausted, when the soils shall have been still further impoverished and washed into the streams, polluting the rivers, denuding the fields, and obstructing navigation?" In 1908, there were fewer than two billion people on the planet. In 2012, the number topped seven billion. Certainly, in today's world, the alarm is sounding louder.

Today, we face an amplified version of the same problem. In Roosevelt's day, the government accepted the role of conservation—the keeper of the gate. The government, through legislation, has set guidelines for sustainable practices that encourage conservation and stewardship of our resources. Yet our world economy is becoming increasingly consumptive, and the United States remains the premier consumer in today's world.

The health, quality, and availability of water are at the heart of the conservation discussion. Changing climates around the globe are causing droughts and water supply problems in some regions, while storm patterns are becoming more intense in other regions causing flooding and disasters. Utilities are wrestling with resiliency issues to guarantee future water supplies or flood control measures that can meet the challenges of today and tomorrow. New water regulation discussions emerge on an annual basis. Nutrients, pharmaceuticals, microbeads, and other emerging contaminants continue to challenge water utilities that still struggle with old infrastructure repairs and must meet sanitary/combined sewer overflow consent decrees with limited funding options. The Clean Water Act (CWA) is ever expanding with initiatives to move toward non-point source regulations that fall on the backs of regulated point source dischargers, farmers, or underfunded stormwater utilities.

When the CWA was passed in 1972, the waters of the United States were in serious trouble. Before and after, pictures of bays and rivers throughout the country display the successful implementation of the CWA. The Cuyahoga River, located in Northeast Ohio and feeding Lake Erie, is famous for being "the river that caught fire." The CWA has been the number one quality restoration initiative undertaken by the federal government. The CWA resulted in the establishment of secondary treatment facilities, regulated industrial discharges and restored waterways. Tremendous strides were made throughout the 1970s and 1980s. Wastewater agencies popped up in communities across the country, and the stage was set for our current day operations.

Water crosses many boundaries and never more than today. Agricultural, industrial, and public demand for water is at a premium. Water is at the heart of all economic activity; water is life. Water flows across geographical and political boundaries. Yet water utilities and protection are managed, for the most part, in very small regions—primarily at the municipal level. This results in relatively small constituent or customer bases that are called on to resolve very large problems. Small numbers funding large dollar expenses result in slow responses to serious resiliency problems. In fact, there are approximately 54,000 water utilities across the United States.

As the industry struggles with droughts, intense storms, rising sea levels, nutrients, and emerging contaminants, the question needs to be asked whether the current formula works effectively to solve these problems. Perhaps several questions need to be asked. Can our current local authority network adequately address multi-regional problems? Where does the money come from to invest in these issues? Is the boundary of the utility wide enough to address issues outside the fence? Are water problems local, regional, statewide, multistate, or national? Does our utility model advance technology and entrepreneurship?

Before answering these questions, it is important to understand the thoughts from which the answers are based. There is more than one solution to any problem. The best solutions will come from analyzing the problems and applying direct solutions. Effective and efficient action is a result of a well-defined and funded mission. A well-known example of such thinking is putting a man on the moon. To accomplish this task, the National Aeronautics and Space Administration (NASA) was created in 1958 and funded to win the race to the moon. They accomplished the mission.

The CWA established the same dynamic for water utilities. As a result, almost all local water utilities are extremely successful at providing high quality potable water and treating used water to specified quality limits. The mission is clear. Step 1: Take water in. Step 2: Treat water to specified quality control limits. Step 3: Distribute or release. Funding was provided to add fuel to the rocket and bring the programs off the ground. Water bodies across the United States experienced significant improvement from work performed in the 1970s and 1980s. Water utilities have done a fair job of acquiring funding, adjusting to new "in fence" regulations and even addressing infrastructure needs in collection and distribution systems. Although the complaint about unfunded mandates arise, utilities have raised rates and put together programs that achieve outstanding in fence results, and at the end of the day, the mission is accomplished.

The new water issues expand beyond the fence. The problems of today are outside of the traditional issues utilities have faced. Existing stormwater systems are designed to prevent flooding and move water away from dwellings. In general, stormwater activity is significantly underfunded, and projects are targeted at increased wet weather activity and flood protection. Non-point source pollution is the biggest contributor to the remaining pollution loads across the country. These issues preside outside the fence of the local utility. Utilities are stretched to fund existing infrastructure and regulatory needs. Therefore, it can be overwhelming to contemplate taking on these much broader problems. Water supply utilities have done a great job with ensuring sufficient source water, but with drought conditions arising in various parts of the country, this problem is breaking through traditional fence lines.

Water utilities need to engage in today's issues in order to fulfill their current mission. However, it may be time to step back and consider another alternative. Can we create organizations that have a broader mission and can work at these problems on a macro level? Again, effective and efficient action is a result of a well-defined and funded mission.

It should be clear that water utilities are functioning well within the parameters of their original mission and will be needed regardless of consideration of a new model. The local model is working and should continue. Cleaned and recycled water is provided to the environment. The regulators at the federal and state levels provide oversight. This too has worked well and should continue going forward.

It is the larger problems that span multiple communities, including public and private sector interests, where progress and goals are falling short. In order to resolve these issues, it may be time to consider the need for another utility. In the recent "Report of the Mississippi River Nutrient Dialogues" convened by the U.S. Water Alliance in 2013–2014, this concept is presented as a Watershed Protection Utility.

The utility as envisioned in the report would be established as a private company. This idea is founded on the following rationale. The span of service would be at a state level, if not multistate or national. It would be established with the ability to charge residents a fee for environmental services. The environmental, sustainability and resilience issues being faced today all point to every human's dependence on clean water and a healthy environment. Roosevelt's urgency in 1908 should be ringing loud and clear today. Since all humans rely on the environment, it is right to contribute to sustaining the environment and address issues outside the fence. The mission would be clear—address major water issues that span multiple communities and jurisdictions from an efficient, big picture approach.

In a world where the average cell phone bill is around $100 per month and television and computer services cost another $100 per month, our environment is significantly undervalued. It is commonly accepted that everyone should have the right to live in a healthy environment in a sustainable world, without the threat of disaster, and clean water services at no cost. These tremendous benefits are not free. In fact, they are starting to be recognized as a tremendously valuable commodity. Certainly, they are more valuable than a cell phone or television. Recognizing and assigning this value would transform our water environment, provide the resources to address the problems of today and tomorrow and change the world. The world is in dire need of sustainable technology and practices. The next industrial revolution will be environmental, sustainable technology. Creating a private market with significant dollars—rocket fuel—driving innovation and solutions would produce incredible mission results. In an economy that needs a new market driver, a $100 per month Watershed Protection Utility fee would launch a $140 billion dollar industry in this country. That is a lot of fuel and energy that could be harnessed for the environment and for the economy. Like NASA, the technology advances would multiply the economic opportunities.

The world is at a crossroads in terms of being stewards of the planet. In order to sustain life and adjust to the changes in catastrophic weather events, we will need to create a focus on sustainability and reduce consumption. I heard in a speech that the mass of ants on the planet far exceeds the mass of human life. Despite their tremendous mass, ants manage to add benefit to the Earth and leave the soil in a better state than if they did not exist. Humans need to figure this out. The time is now and the needs are known. There is more than one way to solve the problems we face. This short chapter represents a possibility. Hopefully, it inspires the thought that there is a new horizon for water.

MICHAEL DEANE
EXECUTIVE DIRECTOR
NATIONAL ASSOCIATION OF WATER COMPANIES

Crucial Conversations About the Value of America's Water Infrastructure

During the last 100 years, the water industry has done such an effective job of invisibly and reliably delivering drinking water to the tap at a reasonable cost that we inadvertently diminished the value of the water systems that deliver it. Today's homeowners, businesses, and industries should expect, but not take for granted, that their tap water is clean, safe, and readily available for drinking, cooking, bathing, firefighting, farming, manufacturing, and recreation—24 hours a day, all year long. Water saturates every aspect of our life, and it stands to reason that the systems that deliver water are as valuable as the water itself.

Although water is a natural resource, the simple fact is that untreated water from rain, lakes, streams, rivers, and springs does not meet EPA water quality standards. Water utilities essentially add value to the water when they treat it to make it drinkable and usable. Safe drinking water that meets or exceeds the U.S. Environmental Protection Agency's (USEPA) water quality standards in the Safe Drinking Water and Clean Water Acts requires a vast, well-maintained infrastructure to treat and deliver water. If America's complex system of pipes, valves, pumps, tanks, and treatment facilities continues on the current course, water quality could be severely compromised.

In many communities across the country, unfortunately, water systems have only received a fraction of the investment needed for proper maintenance and replacement. Much of America's water infrastructure is outdated, overused and underserviced. As we talk about the value of water and the systems that deliver that value, there is one indisputable fact. It will cost a lot of money to fix this problem. USEPA's *2013 Needs Assessment Survey* states it will cost $384 billion to repair and replace our nation's drinking water infrastructure by 2030. That averages out to about $24 billion a year ($2 billion a month) for the next 16 years if we start today. It is also important to note that today's water infrastructure challenges rely on today's assessments. What about tomorrow's assessments? These costs are daunting whether you are counting dollars or days.

By contrast, water service is normally the lowest percentage utility cost for households and businesses compared to gas, oil, telephone, and electricity. When one considers that it takes more money to build and replace water infrastructure than it does infrastructure for gas, oil, and electricity, the value of the infrastructure that delivers drinking water is even more profound. The *ITT 2010 Value of Water Survey Report* states that 95% of American voters believe water is the most important service they receive.

Consumers of water and public officials do not want to pay more for things they do not understand. That is why it is time for the water industry to have crucial conversations that result in meaningful actions to fix our water infrastructure and deter a national crisis. Crucial conversations that lead to action need to start with the basics about water so Americans and their elected leaders in communities throughout the country have a context for understanding the tenuous condition of a given water system and the threat it imposes to our quality of life. It is time to have ongoing, crucial conversations with people outside the water industry about water and the water systems that have been neglected for too long.

If we lived in our homes and worked at our businesses and rarely, if ever, did any general upkeep for 50 or 60 years, what would happen? Would they work properly? What if you were required to own one car for the first 50 years of your life and you rarely maintained it properly?

Today's water consumers' and public officials' understanding of the basic facts about water and water systems can lead to action. Just because people turn on the tap does not mean they understand where water comes from and how it got there. More than three quarters of Americans, excluding those receiving well water, cannot accurately identify the natural source of water used in their homes.[1] The fact that there is a finite amount of water on the earth is a good place to start having crucial conversations with today's consumers—water is irreplaceable, and we cannot reproduce it.

The quality of our nation's water systems is essential to growing businesses and industries that attract and keep jobs. When every $1 billion invested in water infrastructure creates 26,000 jobs,[2] it is easy to see the value of water and the systems that provide it. Each job created in the water and wastewater industry at the local level creates 3.68 jobs in the national economy.[3]

---

[1] The Nature Conservancy. (2011, March). *More than three-quarters of Americans do not know where their water comes from.*

[2] 2009 Report, Clean Water Council & National Utility Contractors Association.

[3] 2008 U.S. Department of Commerce, Bureau of Economic Analysis.

The quality of the water we drink is the highest priority for any water utility. Water utilities have played an important role in the establishment of federal and state water quality standards, working closely with the EPA and other organizations to ensure that treated water and its by-products are safe for their customers and technicians.[4]

We need to continue to leverage the expertise and resources of all water utilities to deliver sustainable, consumption-based strategies and technologies designed to manage the delivery of the right quality of water for the intended purpose—drinking, toilets, watering lawns, farming, and manufacturing. When America's water utilities start working together, proven solutions that can attract $384 billion in capital will emerge—but we need to accelerate the process that leads to capital investment. The capital to solve our water infrastructure problems is in the marketplace looking for the right public–private partnership project with the right solution for each community. Further, leveraging the strengths of all water utilities to identify ways to finance new infrastructure, we can also combine our talents and expertise. Water utility professionals from the private sector, together with the public sector, can solve the problems we face today.

As we mobilize our efforts to have crucial conversations with people and elected leaders outside the water industry about the value of water, we need to promote the message that water's value is achieved and sustained when our water systems are well maintained. Well-maintained water systems connect us, grow jobs, keep us safe and healthy, and sustain our environment.

Crucial conversations with America's water consumers and elected leaders start with the undeniable truth that water *connects us* all. What we do with water and the systems that deliver that water affects someone somewhere. As we inform more and more people about the realities

---

[4] NAWC. (2014, July). *Water challenges: Health and environment.*

of our water infrastructure challenges, we have the opportunity to perpetuate new values and ethics about the use of water.

Crucial conversations about water infrastructure mean telling stories about real people who have *jobs* and careers in the water industry. Where there is water, there is *opportunity*. A job in the water industry means you can go home knowing you did something meaningful as part of a team that delivers quality water from the source to the tap. Jobs in the water industry are essential to creating robust local economies and stimulating new ventures.

Crucial conversations about water infrastructure mean we have the opportunity to show how the community of water professionals across this country can come together and tackle major threats to our *safety and health*. When Hurricane Sandy flooded coastal communities and inland cities, the water utilities worked together with the Red Cross, FEMA, and other water professionals to ensure clean water was there when it could not come through the tap. When you drive down a street and see new pavement or concrete, consider the possibility that your water professionals fixed a problem in the cold of the night or the heat of the day to restore someone's water service.

Crucial conversations about water infrastructure must always include the importance of *protecting our environment* by keeping rivers and streams free of debris and trash. Many water utilities have employees and community-minded citizens who take a day of their weekend to clean up water sources. The Clean Water Act was designed to control and restrict the release of unlawful pollutants and discharges like sewage and chemicals.

Our water quality is better than it has ever been, but that will not continue without immediate, sustained investment in the water infrastructure.

Let's elevate our effort to change the course we are on and have crucial conversations with people outside the water industry about the value of water and water infrastructure. America's quality of life depends on it.

SUSAN N. STORY
PRESIDENT AND CHIEF EXECUTIVE OFFICER
AMERICAN WATER

The Science of Water

More than one year ago, I left a 31-year career in the energy industry to join American Water. It was the toughest yet most rewarding professional decision I have ever made. The reason I took the leap was simple, the story of water is utterly compelling to me. Our country is at a crossroads when it comes to a reliable water supply, as well as the infrastructure used to deliver it. I did not want to be on the sidelines; I wanted to be with a company that could help the United States find solutions.

With each new career comes new learnings, and my switch to water did not disappoint. One of the more exciting things for this former nuclear engineer was to learn the role innovation is playing in tackling our water and wastewater challenges. The diversity of my formal education and my array of experiences in the energy industry has been a boon to my career, giving me both the technical know-how and the business acumen to run an efficient operation. However, most people do not understand or even think about how scientific and technological the water industry is. Many people look at our industry and imagine pipes and pumps—very slow and far from high tech, when the opposite is actually the truth.

There are two overarching concerns when it comes to water and wastewater in the United States. First is the critical need to upgrade the nation's water and wastewater infrastructure, and second are the issues we are facing around water supply. There are one million miles of water pipe in the United States, and many of those miles are aging. A major water main breaks every two minutes with two trillion gallons of treated water lost every year at a direct cost of about $2.6 billion. Oftentimes, these water lines rupture underground where it is not visible—risking major damage to roadways and structures. In addition, with the 700,000 miles of sewer mains, over 900 billion gallons of untreated sewage is discharged in the United States every year.

Given these facts, the entire cycle of the water process is affected. Restoring existing water systems as they reach the end of their useful lives and expanding them to serve a growing population is estimated by the Environmental Protection Agency to cost over $650 billion in the next 20 years. The American Society of Civil Engineers estimates that $1 trillion is needed over that same time frame.

Related to the challenge of infrastructure is the challenge of a limited water supply. Obviously, this is a big challenge in California and Texas right now, but it goes beyond these traditionally dry states. As the previous summer's drought showed us, water utilities across the country need to plan for their systems to be sustainable in times of reduced supply. The recently released *Report on Freshwater Supply* from the Government Accountability Office (GAO) states that according to state water managers, experts, and literature GAO reviewed, freshwater shortages are expected to continue into the future. In particular, 40 of 50 state water managers expected shortages in some portion of their states under average conditions in the next 10 years.

These are daunting challenges, but ones that can be met. Innovation is key, and while technological innovations will be required, the challenge is bringing innovation to the marketplace.

A few years ago, American Water formed our Innovation Development Process to specifically look for new technologies and accelerate their validation and acceptance within the water industry. This approach to innovation has helped to permeate an "innovation philosophy" throughout the organization and industry.

From a technology perspective, we are working on a smart water grid—not just pipes, not just valves, but we are looking at flow monitors, pressure monitors, smart meters and SCADA devices in water plants so we can monitor water to ensure it is at the highest quality, and we can deliver it reliably.

We are particularly focused on acoustic monitoring, which helps identify cracks before they become a more acute problem. If we catch cracks early, it is up to 10 times less expensive to repair them. Two of the technologies that we use are FCS Permalog sensors, which are used on water main valves to record sound vibration data that can be downloaded and analyzed periodically; and Itron MLOG technology, which allows for continuous monitoring. Reducing water pressure can also reduce leakage. American Water is a partner in a two-year award from the Israel–U.S. Binational Industrial Research and Development (BIRD) Foundation along with Stream Control Ltd., an Israeli start-up company, for the development of an advanced pressure management system. International efforts to reduce leakage have confirmed that reducing excessive pressure not only reduces the volume of leaks through pipes but also reduces the frequency of pipe failures.

Last year, we signed an agreement with a company that developed a standardized communications platform that creates interoperability among meter manufacturers. In addition to seamlessly integrating different types of meters, the SET platform is able to receive many kinds of data from the water distribution network including pressure, water quality, leak detection and flow, not just meter data. This makes for a powerful tool, not only for meter reading and billing purposes, but also for the collection of real-time system data so that we can better manage and operate the distribution network.

Reducing energy also plays a role in saving water. About four percent of the electricity consumed in the United States is used for collecting, treating and moving water and wastewater. As such, American Water is partnering with ENBALA Power Networks to use demand response practices at our water pumping stations. This way, we can work with local electric utilities to slow down or speed up pumping as part of smart grid programs; returning power to the grid during peak periods.

Another example involves a process called NPXpress, patented in September 2011, which dramatically reduces the amount of energy needed for aeration activities at wastewater treatment plants. American Water has been awarded three patents for NPXpress to reduce aeration energy consumption by up to 50% and supplemental carbon source by 100%. This technology has been implemented at seven full-scale wastewater treatment plants in New Jersey and New York and is currently being implemented at a system in California as part of the company's overall initiative to achieve sustainable, energy-neutral wastewater treatment.

Turning to water supply, water utilities across the country need to plan for their systems to be sustainable in times of threatened supply, which is yet another reason to ensure the water that is being treated and pumped is actually making it to homes and businesses. There are not many sources of water. There is groundwater and surface water. If those are not adequate, we need to look at efforts like reuse and desalination.

Over 90% of the treated wastewater in the United States is not recycled. American Water sees this water as a valued resource and has been at the forefront of research to study and promote reuse. Since 2006, American Water has conducted 11 research projects sponsored by the WateReuse Research Foundation. These projects have examined issues dealing with water quality, public health safety, best management practices, treatment process, and energy efficiency. These studies support the approximately 40 reuse systems owned or operated by American Water and provide the strategic groundwork for future growth in this area.

American Water also operates reuse systems in five high-rise buildings in Battery Park City, Manhattan. It uses segregated piping systems to collect, treat and recycle wastewater and stormwater for a variety of purposes, including toilet flushing, air conditioning and irrigation for rooftop gardens and an adjacent park. By reusing wastewater for non-potable applications, these buildings' potable water needs are reduced by nearly half. Together, these five buildings save approximately 56 million gallons of water per year.

In addition, American Water operates the water reuse system at Gillette Stadium, the home of the New England Patriots. The facility's double piping system treats recycled wastewater from the stadium, as well as from adjacent office complexes and stores, saving 250,000 gallons of water for every major event.

As such, reclaimed water need not only be confined to wastewater; highly saline sources, such as ocean or deep groundwater, can also be treated. The process of water reuse can involve desalination, where the salt content is removed, and membrane filtration, where contaminants are removed via a membrane process. Furthermore, these technologies are continuously being streamlined, becoming more cost effective and energy efficient.

Lastly, reuse and desalination technology can help us look at water differently. American Water is challenging people to think about the broader notion of "One Water." This term describes the company's long-term strategy of not thinking about individual segments of water but rather thinking that it is all water, and it is all a resource. It is thinking about the system holistically, from the start of the watershed through to the various points of use. For example, stormwater is often a valuable water supply source. Yet in many locations, it is treated and managed as if it were a waste or a problem.

Where water is scarce or of impaired quality, discussion tends to focus less on overcoming the "yuck" factor and more on providing the flexibility to match water quality to a specific use. According to a GE consumer survey unveiled in October 2012, two thirds of Americans (66%) feel positive about water reuse. In addition, although the majority of Americans hesitate at the concept of "toilet-to-tap" recycling, more than 80% of Americans surveyed indicated that they support using recycled water for many "toilet-to-turf" uses—activities that require significant amounts of non-potable water, such as agricultural irrigation, power generation, landscaping, industrial processing and manufacturing, toilet flushing, and car washing.

As new challenges in the water industry arise, so will the opportunity to increase collaboration and innovation. Water is not a low technology industry. In fact, American Water uses its expertise and research capabilities to evaluate new technology and its facilities to pilot test and become early adopters. As a result, the company is not only benefitting from an innovation, but also helping to bring a valuable new technology to the rest of the water industry. Through innovation and by embracing the powerful combination of public service and private enterprise, we can build the water infrastructure our communities need to thrive and to be healthy. We need to focus on smart solutions that are resilient, sustainable, and affordable.

If nothing else, it is our job in the water industry to remember that what we do changes lives. It provides for health. It enables energy production and electricity generation. It grows food.

Our economy runs on water. We must provide clean, safe, reliable, and affordable water to our customers today, tomorrow, and into the future.

KAREN PALLANSCH
CHIEF EXECUTIVE OFFICER
ALEXANDRIA RENEW ENTERPRISES

Water – Maintaining the Miracle Molecule

arlier this year, the World Economic Forum's Annual Global Risks Report identified the most dangerous threats to our fragile planet. Three of the top ten was water-related: The failure to address climate change, extreme weather events like floods and droughts, and freshwater scarcity and water pollution.

For us, these problems seem far away. Here in Northern Virginia, we have a reliable source of freshwater. Water pollution is largely under control. We assume that there will always be a plentiful supply of clean and safe water. City residents are to be applauded for conserving water use in their day-to-day lives, much as they do electricity and natural gas.

However, this does not mean we should not be concerned. We as a national community need to recognize that greater stress is being placed on our freshwater supplies as our population grows—after all, the city is a great place to live—and as we reinvigorate urban living.

Lest we forget, Virginia is not immune to droughts. Think back to 2002 when then-Governor Warner banned lawn watering and washing cars in most parts of the Commonwealth. Alexandria had voluntary restrictions. Given the wild swings in weather brought about by climate change, can another major drought be ruled out? Perhaps not.

That is why we owe it to ourselves to identify and mitigate the inherent risks and uncertainty associated with water. We need to be vigilant and forward thinking about how we manage our precious water resources. If we are, we can turn a big challenge into a big opportunity for progress and prosperity.

Water is truly the miracle molecule. More than sustaining life and helping to grow the foods that nourish us, water and a reliable water infrastructure fuel our economy, spur job growth, and help build stronger, healthier communities.

Sometimes, it is hard to see the connection in a modern urban setting like Alexandria whose water-dependent light industry and much of its power generation plants are largely a distant memory. The city's 1949 Bicentennial Booklet extolled the Mutual Ice Company plant and railroad car icing station as the largest of its kind east of the Mississippi River. Approximately 58,000 cars of perishable foods were iced there annually, using 100,000 tons of ice. That is a lot of water.

Water still plays a big, though less visible, role in today's economy. The many associations, government agencies, and businesses that call the city of Alexandria home would not be here if we could not supply the freshwater they need and clean the dirty water they produce. Visitors flock to our Old Town area, boosting the local economy, and in turn, generating revenues for important government programs. However, none of this would be possible without freshwater and the transformation of the Potomac from a health hazard to a tourist and recreational magnet.

Indeed, the city has certainly come a long way from the days when outhouses were perched at the end of Prince Street over the Potomac. The Alexandria Sanitation Authority began receiving and treating wastewater in 1956 and today, Alexandria Renew cleans dirty water to stringent federal and Commonwealth standards unimaginable back then. The journey was worth it.

However, there's a flip side to water. Reagan National Airport's rain gauges have been getting a workout of late, but a lack of water thousands of miles away can hit you in the wallet when shopping locally. For example, the current drought in California is laying waste to farmland that produces nearly one half of the nation's fruit, nuts and vegetables. This is causing a spike in food prices that all of us will feel—from Alexandria, Virginia, to Alexandria, California.

Water uncertainty could also affect your 401(k) and other investments. Huge multinational corporations are for the first time viewing climate change and extreme weather as real threats to their operations and balance sheets. As freshwater sources dry up, so does the ability of these corporations to expand their businesses and global markets.

So when it comes to water, what should we do, and just as importantly, what can we do? I believe that a holistic approach to meeting both freshwater and water cleaning challenges is the best strategy. That means conservation alone will not solve local, national, and global freshwater shortages. With growing populations, we cannot conserve our way out of the problem. We must better manage our current and projected freshwater use, which makes using safe, reclaimed water for irrigation, industrial, business and other purposes, a must-have.

At Alexandria Renew, we have already partnered with developers, government, and industry to extend purple pipes carrying reclaimed water from our campus directly to their doorsteps for a variety of approved purposes. We are also constructing a reclaimed water pump station so that tanker trucks can fill up, rather than hooking up to a fire hydrant or spigots that are connected to freshwater lines.

We must also encourage the growing conversation about how and where we should invest our precious water dollars. Should they go toward constructing more brick and mortar facilities like dams, reservoirs, and storage facilities? Or would that money be better spent on enhancing reclaimed water production and use and taking water conservation technology to the next level? It many cases, it will be a combination of both, and that is a good thing.

No one body, group, sector or interest can solve the many water challenges we confront today and will continue to face in the future. We must take steps together. There must be collaboration between the community members, our public servants, and our private enterprises. Our communities, urban and suburban, need and deserve great water quality, delivered by great water infrastructure. Investment in the miracle molecule is investing in a better future for our children and our nation.

LISA SPARROW

PRESIDENT AND CHIEF EXECUTIVE OFFICER
UTILITIES, INC.

With Knowledge Comes Responsibility – The Intersection of Being a CEO of a Water Utility and a Mom

The value of water? It is an interesting question that can be answered in many ways. I'm an engineer, so I cannot help but think of answers in terms of $z = x + y$. But as a mom of young boys, I also cannot help but think of it in terms of softer issues—issues that I largely take for granted as my family moves through its day. In my head, the intersection of those two thoughts goes something like this:

Value of Water = Value of Supply + Value of Convenience + Value of Confidence in Safety and Reliability + Value of Life

Let's start with Value of Supply. I recently watched a TED Talk given by Brene Brown where she mentioned that during her research when people were asked about topics of abundance, they instead responded with their stories of extreme scarcity. Fascinating, and I think a very good concept for all of us to contemplate. The earth is made up roughly of 70% water. We are "good to go," right? Not so much really. Ninety-six percent of the water is contained in our oceans and has a salinity that renders it unhealthy. The cost to desalinate is astronomical, although desperate communities have spent millions of dollars to do just that. Citizens of Toledo, Ohio, are probably well suited to talk about the scarcities of water right now following a toxic algae bloom that left them without any potable water. Or citizens of Atlanta when Lake Lanier dried up a few years ago. Or citizens of California who have experienced extreme drought for multiple years in a row. Or users of Lake Mead that have watched the Lake go nearly dry.

However, those are exceptions we tell ourselves. They may be today, but the reality is that conditions exists nationwide (aging infrastructure, lack of public priority to address it, changing weather patterns, etc.) that make these exceptions more and more common. Water seems like it is everywhere, but access to and the cost of this scarce resource are huge limitations.

What about Value of Convenience? What is the value of water at our kitchen tap? Or factory floor? Or farm irrigation systems? Or power plant cooling tower? Convenience is the variable and the answer is nearly immeasurable. What does our life look like with and without central water service?

My average day as a working mom looks loosely like the following: Wake up, get kids ready, get self ready, feed and drop said kids at preschool, work, come home, feed and get kids in bed, catch up on e-mail, and sleep. All of that assumes and depends on a clean and readily available water supply that is as easy as turning on the sink or tub or shower faucet without giving it another thought. What if it was not quite that easy? How would my day look if I had to provide my own water and wastewater service? I'd get up, shovel the foot of snow from my side-walk to the outhouse, get my kids dressed in their winter gear to take them to it, I'd hand draw some water from my well or rain barrel (and then boil) for my kids' breakfast, spend time throwing on/off winter gear and head in/out of our workplace to go to an outhouse or latrine, draw water to make dinner, draw water for my kids' bath, and bathe in their water to conserve. I would need to modify my habits around wash-ing dishes, hands, floors, and clothes because the water I collected would not be pressurized and thus have no ability to flow. I would then also need to collect that water and carry it back outside to dispose in my yard. I'm thankful I do not live in a high rise. I would also likely then spend some of that day worrying about whether my children have contracted any illnesses from the untreated water we used.

So compare a life with and without water and wastewater service and that adds a lot of time! I think my life is busy and that I worry about my children now, but it is absolutely nothing compared to what people in societies without safe, reliable drinking water and wastewater collection service deal with every day. And that description was just a "basic" day. Imagine one filled with trying to navigate in/out of security to use out-door facilities at an airport, or you have a loved one in a hospital with healthcare workers unable to wash their hands each time they move from patient to patient, or heaven forbid your or a loved one's house is on fire.

I will confess in my real life, even as I know what a scarce resource water is, it is possible you will find my kids playing at the sink, while I use the faucet as a "babysitter." A true sign of ultimately taking it for granted that I know the opportunity cost; yet I continue using it as a babysitter.

So what is the issue with convenience? Well, water is a heavy prod-uct with heavy costs to move it from Point A to Point B. While we can, and should, work to ensure the least able among us have access to affordable drinking water, the reality is there is a price for that convenience. When we see a UPS truck full of Amazon products driving down the road, the cost of that delivery is palpable. Would we expect Jeff Bezos to deliver us a couple of thousand pounds of products to our homes, every day, every year for $1–$2 a day? Of course not. Yet the unseen and hidden infrastructure that brings water to us reliably every day supports the long held idea that water somehow requires "less" to move it. Simply not so. We can debate the issue of who pays for that infrastructure, maintenance, and resulting reliability (and we should have that debate), but it costs a lot of money, period.

Groups such as the U.S. Environmental Protection Agency (EPA) and the American Society of Civil Engineers, among others, have estimated that the cost to replace the aging and potentially dangerous water supply infrastructure is currently in excess of one <u>trillion</u> dollars just in the United States. An honest discussion about the value of water cannot occur without this in the assumption column.

The next variable is the value of confidence in the safety and reliability of our water service. For better or for worse, our EPA provides us strict regulations to ensure public health and safety. They also regulate the safe collection and return of wastewater to our natural environment. Although the "Google mania" world we live in would lead one to believe we can be experts at anything with enough Internet research, the fact is that it takes time, commitment, resources, knowledge, and expertise to determine the effects of contaminants in water. We live in a world (today) that is largely driven by lack of good information, worse yet misinformation, and a willingness to accept headlines that belie the facts beneath them.

For example, if I relied on the Internet: Lead pipes = bad. However, thanks to good science, we now know that disturbing lead service lines actually increases the lead level in water samples, which is a serious issue for young children with developing brains. We have the absolute luxury to live in a time and place where we have scientists who work hard to keep us safe and certified, professional utility personnel at companies like my own who follow scientists' recommendations to ensure a safe water cycle from the aquifer to our taps and back.

Last but not least is the Value of Life. I would not presume in any way to define what value means for anyone's life. However, as a wife to an amazing husband, mother of two of the sweetest boys on the planet (fair enough, I'm biased), sister to two of the best siblings I could ask for, daughter to parents I can only hope to model, and CEO to an experienced organization that cares deeply about the customers to whom they provide service, I have had the luxury of knowing what an incredible life is available, but none of it can be had without water.

So what can be done about some of the issues that face us in regard to the very real scarcity of this precious resource and the prospect of ever-increasing costs headed our way? Let's look at some great examples. The Florida Public Utilities Commission has been pricing water for years recognizing the scarce resource it is.

Specifically, they set a structure that the more you use, the higher the price. The so-called "tiered pricing" acknowledges the scarcity of supply, the "well to tap" convenience, the critical importance of safe and reliable service, and obviously, the value to a better life that water allows, and they have even gone a step further. Consumers and leaders in the state of Florida completely understand the necessity for and value of reusing water for irrigation, car washes, and so on, to protect their potable water supply. They truly "get" the need for conservation. It is not just a go-green bumper sticker.

This in stark contrast to some desert communities that have actively resisted using reclaimed water in their water starved areas—likely because of the perception that potable water will somehow always be there. So that is how I think about the Value of Water. Innovative pricing models, conservation methods, and more ways of communicating the Value of Water are needed to solve these issues. Our society needs the courage and commitment to have difficult conversations and make difficult decisions. These issues are not easy, but they are solvable.

PATRICK DECKER

PRESIDENT AND CHIEF EXECUTIVE OFFICER

XYLEM INC.

A Tale of Two Cities

n October 1848, residents of Boston gathered in Boston Commons to witness the unveiling of the city's first public water system, one of the first in the United States. The event prompted the *Daily Evening Transcript* to write, "The value of such a blessing, freely dispensed throughout our city, is not to be calculated in dollars and cents; for it has relations inestimable with the moral and physical welfare of generations present and to come."[1]

This attitude that water is a blessing, freely dispensed and not to be calculated, has guided the role that water has played throughout the last few centuries in the developed world. Prior to that celebratory day in Boston Commons, there had been heated debate over whether the water supply should remain private or become a public service. The latter lobby won out, and water became an urban blessing in Boston. Today, in

---

[1] Retrieved from www.bostonglobe.com/ideas/2013/05/04/boston-water-public-private/ Jzj88ifSRYs9DEcU2m0tKJ/story.html

the developed world, unlike almost every other finite resource, water is cheap and almost always available.

The perception of unlimited availability, however, is a mirage. In just one generation, by 2050, 6.4 billion of an estimated 9.6 billion people on the planet will crowd into cities, placing unprecedented demands on limited water resources.[2] Against this context, the second wave of urbanization will divide the world into two futures, which we will explore through the story of two fictional cities: Alpha City and Omega City. In 2050, Alpha City is shrinking, destitute, bleak, and a parable of urban decay. By contrast, Omega City is thriving, densely populated with healthy and prosperous citizens. In 2050, the success of all cities will be determined by one factor: How they have governed and managed their water.

Alpha City is an urban metropolis that in 2050 is suffering from the human and financial costs of an old, degraded, leaky, dirty, and dysfunctional water system. Despite determined efforts each day, its managers struggle to provide water to their customers. Water, already naturally scarce, leaks freely through dilapidated pipes not unlike Dhaka, Bangladesh, where two out of every five gallons of water pumped into the system bleed out through corroded pipes.[3] Water quality is compromised by aging pipes operating at partial pressure that permit sewage and contaminants to infiltrate into the drinking water supply, a phenomenon not unfamiliar to the residents of Mexico City, where tanks made from asbestos still serve low-income areas and rusty, moldy pipes deliver yellow water to the city at large.[4]

Alpha City's residents are also concerned about environmental quality. In this, they are not alone. A few examples illustrate the point. In

---

[2] Retrieved from
www.who.int/gho/urban_health/situation_trends/urban_population_growth_text/e/
[3] United Nations Development Programme. (2006). *Human development report, 2006: Beyond scarcity.*
[4] Retrieved from www.theguardian.com/cities/2014/feb/05/mexico-city-water-torture-city-sewage

China today, 70% of rivers and lakes are polluted past the point of being drinkable and two thirds of the country's 700 cities suffer shortages.[5] Lake Tai, a large freshwater lake near Shanghai, once lauded in Chinese poetry for its beauty, has become a dumping ground for wastewater and garbage. Government efforts to clean up the lake have failed in the face of vested economic interests, rendering it unusable and dangerous. Even in more affluent communities, the problem is evident. Lake Erie, for example, suffers from rising levels of phosphorus from fertilizer and septic systems; yet only after Toledo, Ohio's water supply was threatened does talk of change begin in earnest.

By 2050, the most obvious symptom of Alpha City's water insecurity is the city's economy, which has been in decline for decades.[6] City managers realized too late that the city's unreliable water supply was materially diminishing its citizens' quality of life and the ease of doing business. By the time they were able to act, those businesses and families who were able to leave had already done so.

At first read, Alpha City's experience may seem unrealistic or imaginary—but even today, water is becoming a driver of locational decisions for manufacturers. Today's manufacturers must already factor water availability into their operational planning. One Silicon Valley technology firm manufactures microchips in water-scarce China, using 3,400 gallons to manufacture a single chip. JP Morgan Global Equity Research estimates that a "brief water-related shutdown at a manufacturing plant could compromise all material in production for an entire quarter."[7]

Alpha City's experience is a cautionary tale. Once a thriving urban hub, the city withered from its inability to manage its water resources and infrastructure. Warning signs such as pollution and water delivery failures were visible, but decision makers continually deferred invest-

---

[5] United Nations Development Programme. (2006). *Human development report, 2006: Beyond scarcity.*

[6] Retrieved from www.nytimes.com/2014/07/04/opinion/going-without-water-in-detroit.html?_r=0

[7] Retrieved from http://pdf.wri.org/jpmorgan_watching_water.pdf

ment and delayed action. In 2050, the challenges are undeniable, but it may now be too late.

On the other hand, Omega City anticipated, embraced, and invested in the right kind of change for its water infrastructure, guided by three interdependent and measurable priorities: Water productivity, quality, and resilience.

Water Productivity

Omega City's planners knew that while citizens had little awareness of water scarcity, the city's rapidly growing economy would soon run up against real constraints in water supply. Their first focus, therefore, was to increase Omega's **water productivity**, the efficient delivery and use of clean, processed water. By aggressively investing in efficient water infrastructure and demand-side conservation measures, Omega City dramatically reduced water losses and waste, as well as chemical and energy consumption. These investments enabled the city to support an expanding economic base while sustaining a thriving natural environment, in turn supporting a rich variety of ecosystem services including water sports, tourism and water-front development.

Omega's City's managers turned water productivity into a daily obsession, because they noticed a virtuous cycle connecting infrastructure and ecosystem renewal, economic growth, and reinvestment into the community's future. Today's leading cities are already driving similar gains, and water solution companies such as Xylem are helping them design energy-efficient and water-efficient systems that set the stage for meaningful gains in water productivity.

Water Quality

Omega City's planners then turned to the goal of improving **water quality**, which they defined as the efficient and effective management and renewal of wastewater. The city noticed that its wastewater management systems were outdated, consuming significant energy and far from world class in effluent quality. Rather than treating nutrient-rich and energy-rich sludge and biosolids as waste, planners in Omega City see them as valuable resources that contain 10 times the energy needed to treat them. They recognize that it is technically feasible to recover energy from sludge and that renewable energy can be directly used in wastewater treatment, reducing the city's dependency on conventional electricity. The greater the quantity of energy produced within the industry, the more the industry can help reduce emissions of greenhouse gases. Omega City's systems are designed to unlock the value of these natural assets by driving greater water efficiency, energy efficiency, nutrient and energy recovery, and water reuse.

To maximize their ability to reuse water, Omega City took a cue from Singapore, an island nation and megacity with little land available to collect and store rainwater. Singapore had the foresight to invest in research and technology and found an integrated way to turn crisis into opportunity. In a bilateral agreement, Singapore buys raw water from larger neighbor Malaysia, purifies it, uses what it needs and sells back the surplus, sometimes at a profit. A third of the nation is served by four NEWater plants, which produce "high-grade reclaimed water purified using advanced membrane technologies and ultraviolet disinfection, making it ultraclean and safe to drink." The technology and approach adopted by Singapore can be adapted by any aspiring Omega City. Many cities have adopted variations on the cost-effective return of treated wastewater to its source.

Water Resilience

Finally, Omega City's planners realized that the city faced a range of unpredictable water risks, ranging from drought-induced shortages to storm-induced flooding. They worked with local partners to design a **water resilience** strategy that includes investments in both preparation and response. Preparation included hardening the city's infrastructure to increase resistance to the most common challenges, as well as building redundancies and backup systems to contain the impact of any system failures. Omega City prepared for torrential rains and subsequent runoff by updating its pumping stations to be able to handle these excesses and also by using sophisticated analytical instruments throughout the local water infrastructure that alert authorities in real time to mounting water threats, including natural disasters and contamination.

A recent example of how vital resilience is to today's modern city is Hurricane Sandy. The massive flooding and power outages brought on by the Superstorm in 2012 caused billions of dollars' worth of damage. Yet, the situation could have been worse. Leading up to the storm, through the use of analytical instruments and sophisticated monitoring equipment, teams were able to track the storm and plan and prepare for the recovery efforts. Similarly, during and immediately after the storm, New York City teams stockpiled and distributed dewatering equipment, including 200 Xylem submersible dewatering pumps to pivotal infrastructure caught in the hurricane's projected path. The powerful pumps ran without electricity, moving massive amounts of water to minimize— or eliminate—flood damage at their operations. The rapid response raised the bar for how any Omega City can manage the unavoidable and prepare for the worst. Resilience requires translating the lessons of recovery into a new round of preparation by identifying and addressing potential failure modes to prevent future impacts.

From Alpha to Omega

What explains Alpha's failure to adapt even as Omega thrived? Omega City recognized the importance of three critical factors—early and strategic investment, the creation of public–private partnerships and innovation.

Early and Strategic Investment

One notable current-day example of meaningful investment is in Colombia, where 17 urban centers (with a total population of 1.2 million people) hired local firms through long-term contracts to operate water supply systems for the poor, with positive economic and service delivery outcomes. Another good example is in the state of California, where 100,000 people still lack basic water access. In this instance, a new state mandate supporting human right to water is met by cross subsidies: Productive firms that demand more water and pay more for secure flows in a rising rate structure, rewarding investments in per-unit efficiency and ensuring all users are more equitably served.

Through these kinds of inclusive, collaborative, and locally scaled approaches, Omega City turned what was formerly an impoverished system into a virtuous cycle.

Partnerships

To achieve Omega-level water productivity, quality and resilience by 2050 will require a united front and collaboration between funding agencies, regulatory bodies, voters, large companies, entrepreneurs, and water consumers. Partnering across sectors is the ultimate catalyst to water security. No one party can bridge the 40% water gap between future water demand and capacity.[8] Omega City was successful because it combined investment with leading innovation and informed policy.

Governments must look for partners, understanding that there is often a business case for collaboration to fill portfolio gaps or take bets on new opportunities. Cities around the world are striving toward that balance today: a tour around the world's prospective Omega Cities reveals that invention, collaboration and commitment are creating improved urban environments.

In just the last few decades, the government of Quito, Ecuador realized that preservation of the "natural infrastructure" in upstream headwaters presented a clear financial value proposition. Forward-thinking officials prepared a rational prospectus for the water and electrical utility

---

8 Retrieved from
www.mckinsey.com/client_service/sustainability/latest_thinking/charting_our_future

and a brewing company, all heavy water users, and persuaded them to combine their resources in a trust fund—the Water Protection Fund for Quito—which grew 250-fold over eight years from $21,000 in seed funds to $5.4 million in interest-bearing capital. The basis for this dramatic shift was to see water as not only a political or social good and human right, but also an economic force unto itself. With that priority in place, investing in the source—the watershed as a service—was the next logical step.[9] Within a decade, two million people were benefitting from the protection of secure water, and the model has been replicated in 13 more water funds throughout the Andes.[10]

The private sector has a critical role to play. Specifically, companies can apply innovation to upgrade early warning capabilities. The faster we identify where storms are likeliest to hit, the better we can target efforts to prevent and respond to damage. Technologies that link sensor networks, large-scale data analysis, and communication systems provide decision makers with timely information to guide response. We already have many of the ingredients needed to build resilient operating systems in cities around the world; now, it is a question of affordability and coordination.

Innovation

For decades, Singapore has worked to establish itself as a hydro-hub, testing and implementing new technologies on a large scale, backed by government support with a high degree of public awareness. These technologies work best in collaboration with other like-minded parties. As such, in partnership with Xylem, Visenti, a Singapore-based company that supports the water sector with technology for monitoring water networks, is providing a system that will enable the country's national

---

[9] Retrieved from
www.fondosdeagua.org/sites/default/files/WATER%20FUNDS%20spreads%20alta%2FINAL.pdf
[10] Retrieved from www.naturalcapitalproject.org/pubs/TNC_Water_Funds_Report.pdf

water agency to utilize energy-efficient technology and smart sensing platforms that reduce energy consumption, maximize water quality, and ensure optimal network conditions around Singapore's water infrastructure. The high-tech system is designed to detect problems with water flow, pressure and quality, sending wireless signals that sound early alarms that allow the water agency to address leaks, clogs, low-flow and water quality issues quickly—and avoid some of them altogether.

A surprising hydro-hub is Milwaukee, Wisconsin. Although it sits on one of the world's largest and most pristine natural reservoirs, Lake Michigan, it has galvanized political, commercial, and public support in response to hardship, in its case, economic adversity.

The "Rust Belt" postindustrial city decided that in order to compete with other urban areas, and to lay groundwork for a renaissance, it needed to develop core competencies. Hence, a progressive coalition of public officials and private companies like IBM and Badger Meter chose to focus on water, investing in education, networking events, business venture incubators, and strategic alliances enabling the region to become a World Water Hub for freshwater economic development and education.

These are a few examples of cities that are positioned to be Omega Cities in 2050. Unlike reactive Alpha City, they proactively developed their capacity for water productivity, quality, and resilience by cooperating across sectors. They offer more than hope—they offer practical, successful models for what other cities can do—no matter where they are located, their size, or their stage of development.

A Cautionary Tale

This tale of two cities is less cautionary than it is reality. Success in 2050 will depend on the choices made today. Any urban center has the power to become an Omega City. It requires significant recognition by public and private leaders alike that water is the matrix of urban life. To continue to ensure water quality and its availability will require continued investment.

The days of freely dispensed water without regard for the monetary cost are drawing to a close. The launch of the public water system in Boston marked the official transition from wooden to iron pipes, an important technological advancement.

Today's critical transition must be the move from a system of temporary stopgap solutions and reactionary measures to a more complete collaboration across public and private sectors to ensure the welfare of generations to come.

KEN KIRK
EXECUTIVE DIRECTOR
NATIONAL ASSOCIATION OF CLEAN WATER
AGENCIES

The Value of Water and the Utility of the Future

Since passage of the Clean Water Act in 1972, clean water utility leaders have amassed more than four decades of experience implementing the Act's complex requirements. These leaders have developed a level of sophistication that could not have been contemplated even 10 years ago.

Although traditional public health and environmental objectives will always be central, the model of the Water Resources Utility of the Future (UOTF) is evolving in new and exciting directions. The UOTF separates, extracts, reuses, and generates valuable water, energy, nutrients, and other commodities from wastewater while using utility assets in innovative ways to reduce costs, increase revenue, and strengthen the local and national economies.

Clean water utilities have become so dependable, effective, and efficient over the last several decades that for most people, they are largely "out of sight, out of mind." In my view, water is ever present and in everything we do—we can bathe ourselves and our children, drink from taps and water fountains, flush our toilets, go to the beach—all while virtually never having to worry about it. In short, the value of water provides everyone in this country with an inestimable and incalculable "peace of mind." This peace of mind constitutes the true value of water. This peace of mind constitutes the true power of water.

Historically, clean water utilities sought to collect human and industrial wastewater and pipe it as far downstream, as quickly as possible, to central treatment works to remove harmful constituents so that receiving waters would meet applicable environmental standards. For decades, that model worked well. Today, more than 90% of the U.S. population enjoys such services through more than $500 billion in public assets into which the nation as a whole invests more than $55 billion a year to remove more than 90% of organic inputs, an estimated 55% of nutrients, and nearly all harmful bacteria. Environmental outcomes are equally impressive—according to the U.S. Environmental Protection Agency (EPA) and state analyses, municipal wastewater discharges account for less than 10% of the remaining water quality impairment of the nation's rivers, streams, lakes, reservoirs, and coastal shoreline and only about 30% of impaired estuaries.

What Are the Forces Behind the UOTF?

In large part, the UOTF is emerging today in response to a series of unprecedented challenges. Costs of removing the initial few increments of pollutants from wastewaters in the 1970s and 1980s—even in the 1990s—were relatively low compared to the current and future costs of advanced treatment to remove nutrients and to store and treat wet weather flows. Compounding the financial situation further, much of our existing infrastructure is old and must be replaced over the next several decades. For an increasing number of utilities, these combined costs are proving untenable.

Funding for clean water has shifted dramatically over this period from a shared, intergovernmental approach to an almost exclusively local, user-financed approach. According to the U.S. Bureau of the Census, the local share of investment in clean water capital works increased steadily from about 50% in the late 1970s and early 1980s to more than 95% today (operations and maintenance costs have always been locally financed). Over this period, the doubling or tripling of sewer costs raises questions of affordability for many types of ratepayers in more and more utilities across America.

Delivering Value to Ratepayers

There is no standard for a Utility of the Future. Every UOTF innovates around its own regulatory, fiscal, and community conditions. Yet all UOTFs create value in the form of reduced operating and capital costs, increased rate and non-rate revenues, and/or stronger communities that in turn lead to a stronger utility bottom line and reduced rates charged to households and businesses. They do this through energy and operational efficiency; energy recovery, and energy generation; water and materials reuse; green infrastructure; and community, and other partnerships.

The Energy–Water Nexus

Energy costs represent nine to 12% of clean water utility operating budgets, on average, or about $2.5–$3 billion a year across the nation. Even a relatively modest reduction of three to five percent in energy use from routine energy efficiency activities, such as improving blower or motor efficiency, use of heat exchangers to capture waste heat, or motion-sensitive lighting, can reduce annual energy costs for this sector by $100–$150 million.

There are more than 1,000 clean water utilities across the nation engaging in energy efficiency and production activity. Many are now co-digesting by taking in food waste, which boosts electricity production even further. According to the EPA, if only half the food waste generated each year in the United States was anaerobically digested, enough electricity would be generated to power more than 2.5 million homes for a year. That represents about $2.6 billion in electric savings and/or new revenue for clean water utilities and the economy.

If clean water utilities in the United States reduced electricity demand by 50% through a combination of efficiency, methane-driven microturbines, and renewable energy generation, we would as a sector reduce total CO_2 emissions by some 28 million metric tons a year, or about 0.5% of total national emissions of CO_2. That is the equivalent of taking about six million cars off U.S. roads, or about two percent of all registered cars in this country.

Similarly, clean water utilities are capitalizing on their horizontal assets like land and building roofs to install solar photovoltaics (PV) and, in many locations, they are taking advantage of prevailing winds by installing windmills to generate supplemental energy.

Water Reuse and Recycling

Water is one of the most valuable commodities in many parts of the nation, especially with key regions facing historic droughts. As a result, many clean water utilities actively market their effluent for industrial cooling, industrial processing, landscape and agricultural irrigation, firefighting, ecological enhancement, and groundwater recharge. Aside from de-facto indirect reuse, which occurs across the United States when drinking water utilities intake river water mixed with discharges from upstream clean water utilities, a huge upsurge in indirect and even direct potable reuse appears inevitable.

The economic benefits to clean water utilities and their ratepayers are obvious—every gallon of reused wastewater represents new income, or offsets the cost of potable water supply for which recycled water substitutes. However, this revenue stream is still largely untapped. Although non-potable wastewater reuse has doubled over the last decade to about two billion gallons a day, this represents only about five percent of total municipal wastewater discharged, according to the WateReuse Association. The potential for additional reuse, and with it, generation of new revenue, is significant. According to the National Research Council of the National Academy of Sciences, some 12 billion gallons of municipal wastewater effluent is discharged each day to an ocean or estuary (where water rights issues do not impair reuse). Reusing these coastal discharges would be the equivalent of adding six percent to the total U.S. use of freshwater or 27% to public supplies.

Resource Recovery

America's clean water utilities are also reclaiming and reusing materials, which both reduce processing and disposal costs of residuals and create opportunities for new revenue streams. Capturing phosphorus and processing it into fertilizer is one of the best examples. This process enables utilities to meet stringent nutrient discharge regulations with little or no capital investment, create new revenue from a marketable commercial fertilizer, and increase overall plant operating efficiency.

Dried biosolids can be used as a substitute for oil, gas, and especially coal because its calorific value is identical to that of wood. Cement kilns are being used to convert the biosolids into fuel in place of coal. Dried pellets also may be used as a fertilizer/soil amendment.

And research efforts are underway in the United States, Europe, and China to commercialize processes that will recover valuable metals, inorganic chemicals, and other materials from "wastewater."

Green Infrastructure and Watershed Approaches

Green infrastructure uses vegetation, soil, and other simple mechanical methods in upstream community locations to trap, store, and purify stormwater (or solve other water quality impairment issues) before it enters combined and storm sewers for more costly central treatment downstream. Communities can save tens of millions of dollars using an appropriate balance of grey and green infrastructure. NACWA refers to this balanced approach as "sustainable infrastructure." Beyond water quality, cities are increasingly improving the ways people live, work, and play in urban environments by embedding green infrastructure within broader initiatives to green the urban landscape.

Across all watersheds, utilities are reaching out through innovative collaborations to farmers and vice versa. Agricultural sources cause three to four times more impairment due to nitrogen and phosphorus than municipal sources. Even if nutrients were eliminated completely from utility discharges, nutrient contamination in these watersheds— and in many cases, far downstream into near-coastal waters—would persist. Further, pound for pound, the cost to remove nitrogen or phosphorus from farm runoff and drainage is typically four to five, sometimes 10–20, times less than the cost to remove the same amount from municipal wastewater or stormwater leading to new partnerships to address a vital water quality problem.

The Value of Water—Property Values, Jobs, and Development

Some types of value can be estimated, even measured, relatively precisely. In one of its earliest analyses, EPA case studies of various watersheds showed that clean water increased the value of single-family homes up to 4,000 feet from the water's edge by up to 25%. Since that time, many others have documented similar effects: A six percent increase in waterfront property values associated with meeting bacteria standards along the western shore of Maryland's Chesapeake Bay; three percent to 13% higher property values along seven restored stream in California compared to similar homes on damaged streams; an estimated 10 percent increase in the value of homes that abut a proposed $26 billion Great Lakes water quality restoration project; and, two percent to five percent increase in property values in Philadelphia associated with green stormwater infrastructure.

Clean water utilities create indirect value through changes they cause in local economies. One such change is in the local workforce where utility operations create demand for qualified workers in such fields as engineering, construction, management, and finance. Each $1 billion invested in clean water infrastructure generates 20,000 to 30,000 such jobs (effects vary from place to place), many of them local. A $305 million stormwater management program in Montgomery County, Maryland, for example, employs 3,300 local construction workers. All stormwater programs in the Chesapeake Bay watershed over the next five years will employ roughly 36,000 construction workers in Maryland, 10,000 in the District of Columbia, 80,000 in Pennsylvania, and 52,000 in Virginia.

As utility expenditures for labor and materials filter through local economies, their value multiplies. According to the U.S. Department of Commerce's Bureau of Economic Analysis, for example, for every job serving the clean water industry, another 3.68 jobs are created to support it.

Wages from these workers create demands for goods and services across the economy, much of it local, for food, gas, transportation, housing, and other necessities of life. Every $1 billion invested in wastewater infrastructure, for example, results in between $2.62 and $3.46 billion (varies from place to place) in such demand.

The $45 billion commercial fishing and shellfishing industry depends on clean water to sustain fisheries and deliver products that are safe to eat. Our commercial fishing fleet delivers fish and shellfish products worth about $4 billion annually, a value that increases tenfold or more in the retail marketplace. The industry employs 250,000 people harvesting over 10 billion pounds of fish and shellfish from the Great Lakes, Gulf of Mexico, Puget Sound, and other water bodies.

Our collective investments in 16,000 clean water utilities across America also provide a network effect in the form of environmental equity and productivity of labor and capital. People and businesses that move from place to place can do so with confidence that they will receive at least a standard set of clean water services regardless of location. Mobility in the workforce and in industrial location enables unconstrained deployment and redeployment over time of labor and capital to the most productive sectors of the U.S. economy in the most productive locations across America.

Nowhere is the relationship between clean water and industrial value added more striking than in the soft drink and beer sectors. A recent National Soft Drink Association analysis found that the soft drink industry, which relies on clean water to produce its product, employs 175,000 people, creates 1.6 million jobs, generates $8 billion each year in salaries and wages, and pays $17 billion in federal and state taxes. According to the Beer Institute, the U.S. beer industry adds about $275 billion in value to the economy. The beer industry directly or indirectly employs some 2.5 million workers, who earn $60 billion in wages and benefits.

Achieving the Full Potential of the UOTF

The market is beginning to reflect the shift to the UOTF; according to the Cleantech Group, which tracks global investment in technology by sector, investment in water and wastewater technology companies more than doubled from $181 million (36 deals) in 2007 to $410 million (82 deals) in 2013, despite the economic downturn.

The full potential of the transition to the UOTF will be unleashed when regulators and governing boards acknowledge the substantial returns associated with making this transition and, based on that, support new ways of doing business. Much of this support will require only administrative and procedural changes with few or no changes to laws or regulations.

By offering the right incentives and removing unnecessary barriers to innovation, the nation can help utilities be more efficient stewards of the environment and suppliers of public health services, all the while generating high rates of economic and social return.

In short, by reexamining current policies from the perspective of the UOTF, we can further enhance environmental and public health outcomes while enabling emerging objectives like resource recovery, water reuse, energy efficiency, and sustainable communities. This, in turn, will help the water sector as a whole tell a compelling story about the true value and power of water.

*All data, citations, and quotes for this article are drawn from NACWA's July 22, 2014, white paper titled *Today's Clean Water Utility . . . Delivering Value to Ratepayers, Communities and the Nation*. The white paper is available on NACWA's website at www.nacwa.org.

CHUCK CLARKE
CHIEF EXECUTIVE OFFICER
CASCADE WATER ALLIANCE
RAY HOFFMAN
DIRECTOR
SEATTLE PUBLIC UTILITIES
LINDA MCCREA
SUPERINTENDENT
TACOMA WATER

Resiliency – Planning Individually and as a Region for Tomorrow

Water—we use it every day. Because it is always there, we seldom worry about it. We use it to brush our teeth, to take a shower, and to make that morning cup of coffee. Our growth and economic development depend on it. Water's value—priceless. That is why we in the Pacific Northwest are working together to use available water before making any additional investments. Our goal is to protect the supply we have to provide the same ongoing water value.

Together, our three utilities provide almost two million customers in the central Puget Sound region with drinking water every day. Our water comes from the rain and snow that falls on the west side of the Cascade Mountains, and our forecasts show that we have enough water for decades to come.

But what if something outside our control prevents us from providing that water? Recent experience in other parts of the country shows us that when disaster strikes, people are willing to go without water from their tap for about two weeks. After that, they might leave the area. And many do not return. The impacts of that, from the effects on the economy to the very heart of a community, are long lasting.

We know disasters do not stop at a jurisdictional boundary or a utility service area. With all these sobering realizations in mind, our three major utilities know that no matter how much we do individually; there are benefits in planning and preparing as a region. Each of us is making major decisions and investments, and the more flexible and proactive we can be individually and collectively, the more responsive we can be. To start, we have come together to explore answers to these questions:

- How well will our water systems perform when—not if—the next major earthquake hits?
- When the next drought occurs, how much are our customers going to reduce water use when per capita water demand is already so low?
- How significant will the impacts of climate change be on water supply and on infrastructure located near our saltwater shoreline?
- How will volcanic ash or a fire in our forested watersheds impact our water quality?

The following illustrates what we are doing individually and the effort that we are undertaking as a region to be ready for natural and/or man-made changes the future may bring.

Seattle Public Utilities

In 1889, the Great Seattle Fire left downtown in ruins. Seattle's water supply, provided by a privately owned company, could not provide enough pressure to put the fire out. Meanwhile, residents were left to drink contaminated Lake Washington water, resulting in local typhoid fever outbreaks. Afterwards voters overwhelmingly approved a bond issue to provide clean, mountain water from the Cascades and build reservoirs throughout the city. That solved the city's drinking water and fire protection challenges, and a focus on resiliency and reliability was born.

Today, Seattle has some of the safest and best-tasting water in the nation with sufficient pressure to effectively fight any future Seattle fires. Residents take conservation seriously and consume less water now than in the 1950s when the population served (both retail and wholesale) by Seattle was about half the size it is today.

Water supply is expected to meet customer needs well into the middle of this century. Customers include Seattle residents, along with 19 municipalities and special purpose districts, plus the Cascade Water Alliance, who are all served through wholesale contracts.

Water for a service area population of 1.3 million people comes from the Cedar River and South Fork of the Tolt River in watersheds surrounded by over 100,000 of protected acres in the Cascade Mountains. These watersheds also provide habitat for endangered salmon and other animals and plants.

Climate variability and climate change are among the uncertainties that Seattle Public Utilities (SPU) considers in ensuring that current and future water demands for people and fish are met. SPU is focused on staying engaged with the climate research community to pursue tailored analysis that addresses issues of direct concern to the utility. Rising sea levels and "King Tide"[1] events are also being carefully considered, as they are issues critical in a city with 50 miles of tidal estuarine shoreline.

Seattle's industrial core and water supply infrastructure in the Duwamish Valley are vulnerable to rising sea levels, as well as damage from earthquakes. As SPU considers new water distribution pipeline investments there and throughout the system, there is recognition that the pieces that are built and operated today will be subjected to different conditions over the course of their lives.

Tacoma Water

Over the years, Tacoma Water—one of the nation's oldest municipally owned water systems—has grown with the region it serves by investing in new supplies and water delivery systems. By continually planning for and adjusting to a growing and changing community, Tacoma Water has met the demands of consumers and helped the region prosper while taking care to protect the natural resources we all depend on.

When the valves at the J St. Standpipe in the center of town were opened just over a century ago, allowing water from the Green River to flow into Tacoma, a clean, reliable water source was finally available. With typhoid running through the city, and an infrastructure built of wood, it is hard to imagine what resource the city could have needed more at that moment.

In recent times, the utility has expanded the supply from the Green River by constructing the Second Supply Pipeline in partnership with three South King County utilities. This project not only provides increased supply to the region but also enhances reliability and interconnectedness. As a result, access to water from the Green River is now

---

[1] King tides are the highest tides of the year. They occur naturally when the sun and moon align, causing an increased gravitational pull on the Earth's oceans. In Washington, king tides typically occur in December and January.

available to more than one million people in the South Puget Sound region.

Although Tacoma owns only 11% of the 231-square-mile Green River watershed, it vigorously protects the water supply by controlling access to the entire watershed, patrolling lands and maintaining agree-agreements with the other landowners. Tacoma Water is furthering its water quality protection by building a filtration facility on the Green River that will not only improve water quality, but also allow greater use of the river during periods of turbidity.

Although the Green River is Tacoma's primary water source, more than 20 wells in and around Tacoma provide groundwater for peak summer demands, emergencies, and future needs. A Groundwater Protection District protects this critical source by establishing policies and protective boundaries around the wells to prevent contaminants from reaching the aquifer.

Tacoma's system is well engineered and made to last. As it ages, asset management principles and programs will inform decisions on where and when investments in its infrastructure are made, including completing condition assessments, likelihood and consequences analyses, financial models, and maintenance plans. The utility is also engaging customers in determining the level of service they expect for resiliency and what they are willing to pay.

With its diverse supplies (adequate to meet regional growth needs for the next 50 plus years), redundant infrastructure, and protected watershed, Tacoma has built resiliency into its system. Looking forward, regional resiliency planning will supplement efforts within the utility to prepare for climate change, aging infrastructure and natural disasters.

Cascade Water Alliance

Formed in 1999, Cascade provides clean, safe, and reliable water every day to 350,000 residents in suburban Eastern and Southern King County. Members include the cities of Bellevue, Issaquah, Kirkland,

Redmond, and Tukwila; the Sammamish Plateau Water and Sewer District; and the Skyway Water and Sewer District. Cascade, which is governed by a board of elected officials representing members, has current agreements with Seattle and Tacoma for short-term water supply.

In 2009, Cascade purchased Lake Tapps in adjacent Pierce County for long-term water supply, securing one of the most significant new municipal water rights issued by Washington State in a decade.

Planning for the future is being driven institutionally through landmark agreements with the Muckleshoot and Puyallup Tribes, Seattle, Tacoma; and the local municipalities of Auburn, Bonney Lake, Buckley, and Sumner; and homeowners around Lake Tapps. As a result of these agreements, there will be sufficient water in the White River (which feeds Lake Tapps) for fish and to satisfy the future water needs of four nearby cities. Working together, this provides a framework for regional partnerships and collaborations.

Because there is sufficient water for current needs, Cascade is now planning to use its Lake Tapps water supply only after determining what future regional needs are and will be. Together with its partners, Cascade is investing in its region's water future, working together to have a plan so that if there is an emergency or a need, Lake Tapps will be there as a future water supply. This allows the region to maximize its future water supply.

Looking Ahead Together to Ensure Resiliency for the Region's Water Systems

Individually, we are preparing for the challenges each of our utilities face. Thankfully, there are no urgent crises facing us in the central Puget Sound Region that require an immediate or emergency response.

However, we are aware of what it means to *not* be prepared for extreme events and what it could cost the region to recover. Our utilities have come together to understand what could happen and to determine together how we might respond as a region.

We are studying regional water system vulnerabilities with four key focus areas: drought, earthquakes, climate change, and water quality. Our next steps together will be as follows:

- Identify gaps in our water systems' resiliency risk areas for the region
- Identify and assess tools for management of risks, including synergy of solutions across the above listed four focus areas
- Identify and assess potential response plans and strategies should an adverse event occur
- Create a needs assessment and action plan for both regional and local actions that would mitigate identified risks
- Provide educational forums, communication strategies and outreach efforts for water utilities and other key stakeholder about risks, plans, and strategy

Our planning together is aimed at finding broad regional solutions. The project is underway, with a completion date expected by late 2015 or early 2016. We anticipate our findings to generate regional solutions for consideration by an array of decision makers and stakeholders throughout the Puget Sound region and Washington State.

ROBERT J. SPROWLS
PRESIDENT AND CHIEF EXECUTIVE OFFICER
AMERICAN STATES WATER COMPANY

Building a Secure Water Future

On the fabricated oasis that is California's fruited plain, a desert has been reclaimed by a combination of money, labor, ingenuity and irrigation. There are very few places where water has played a role more consequential than here. The elements have been overcome in California to a formidable end—today the world's eighth largest economy, including one of the most productive farm regions on earth.

However, if its history can be seen through chapters that evoke rich tradition and unbridled promise—the Mission Period and transcontinental railroad, the Gold Rush and technology boom—the California experience now runs the risk of a future dominated by an Era of Water Insecurity.

Like food insecurity among the less fortunate, where the staple may exist in one's surroundings but it is not known if or from where the next meal is coming, a succession of dry years, the long-term impacts of climate change, and inadequate funding for water management threaten to impose a similar psyche on water users from every station in life.

Persistent drought has only exaggerated the obvious—that water stewardship demands vigilance. We know that waiting for rain is a strategy destined for failure, and that a range of solutions is required—but the fact is nearly all roads lead to one overwhelming need: Infrastructure.

Even if its condition is severe by comparison, California is certainly not alone: A study by the U.S. Environmental Protection Agency (EPA) pegs nationwide water infrastructure needs at $384 billion, with water transmission and distribution lines cited as most pressing. The American Society of Civil Engineers gives the nation's water delivery system a dismal D grade, citing the occurrence of nearly a quarter million water main breaks annually; replacement costs are estimated at more than $1 trillion over 25 years.

Among the states, the EPA survey found California to have the greatest water infrastructure needs, at more than $44 billion.

While focusing on the influence of weather patterns, we are prone to accept the role of water's handmaiden, forever vulnerable to the impact of its scarcity on our lives and livelihoods. However, the fact is, we have already demonstrated the solutions are within our grasp. In decades past, Californians impressively marshaled technology, tax revenue and public works to amass and manipulate water.

While our investor-owned company spans across many states and military installations, our largest footprint is in California—and it is through our California operations we see most vividly the challenges our nation faces, what we risk by inaction, and the rewards of becoming drought resistant and water secure.

No matter where we operate, reliability is the cornerstone of a water utility's value. Because there is no alternative to water, for us there is no substitute for the reliable storage and movement of water from where it is to where it needs to go. Fundamental to this is maintaining our infrastructure—not every so often, or in the wake of a crisis, but unceasingly. Over the most recent five-year period, we have devoted $375 million to repairing and replacing pipeline, wells, pumping plants, and other facilities used to provide water to more than a million customers.

Moving vast amounts of water is not easy. Unlike natural gas, for instance, water is a heavy substance difficult to transfer long distances. Preventing water loss from pump to tap, especially important in dry regions, demands regular maintenance and timely replacement of hardware.

Because we operate transparently, at the place where market drivers and the public interest intersect, we have a built-in, forcing function to take the long view—to look beyond today's demand and make prudent investments that will enable us to dependably serve the needs of growth. Where this approach is replicated elsewhere, it is certainly justified.

Much of California's water storage and delivery infrastructure, for example, had been built by the 1970s, when the population was roughly half what it is today. A network of pipes, aqueducts, reservoirs, dams and more, funded by past generations for our benefit, are showing signs of age. Some lines meant to last 40–80 years are now a century old and in a state of disrepair.

Even the call for action is getting a little long in the tooth: It has been nearly a decade since the state's water authority concluded, "California must maintain, rehabilitate and improve its aging water infrastructure."

Compounding the challenge are a growing population and expanding economy, which further increase water demand. And of course, there is the fact that water is a basic human right, and that improved infrastructure offers the best hope of making safe, affordable water available to everyone.

We also serve a public that rarely embraces the true nature of the problem—which is to say they see the problem largely in nature, such as the strength of the next El Niño. The irony is that even in California—where the news media routinely document the state's drought conditions—the public is largely shielded, whether by subsidies that hide the true cost of their water or by the strong performance of utilities to keep an aged infrastructure operating.

The long pole in the tent is, of course, financing. Whether bonds, taxes or user fees, absent a visible crisis, it is difficult to get far before sticker shock trumps long-term planning. We will best succeed through fiscal approaches that do not rely on the fear factor of enduring drought, the austerity of rationing, and the economic distress of water scarcity. Lawmakers and others who answer to the public have our empathy: As a utility provider, we find it necessary to align our repair and replacement schedule to incremental rate increases that customers are willing to absorb.

There is a lot of work to do, and I would offer three fundamental things that need to happen if we hope to master our water destiny.

First, elected leaders and policy makers must adopt the priority of infrastructure and speak to that priority with verve and seriousness that reflects what is at stake. Nowhere is it more important for public servants to be honest with the people, even where the message may not be popular. Infrastructure is the wise and necessary approach, and there is no getting around the reality that it requires the commitment of money.

It is not easy to tell customers that they need to pay a little more to keep the pipes sound and the tap running—but it is something we and many others do as a matter of necessity. In the broader context of public policy, lawmakers must be willing to talk straight with their constituents and make them understand that our water future is not just in the hands of the planners and engineers but in theirs as well.

Second, private investment must be embraced as part of the solution. It certainly would not be the first time that a public–private approach delivered the path to a better, stronger tomorrow.

In the case of water, it is an opportunity to help fund infrastructure improvement, and frankly, to alleviate pressure on political leaders. Attracting more private capital for public water infrastructure could provide a more attainable funding source to supplement comparatively unpopular taxes and bonds.

Third, the time has come to muster the innovative spirit of our technology sector to find better and more efficient ways to strengthen infrastructure. We can create and expand the footprint of "smart water infrastructure" through partnership with the best and the brightest on our tech landscape.

Some of this can happen organically; where there is a compelling need, the market often inspires efforts that leverage new thinking and emergent technology—and this drive should be no less evident than with the life-giving resource of water. Again, society benefits from a re-sourced public–private cooperative; we see it in our everyday lives, from the Internet to aerospace to medicine to other public works.

Conservation is also worth mentioning, because it is important that we drive solutions on the demand as well as supply side. It is happening in both residential and agricultural sectors, though more can be done. In the Western region of the United States in particular, reconsideration could be given to the harvesting of highly water-intensive crops during especially dry periods.

In addition, we should make permanent the kind of tougher temporary measures that consumers generally accept once they accept the severity of the problem. There is nothing draconian about watering one's lawn short of wasteful runoff or washing the car with a shutoff valve, or sweeping leaves from the driveway with a broom instead of a hose.

Such important and meritorious efforts, however, cannot nearly compensate for the neglect of infrastructure.

There is an adage in Hollywood that holds you will only know you have produced too many sequels of a hit movie when the latest one bombs at the box office—because only then is all doubt removed that everything has been extracted from that franchise. The money and brand luster sacrificed on the altar of certainty is deemed an acceptable tradeoff.

That may pencil out in the film industry, but it is hardly suitable for the water franchise: The infrastructure needed to store, conserve, protect, and deliver the world's most precious resource.

Of all its achievements and for all it is renown, conquering the desert may be the most descriptive metaphor for California's aspirational persona. There is no reason to turn back now. If the best we can hope for with Mother Nature is détente, then let's accept that rather than merely awaiting her deliverance.

The good news is we do not need to do that. We mastered our water destiny in generations past, by building the architecture to manage water for society's benefit. With advanced technology, measures to conserve usage and protect habitat, and the will to put resources to the challenge, we can look to a future of water security, rather than merely looking to the skies.

ERIC W. THORNBURG
CHAIRMAN, PRESIDENT, AND
CHIEF EXECUTIVE OFFICER
CONNECTICUT WATER SERVICE, INC.

Water Changes Everything

ater changes everything! I thought that I knew what that meant! After 30 years in the drinking water industry, I had seen the tremendous impact that safe, high-quality water service had on families and communities in the United States.

Then I went to Rwanda! It was there that I really came to understand that water changes everything!

I journeyed there on a Water for People (www.waterforpeople.org) country impact tour with my daughter and four others. Water for People is an international nonprofit humanitarian organization dedicated to creating reliable, safe drinking water resources, improved sanitation facilities, and hygiene education programs in the developing world.

The lasting image that I came away with from Rwanda was people carrying "jerry cans"—those yellow plastic containers meant for diesel fuel. In the developing world, these cans are a necessary tool for carrying water. The task of trekking to the nearest water source would often take several hours depending on the distance. For a family that needs just five gallons a day for drinking, cooking, and bathing—that means that someone has to carry more than 40 pounds of water—sometimes over great distances—every single day.

The children I saw were sickly. Drinking untreated water and poor sanitation had clearly taken its toll. The women and girls were exhausted from fetching water. The men seemed to lack all hope and avoided eye contact—their very dignity in hiding. It was a desperate situation. As a human being it was truly heartbreaking to see! As a water professional, it was unacceptable! We know how to solve this!

Water for People's approach is to work with the local community to build their capacity to develop, operate, and maintain their own water system, providing a reliable source of clean, safe, and accessible water. To borrow a parable, it is not giving people a fish, but teaching them how to fish!

Once a community has a sustainable water source, human health is vastly improved, and the quality of life takes a leap forward. The difference I saw was incredible. The kids were healthy and attending school. The homes were tidy and commerce was evident. They were optimistic. They had hope. The village was transformed!

Water truly had changed everything! How do you place a value on water, a resource that has the power to do that?

In the "developed" world, where we have come to expect easy access to safe drinking water, water still changes everything. The availability of clean, safe water is critically important to families and communities. We are fortunate, for the most part, that the vast majority of the population in the United States and Canada has access to the safe water that our health depends on.

Safe drinking water for human health aside, a robust water system is an essential ingredient to our quality of life and helps drive the economic development of our communities. Business and industry are much more likely to locate themselves in a community that has a reliable supply of water provided by a financially sound and well-managed water utility. The community also benefits when the water system infrastructure supports public fire protection. The hydrant, which can provide hundreds or thousands of gallons of water per minute, is the sentinel on the corner protecting lives and property.

Again, water changes everything!

Infrastructure Changes Everything

In developing countries, the infrastructure may consist of a well and minimal piping. Public water systems in developed countries often require extensive networks of pipes, treatment systems, control systems, water storage facilities, and backup power supplies.

In either instance, the original infrastructure must be funded and replaced when it reaches the end of its useful life if the system is to continue to provide a reliable supply of water to families and communities. We owe a debt of gratitude to those who had the foresight to develop water systems as far back as the mid-19th century that continue to serve us today.

However, all too often little attention is paid to the pipes and other infrastructure that are necessary to provide water service. As public water providers it is our obligation to plan for the replacement of water infrastructure before it begins to fail, causing water service interruptions, damaging roads, and impairing public fire protection. Further, we must ensure that the water systems entrusted to us to meet our needs today are available to future generations to meet their needs.

Replacing Aging Infrastructure Is Expensive, But It Is More Expensive Not To

In the Northeast, where Connecticut Water and Maine Water serve families and communities, the cost of replacing water main can easily approach $200 per foot, or some $1 million per mile! It is easy to see why public water utilities need to be on a sound financial footing to invest in their water systems. Having access to capital is critical if a water utility is to programmatically replace infrastructure so that the water system can reliably serve future generations.

In the public sector, the funding of water infrastructure and operations and maintenance cost is often entangled in politics. Finding the political will to increase water rates can be a profile in courage. The result is all too often, a steady decline in system reliability due to deferred maintenance or the inability to replace infrastructure that has long outlived its useful life. Further, it is a financial burden being placed squarely on the shoulders of future generations.

Investor-owned water utilities also pay a price when our publicly owned colleagues defer maintenance and delay infrastructure replacement. It keeps their water rates artificially low and does not reflect the true cost of providing water service and adequately maintaining water infrastructure. It also sets a baseline for water rates in a community that investor-owned public water utilities are compared to, especially those that do invest in their infrastructure and have rates that reflect the full cost of providing water service.

As an industry, we need to do a better job of educating the public and public officials about the need to replace to aging infrastructure, and to create a political climate where our colleagues at publicly owned water systems are able to make the necessary investments in their systems.

Being Good Stewards of Natural Resources Changes Everything

Water utilities were perhaps the first green industry. We have long known that the quality of our water source will have a direct correlation to the quality of the water we deliver to our customers. We are fortunate that most communities have enacted regulations that protect public water sources from contaminants, and most water utilities are vigilant in protecting their water supplies.

Aside from the quality, water utilities need to be concerned with the water quantity. Water is a finite and precious natural resource that needs to be used wisely. There are competing interests for available water resources, and as public water utilities, we have an obligation to take no more than is needed by the families that rely on our water. Therefore, we need to work with consumers and promote wise water use. It is the right thing to do. This kind of action helps us to conserve a precious natural resource, to reduce the amount of power needed to pump and treat water (and the associated environmental cost of producing that power), and to reduce the amount of chemicals required in water treatment (and the associated environmental shipping costs).

Unfortunately, effectively educating customers about water conservation has historically had a negative financial impact on utilities. Under the traditional regulatory model, a certain level of water sales to customers is assumed during the rate setting process. The revenue required by the utility to be financially sound, as determined by regulators, is then divided by the assumed sales. By promoting conservation, water utilities are lowering water sales, which in turn means they will not be able to recognize the revenues that regulators approved.

In Connecticut, we are fortunate that our state leaders and regulators understand that dynamic. That is why they have created a Water Revenue Adjustment (WRA). The WRA allows water utilities regulated by the Public Utilities Regulatory Authority (PURA) to promote water conservation without incurring a financial penalty in the form of lower water revenues, which in turn places pressure on infrastructure replacement and operations budgets. The WRA makes it possible for Connecticut PURA regulated water utilities to focus on serving families and communities and not on water sales.

Sound Financial Management

We have an obligation to operate and maintain public water system so that it has the capacity to sustain itself through the replacement of aging infrastructure, implement new technologies that enhance efficiency and water quality, and hire and retain skilled and dedicated employees who are passionate about delivering high-quality water and service. The foundation for such a public water system is built of sound financial management.

As an investor-owned utility, we must always remember that the capital that funds our operation and allows us to build our systems comes from our customers and shareholders, respectively. We have an obligation to both to operate efficiently. It is essential that customers are charged a price for water that reflects the true cost of providing water service. That is the only way we can ensure that the utility is sustainable into the future. Reliability of service and the ability to serve future generations is compromised when a water system does not recover its true costs. The people who invest their hard earned capital with an investor-owned water utility are like most of us who are planning for their retirement or saving for their children's education. We must be good stewards of the capital that they have entrusted to us. It is their capital that makes it possible to build the infrastructure and systems that serve customers.

What Makes Investor-Owned Water Utilities Special?

Investor-owned water utilities are a special breed. We combine an entrepreneurial spirit with a unique and special public mission. Our success and our ability to deliver a fair return to the people that have entrusted their capital to us depends on how well we serve our customers.

Operating in a regulated environment, an investor-owned utility can only thrive when it delivers its customers a reliable supply of high-quality and responsive customer service. The satisfaction of its customers is considered during the regulatory ratemaking process and has an influence on the rates regulators authorize for the utility. By working hard to satisfy customers, regulated utilities place themselves in the best position to provide a fair return to those who have provided the capital to fund the utility's infrastructure.

The regulatory process also ensures that the infrastructure investments made by the utility are prudent and used and useful. Used and useful infrastructure is the only thing that regulated water utilities are allowed to earn a return on their shareholders. This ensures that capital is spent wisely. The operating and maintenance costs of running a utility, such as payroll, taxes, and power are passed through to customers at the utility's cost.

The bottom line is that the success of an investor-owned utility is directly linked to the quality of the water and service delivered to its customers, the prudent investment in infrastructure necessary to serve families and the community, and the ability to operate efficiently within the rates approved by regulators.

Water Does Change Everything

A reliable supply of clean water improves our health, helps business and industry to thrive in our communities, and protects our lives and property from fire. Water cannot do it alone. It can only change everything when we put all of the pieces into place. We need to ensure our water supplies are protected, our infrastructure is sound, and our water systems are sustainable. The water we have on Earth is the only water we will ever have. Water can only change everything if we do our part!

KEVIN L. SHAFER, PE
EXECUTIVE DIRECTOR
MILWAUKEE METROPOLITAN
SEWERAGE DISTRICT

Healing the Sins of Our Past Through Responsible Water Management

When we talk about the value of water, it sounds like we are discussing a commodity. This implies that there is a demand for water. As our instinct tells us, water does have value. We can simply look around the world to see that this is definitely true. Poor drinking water quality and lack of water due to droughts illustrate that we truly do have a demand for clean water. The question is not if water has a value; it does. The question is whether we show this value of water by how we manage it.

Water is a right. That does not mean it is free. In today's world, we need to purify water for consumption, distribute water to the population, and collect and clean the waste that is produced. This costs money, and we should all be willing to pay. This expenditure will make sure that someone else can reuse the same drop of water we just used.

From the outside looking in, if someone were to judge us for the value we placed on water prior to the Clean Water Act, we would have failed. Prior to the Act, we treated our waterways like a backyard dumpster, spewing all types of materials into them, damaging the habitat, the water cycle, and our water future.

We were not good stewards. Prior to the Clean Water Act, we thought that our actions reflected responsible water management. We took natural streams, straightened, and concrete-lined them. We discharged our waste untreated to our rivers and lakes, which became open sewers. We filled waterways not considering the impacts upstream and downstream. We paved our landscape not worried about water runoff. In hindsight, we were very wrong.

If we really value water, then responsible management of the water commodity becomes even more critical. Responsible management of water is the most important step to reflect the value we place on it. Most will think this means making sure we have large enough pipes and treatment plants to move and clean the water, but it is more than that. It requires the management of the manmade and natural infrastructure in the entire watershed.

Watersheds are nature's boundary for how water flows over land. As that water flows, it is used and reused. Responsible management of that water means that we will have to track this path and develop integrated approaches from the most upstream point to the most downstream point. The watershed approach will greatly expand the universe of people that must be reached.

We now know that the most responsible water management is trying to have as little impact on water as possible. Natural infrastructure worked for thousands of years prior to our arrival, and it still will. We have learned that we need to try to mimic this natural approach moving forward.

There will still be the need for water purification facilities, for wastewater reclamation facilities, and for an intricate system of underground delivery pipes. In these cases, I do not believe that we need to change what has been accomplished. We need to continue our great progress toward improved wastewater treatment in the future. Tightening up our old sewer systems so they do not draw in clean water and insuring adequate capacity to manage flows to eventually reach a zero overflow goal is a necessity. New technologies will provide the opportunities to improve these systems, making them more efficient and reliable.

Supplementing this drinking water and wastewater infrastructure with natural or green infrastructure is another step that will help to limit future flooding and to reduce the pollutants that reach the waterways. Along with these benefits, we would also become more resilient to climate change. Installing green roofs on buildings, making parking lots porous, storing water in rain barrels and cisterns, and using bioswales where possible are all steps toward a more natural environment, while maintaining need for development. Through these steps, we will manage water where it falls, reducing the water that reaches our urban infrastructure, and helping purify the water prior to it flowing into a river or lake.

Naturalizing our waterways, removing concrete, and restoring the hydrologic cycle to the extent practicable are some of the many first steps on this road toward responsible water management. These steps would start to heal the sins of our past. Seen mostly in urban settings, this naturalization work will help to restore habitat in urban areas and reconnect those residents to nature.

We also need to continue to address agricultural stormwater runoff. This is the next great clean water frontier. Work with the agricultural community must continue so that we can meet production requirements, while integrating responsible water management to reduce pollutant runoff.

Of course, all these actions will have to be implemented in a world with fewer financial resources and a climate that is changing rapidly. If we truly value water, we need to make sure that sufficient, sustainable funding is available to address the increased needs. Naturalists, politicians, engineers, farmers, and neighbors will all have a say in this expanding discussion.

If we take this approach and expand the dialogue throughout the watershed, then the path to showing how we really should value water will be better defined and end with a more comprehensive result.

DAVID V. MODEER
GENERAL MANAGER
CENTRAL ARIZONA PROJECT (CAP)
CENTRAL ARIZONA WATER CONSERVATION DISTRICT

Developing a Broader Perspective on the Value of Water

Too often, the value of water is evaluated through the lens of the cost of operations and capital expenditures recovered through rates, fees, and bonds. This view diminishes the value that is intrinsic to the water itself. There are a number of factors that make it difficult to readjust this perception. At or near the center of this viewpoint is the regulatory framework that prohibits utilities, particularly small non-municipal water providers, from setting rates above the cost of delivery and a reasonable rate of return. This strictly financial perspective has governed how water is valued for generations.

This perception may be changing, however, as circumstances drive both providers and consumers to take a broader view of the value of a stable, reliable water supply.

Some of this can be attributed to forces and events that go beyond the normal experiences water providers and their customers have grown accustomed to over many decades.

This is particularly true in the Southwestern United States, which, as I write this, is in the midst of the worst long-term drought in the Colorado River watershed in at least 500 years. To paraphrase Benjamin Franklin, people do not know the value of water until the well runs dry.

It is a fact that this long-term drought has had an impact on water supplies in the southwestern states. In light of all of the conversation that is taking place about climate change, or at least changes in weather patterns around the globe and the United States, this awareness has been accompanied by a growing recognition that what we are experiencing may represent only a foreshadow of a future climate regime. Many are asking whether we are experiencing a significant weather anomaly, or if the current drought is only a harbinger of the future.

As a result of increased attention to the climate, water itself has become a more visible issue to the public and the value associated with reliable, affordable supplies is certainly much different than it was 25–30 years ago, or perhaps even 10 or 15 years ago. The issues of increasing water scarcity in some areas and overabundance in others areas has changed those perceptions substantially. There is now a greater acknowledgment and understanding of the broader range of value that water brings.

In the past, public concern about water supplies has largely been a local issue, driven by circumstances at the water utility or community level. It is now become of much more interest to a much broader range of stakeholders. For instance, businesses and industries, even those without a large water footprint, now find it worthwhile to include water availability and not just water cost in decisions relative to starting a business, expanding a business or relocating a business.

In addition, business and industry and agricultural interests have become more sensitive to the value of water beyond the financial bottom line. There is a greater impetus for businesses of all types to examine and incorporate the social and environmental value of this resource in their planning and operations. Whether this pressure is regulatory or stems from greater competition for credibility, the result is that, in the business world, water has a much broader role and a greater perceived value than in the past.

In all of these areas, strong leadership in the water arena is needed to better communicate the value of water. Whether it is retail, wholesale, or managing water districts, the "story" of water brought by a good leader can have a tremendously positive impact on public and stakeholder awareness of water's value and help build support for projects and programs that maintain the reliability of water supplies into the future.

That is particularly true in the West and the Southwest where persistent droughts are more common. A good leader and a good communicator can help people and businesses make better decisions, which in turn benefit community stability and undergird economic activity and regional prosperity.

Our experience at Central Arizona Project (CAP) can help demonstrate that the importance of water to the economic vitality of a region goes far beyond what most water industry professionals may expect.

Although all water professionals know that reliable, safe, and affordable water is extremely important to our consumers, it may be a surprise to note how vital that water is to economic activity in our service areas and the surrounding communities.

In order to help quantify those larger economic impacts, CAP commissioned the W.P. Carey School of Business at Arizona State University to estimate the economic value that the delivery of water by CAP from 1986 through 2010 has generated in Arizona.

In order to calculate the economic impacts of CAP water deliveries, the researchers prepared a baseline scenario of Arizona's annual economy as it has evolved with CAP water deliveries. A "No-CAP" scenario was produced for the same period with water supplies reduced by the amount delivered each year by CAP. The differences between the scenarios for each of 22 sectors of the state economy represents the annual and cumulative impacts of CAP water deliveries on Arizona gross state product (GSP) and employment. The study concluded that the delivery of CAP water produced in excess of one trillion dollars ($1,090,000,000,000) of Arizona's GSP. GSP represents the dollar values of all goods and services produced for final demand in the state.

Other key facts from the study include CAP's contribution to the job market. The study shows that in 2010, CAP is estimated to have generated annual employment of more than 1.6 million jobs. In fact, the government, healthcare, retail, real estate and travel sectors would have lost more than 60% of these jobs had the CAP water supply been unavailable.

Also, the study did not include the recreational benefits and other impacts associated with the operation and maintenance of the aqueduct system and Lake Pleasant. When these factors are added to the water supply analysis, statewide economic impacts of the operation of CAP would be even greater.

The study helped put in context the value of water over and above those normally associated with water supplies. Without the presence of readily available and reliable water Arizona would have lost, in recent years, almost 50% of the economic output of the state.

Certainly, CAP water is not alone in the value it provides to consumers and other stakeholders. Similar studies could be undertaken in other regions of the United States and perhaps in other countries as well. It is likely that these other studies would also reveal that the intrinsic value of having water is of substantial importance to every area of this country.

The study CAP commissioned has proven that the water we provide has a value that far exceeds the impacts of the rates, fees, and taxes our customers pay and, in fact, encompasses the economic well-being of a region much larger than our service area.

This broader and more encompassing view of water's value can be helpful in building support for rate increases necessitated by adaptations to a changing climate or other threats to water reliability, as well as for normal operations. An argument could be made that the impacts of not addressing these needs goes well beyond the realm of finances alone.

For instance, we have known for many years that the Colorado River cannot continue to provide the amount of water we'll need for a growing population in the Southwest. CAP has been preparing to meet the challenges for years. We have been working since 1997 with the Arizona Water Banking Authority to store Colorado River water in underground aquifers in central Arizona where it can be recovered during shortage. So far, the AWBA has stored about 3 million acre-feet to protect CAP municipal supplies. CAP has been working for several years with state agencies and other stakeholders to develop a plan for the recovery of that water.

We have also been actively engaged with the Arizona Department of Water Resources, the other six Colorado River Basin states, the United States, and Mexico to address the long-term health and sustainability of the Colorado River system and the growing water needs of the region. For instance, CAP has been funding conservation in Mexico to preserve Colorado River supplies in Lake Mead and discussing with Mexico the potential for ocean desalination in the Rocky Point region.

All of these programs have a financial cost, which must be absorbed by our customers and the property owners in our three-county service area. Communicating the value of Colorado River water supplies to our region, and helping our stakeholders recognize that these expenditures are necessary to ensure reliable supplies in the future is an ongoing effort. The information provided by the economic impact report is further evidence of how important it is to accurately value the water we deliver.

As issues related to the sustainability of our water supplies become more challenging, it is difficult to predict how well we can alter what nature is providing. However, we can better control our management of those resources. Being more aware of the value of the water we deliver presents opportunities that should not be overlooked.

Our decisions must reflect that broader value to our economy and to our society in general. It is an ideal opportunity for partnerships beyond our own communities and for bringing together disparate interests to ensure we all can have access to secure, reliable, and reasonably priced water supplies in the future.

THOMAS W. SIGMUND, PE
EXECUTIVE DIRECTOR
NEW WATER

The Changing Value Paradigm of a Clean Water Utility

lean water utilities have performed a valuable service in the United States and the world over the last 80 years. In the United States, water-borne diseases have been virtually eliminated and water quality for commerce and recreation has been greatly improved, primarily as a result of improvements in treatment of wastewater that is returned clean to the environment.

Water is one of the earth's most valuable commodities. However, in parts of the United States, we often treat the supply of clean water as limitless and have not given our water supply the respect that it deserves. Clean water utilities are being called on to do more to protect and improve the water supply. As clean water is valued more, the role played by clean water utilities and the value they provide not only to the ratepayers but also to the population in general, will become more important.

Today's utilities have moved beyond the paradigm of treating wastewater to simply meet permit conditions to a paradigm of managers of valuable resources and partners in improving the water environment and economic vitality of their communities. Today's clean water utilities must find ways to improve the efficiency of their operation to reduce operating cost and embrace automation, to recover valuable materials from the influent stream and convert them for maximum economic benefit, and to work proactively in the watershed when those efforts offer the highest value.

The value of clean water utilities today lies in their ability to innovate and take advantage of process and technology innovation opportunities to improve service, and at the same time, reduce cost to the customer. Utility managers are driven to this model as they face increasingly stringent environmental regulations that require expensive treatment solutions, aging infrastructure that must be replaced at considerable cost and the loss of an intergovernmental partnership that historically provided federal and state financial support to help pay for these mandates. Improved cost effectiveness of resource recovery technologies applicable to clean water utilities is allowing those managers to take advantage and implement these innovations to the benefit of their ratepayers.

Utilities are being called on to become more energy and operationally efficient, reuse treated effluent to supplement potable water supplies, recover an increasing large amount of inherent energy from influent and biosolids, recover nutrients and other valuable materials, and work with watershed interests to improve water quality, all while keeping rate increases as low as possible.

Recent industry analyses state that there is enough heat and embedded energy in biosolids alone to meet up to 12% of the U.S. electricity demand and that influent wastewater contains many times the energy needed to run those treatment facilities. The challenge has been recovering that energy in a cost-effective manner. Utilities have generated combustible gas using anaerobic digestion for decades and have used that gas to either generate electricity or heat for use within the treatment facilities or flared the gas to the atmosphere.

As the cost of utility generated electricity has risen, and the technology to generate electricity on-site from digester gas has improved, more utilities are performing a cost-benefit evaluation and finding that on-site generation has an acceptable payback period (10 years or less) and are generating electricity to replace purchased carbon-based fuel utility power. Modern digester gas-fueled engine generators are increasingly more efficient at the conversion of gas to electricity and can be equipped with devices to further recover the excess heat from engine exhaust gas and cooling water to be used within the facility.

Clean water utilities are also finding that high-strength industrial waste can be added to anaerobic digesters along with municipal waste to significantly increase gas and electricity production. In decisions that benefit both clean water utilities and generators of suitable high-strength industrial waste, the material can be transported to the utility and added directly to anaerobic digesters to significantly increase the amount of combustible gas that can be produced. In these business transactions, a nominal fee is charged that is typically less than what the industry would spend to otherwise dispose of the material, and the utility receives value in the form of additional digester gas that can be used to produce heat or electricity, offsetting purchased energy and benefitting utility ratepayers.

NEW Water, the regional clean water utility in Green Bay, Wisconsin has a goal to offset 50% of its purchased energy bill in the first year of operation (over $2 million per year) through generation of electricity and recovery of heat energy. After the initial 10-year payback period, the program will save the utility over $2 million in energy costs every year for an additional 10–15 years. Other utilities have set and achieved goals to become energy neutral or a net exporter of energy.

As little as 10 years ago, utilities talked about the value of nutrients that accompanies wastewater into clean water utilities that were not being recovered for commercial use. Today, many utilities have installed phosphorus and nitrogen recovery facilities that generate valuable products recovered from the wastewater that are sold to and reused by agriculture, and generate significant revenue for the clean water utilities. The phosphorus recovery technology is gaining wide acceptance and has proven to be cost-effective for utilities that have both anaerobic digestion and stringent effluent phosphorus limits.

Research efforts are under way to commercialize processes that will recover valuable metals, inorganic chemicals, and other materials from wastewater. As technology improves and these trace materials become more valuable, clean water utilities will be presented with opportunities to reclaim these materials and sell them to businesses that will incorporate them into new products. These revenues can again be used to benefit the utility's ratepayers.

In addition to the recovery and reuse of materials from the influent, clean water utilities are using solutions focused on improvements in the watershed versus solely on point source effluent controls. Through over four decades of continual improvements in water reclamation facilities, clean water utilities have moved far out on the cost removal effectiveness curve. Incremental improvements at water reclamation facilities to remove small additional amounts of pollutants are very expensive. Opportunities through water quality trading and adaptive management are promised to provide enhanced environmental benefits in the watershed at a lower cost than building the infrastructure at the treatment facilities.

Clean water utilities are looking to partner with others in the community to solve community-wide watershed problems involving nitrogen, phosphorus, and sediment and achieve the greatest environmental benefit at the lowest cost. Across all watersheds impaired by nitrogen and phosphorus, agricultural sources cause three to four times more impairment than municipal sources, underscoring the need to focus the efforts in the agricultural sector, where the greatest return on the investment can be seen.

NEW Water is faced with spending over $200 million to install infrastructure at its two treatment facilities to meet permit-driven effluent limits that will remove less than two percent of the phosphorus and sediment being delivered by the entire watershed to the bay of Green Bay. Under Wisconsin's Adaptive Management option, NEW Water is conducting a pilot test program over the next several years working in conjunction with agricultural producers in the watershed to install and implement Best Management Practices (BMPs) for those producers to meet water quality objectives at the lowest overall cost.

The option to partner with nonpoint sources of pollutants in the watershed is available to some clean water utilities, as a way to achieve desired environmental benefits at the lowest cost to ratepayers. Clean water utilities are entering into relatively uncharted waters as they begin working with urban and rural nonpoint entities, some of which may not be customers of the utility, to ensure that the removals are achieved. In exchange for avoiding construction of expensive gray infrastructure at treatment facilities, clean water utilities support and fund installation of BMPs in rural installations in the watershed.

Adaptive management requires demonstration of eventual compliance with ambient water quality criteria in the receiving water. Adaptive management activities often achieve complementary improvements in the watershed, such as reduction in sediment loadings and improvements in habitat, in addition to the reduction of the specific parameter of concern. Agricultural BMPs can also reduce operating costs for producers because they keep more fertilizer and soil on the land, requiring less fertilizer to be purchased and applied. Clean water utilities are now working collaboratively with the myriad of water quality interest groups in the watershed to achieve these benefits at the lowest cost to ratepayers.

How do clean water utilities today deliver value to their customers and communities? The value is provided far in excess of customer savings from operational efficiency, energy recovery, materials reuse, and the like. Economic value is delivered in the form of improved water quality that makes waterfront land more valuable, draws people to water in urban communities, creates jobs, increases demand for locally produced food and products, and improves entertainment and recreation.

From an economic perspective, the return on investment in clean water is impressive: employment opportunities in family supporting jobs, enhanced productivity in the private economy, higher standards of living, and a more favorable trade balance. These benefits are being provided by clean water utilities, while providing its ratepayers high-quality services at a fair price.

The U.S. Department of Commerce's Bureau of Economic Analysis states that for every job serving the clean water industry, 3.68 jobs are created to support it. For every $1 billion invested in wastewater infrastructure, $2.6 to 3.5 billion of demand is created for labor, goods, and services, much of it locally sourced.

Through enlightened leadership, clean water utilities are transforming how they do business to become much more efficient, extract as much value as they can from the materials they receive, and be as creative as possible, while still providing the highest level of public health protection. This level of sophistication could not have been contemplated as little as 10 years ago. The old paradigm of disposing of waste at as low cost as possible is being transformed by innovative utility managers and technology providers into a paradigm where organizations are using principles once thought to be reserved only for private business. This value paradigm that embraces new technology signals the private sector to make investment in new technology that will further advance this vision.

GEORGE S. HAWKINS
GENERAL MANAGER
DC WATER

H2.0 Innovation

We demonstrate the value of water in the manner in which we deliver it. By constantly improving the effectiveness and efficiency of providing clean water, we both underscore our understanding of its importance and demonstrate to our customers why we deserve their support. Unfortunately, as we know too well, the nation's water infrastructure is notoriously deficient. The critical question is therefore direct: How do we improve water service at a price that society can bear?

In a word, a clear answer is innovation.

Innovation is a word that is used frequently today, mostly with a sense of excitement about something new and fun. Yet in contrast, driving innovation in a large enterprise often seems hard and painful—impeded by a host of obstacles. Arguably, I will write about no more important issue, and no more important concept for a person in a leadership position to master.

Why and Why Not?

To sort out the conflicting characteristics associated with innovation, I suggest that at least three competing realities confront us in the water world.

The first is that many people do not think that innovation applies. Water and wastewater treatment has not changed all that much, and the pipes, valves and fire hydrants out in the street maybe least of all. When people think innovation they think smartphones and smart cars, not drinking water and waste streams. It is hard to support funding for a topic if customers do not associate with your product!

The second reality is that our industry is often stereotyped as being resistant to change. I have argued that part of this perception is true—and for a good reason. When you deliver an essential service 24/7/365 and often struggle for funding, then the incentive to try something new—which might fail—creates a threat to the ability to deliver the service and to the budget if costly remedies are necessary. Moreover, there are those in any industry who fear innovation because it might threaten either their job or their knowledge of how they do their job.

To keep the water flowing, particularly when our customers only seem to notice us when it does not, we tend to stick with what we know works. Innovation is hard when rational motivations cause us to resist change.

The third reality is that while we tend to stick with what we know, what we know is falling apart! Without restating the drumbeat of statistics that have been outlined many times, our infrastructure is near failure. For a service that is both essential to every living organism (water is life) and to every job (water is a necessity at every job site and business) to be given a D grade from the American Society of Civil Engineers is a scandal. Yet our industry faces decades of deferred maintenance, breathtakingly expensive regulatory mandates and a public that is mostly unaware of this potential catastrophe.

Thus, an uninformed public is skeptical at best and opposed at worst to the increase in rates that would allow us to improve our service. Yet sticking with what we have always done will only make the financial and operational catastrophe we face even worse.

What Are We To Do?

My answer is that we capture the imagination of the people we serve, demonstrate that their rate checks are put to good use, and create an incentive to perform better for our staff. Innovation—or the identification of new approaches that can achieve our performance goals at less cost or time or both—is an essential key to delivering on this promise.

Moreover, without innovation we cannot demonstrate that we are wise stewards of our ratepayer dollars. Of course, we need more to fund new capital projects—whether for regulatory mandates or capital replacements of decrepit infrastructure.

Yet we will fail to gain the revenue needed if we cannot demonstrate that every dollar is being spent wisely, and that over time every dollar is going farther. Demonstrating that every dollar goes farther means innovating—systematically decreasing the costs of service through new approaches.

In short, we seek additional revenue not because we are an inefficient bureaucracy that seeks to feed itself—and yes, I have heard this statement over the years. We seek additional revenue because we have much more work that needs to be done, even as we stretch each dollar farther. Innovation must be a principal part of both parts of the equation.

How Do We Innovate?

Although there are clear impediments to innovation, my experience is that most leaders in our industry understand the need. Yet the next question is perhaps the most difficult: How do we structure and manage our enterprise to spur innovation—change for the better—when we know the natural motivations that will rise up to challenge change? Our approach at DC Water is as follows:

1. **Lead**. Everyone in the enterprise needs to know that innovation is a desirable characteristic coming from the top. That starts at the level of the top executive, who must be seen to support and drive change. This commitment must be followed by identifying key leaders who can drive innovation on a daily basis. At DC Water, we have promoted a high-profile research scientist as the "Innovation Chief" in the General Manager's office. He has the visibility, access, and experience to identify opportunities and challenges to innovation and ensure they receive focus from top management. At DC Water, innovation is a priority—and that priority starts visibly at the top.

2. **Engage**. My experience is that there are hosts of good ideas of how to do things better that are pent up in the staff that does the work. Ask staff for their ideas on how to improve on our work and highlight and even reward good ideas. Engage staff-driven ideas first, particularly some visible wins early on, and emphasize that this is about our work and our skills first and not foreign ideas imposed on us. Engaging staff will yield essential buy-in from the folks who actually must change the way they do their work—and can also help overcome one of the most challenging obstacles to innovative ideas. The folks doing the work must first own innovation.

3. **Structure**. The next question is how to structure the enterprise to support innovation. Two models are typically considered. One is to create a program on research and innovation where expertise is identified and built in a stand-alone office. Many private firms have formal R&D offices with their own management and goals. A second model is to have a matrix structure—where innovation leads are identified within each of the existing structures (treatment facilities, water distribution, sewer systems, mainte-

nance, finance, procurement, etc.) and coordinated and led by a chief typically not in any of the specific offices. DC Water favors the second model—so that the folks leading innovation are embedded in the operations and understand implementation realities. The matrix model yields a system where innovation is often harder to start, because it must be integrated from the beginning in operations. However, this initial challenge pays dividends later on, when innovations are owned by operational units and already have internal champions.

4. <u>Research</u>. Even if staff may not know all the answers, they will know most of the questions that need to be answered to improve performance. Develop a log of pertinent questions and start formulating a research strategy. DC Water has a successful and relatively cheap research strategy based on collaboration. The brainchild of our Assistant General Manager Walt Bailey and our Innovations Chief Sudhir Murthy was a project where we collaborated with local universities and businesses to drive dozens of PhD level research projects. The universities and their students get research projects to advance their careers and programs. Private companies join to get in on the ground floor with new products. DC Water gains the benefit of new solutions to old problems. Our largest innovative project—a $460 million dollar investment in a first-of-its-kind biosolid digestion program—was developed after knowledge gained from 40 published papers, secured at low cost in collaborative efforts with three universities and several private firms. Successful research yielding improved performance creates a positive feedback loop that generates the next round of projects.

5. <u>Products</u>. Once the research begins and ideas begin to germinate, we need to develop practices that are standard in the private sector:

a. **Patents:** Protect the intellectual property that is created with the support of ratepayer money

b. **Non-Disclosure:** Protect the confidential nature of special programs and approaches that may become commercialized

c. **Compensation:** Determine how to distribute revenue beyond cost recovery for the inventors of the idea—to create a financial incentive for change

d. **Consulting:** Determine if your own employees may become consultants for others seeking to emulate a new idea—again driving the potential for additional revenue for the enterprise and the employee

The bottom line, in more ways than one, is not only to view innovations as an approach to improve productivity but also to gain revenue by commercializing ideas in the marketplace. Our ratepayers deserve a financial return for what they have invested in up front, and these returns can also fund the next round of innovations and help create a financial incentive for employees to participate.

6. **Business of Water.** Much of the innovation that is relevant to our organizations pertains not just to our unique technical needs, but also the business processes that are common to any customer service enterprise. We need to be as lean and innovative in reviewing permits, responding to customer calls, and planning preventative maintenance. Spurring innovation needs to cover the costs of our business procedures as much as it covers how we manage the streams of water. DC Water is now expanding our successful innovations and research program that focused initially mostly on our technical processes, and specifically focusing on the business of water.

7. **Social Media.** Engagement of employees in the first instance, and then the public in the second, is the best way to capture the imag-

ination of those we need to support our work. Social media—or a fun, interactive web page that allows anyone to suggest a new idea—is tailor-made for this objective. Imagine a virtual suggestion box that can provide an instant forum for ideas, perhaps with fun bells and whistles—like the capability for others to vote thumbs up or down. DC Water plans to launch an innovations website forum to gather ideas. From those ideas, we will select a few each year to be developed into business plans and a smaller number funded for serious pilots and collaborative research. Once we have the system functioning for encouraging internal ideas—and making it fun—we will expand the system to enable any of our customers, or any member of the public for that matter, to suggest how we could do our work better. The sky is the limit, and we are willing to consider a good, new idea from anywhere or anyone.

8. <u>Governance</u>. Innovation, probably defined into particular business areas familiar to the Board, should become a strategic priority for the Board to drive and review, not just become informed of as it comes to fruition. For DC Water, we looped an innovation strategy into our Board-driven strategic plan called Blue Horizon 2020. The areas of innovation that are already on our horizon are integrated into the Board's strategic plan—and are a principal way in that our performance is measured. This is perhaps the holy grail of innovation—when it becomes integral to the performance to our governing body. For DC Water, innovation and Blue Horizon 2020 are now one and the same.

Ultimately, the combination of these steps is designed to capture the imagination! Capture the imagination of our staff, propel a cascade of innovation ideas that keep coming over time; capture the imagination of our governing bodies and rate agencies that govern our future; capture the imagination of our customers who fund our work; and capture the imagination of our political leaders who hold such sway over the entire picture.

What Can Be Done?

Can this work? You bet it can, and it can deliver benefits a thousand times over for every dollar spent. I will end with some examples of how we have embraced innovation at DC Water. Remember as you read them to calculate in your mind how each is helping us take each dollar farther and serve our customers better:

- Innovation in how we communicate with our customers
- Innovation in how we finance our work
- Innovation in how we deploy information technology to keep our customers informed and engaged
- Innovation in how we upgrade water and sewer mains and laterals
- Innovation in how we monitor the status and condition of our assets and deploy preventative maintenance
- Innovation in how we turn wastewater plants to resource recovery facilities to realize value from what has been discarded by others
- Innovation in how we cleanse wastewater to save costs—to electricity, to chemicals, to maintenance
- Innovation in how we partner with private firms to benchmark to world-class standards and improve performance and efficiency
- Innovation in how we communicate with the public when we are working in the field
- Innovation in how we enhance benefits—particularly including local hiring initiatives—to the people and communities that are paying for the work, and where the work is done

The great news is that by diligently thinking about innovation in how we manage our enterprise, DC Water has been able to realize a host of improvements in effectiveness and efficiency. Here are a few brief examples.

Finance. DC Water became the first municipal issuer in the United States to issue century bonds—100 year maturity—matching the financing to the minimum useful life of massive deep tunnels being constructed to clean the city's waterways. In this transaction, DC Water is also the first issuer of any sort in the United States to gain a third party green certification for the century bonds. These steps brought in new investors for DC Water and will more equitably spread costs to ratepayers over the life of unique assets.

Finance and Research. DC Water instituted a nutrient rebate fee on our biosolids, which has funded a research program. Funded research projects have demonstrated that crops grown with biosolid fertilizers are more drought-resistant and produce higher yields—due to the high levels of vital, naturally occurring plant hormones in organic biosolids.

Aging Infrastructure. DC has water mains that have a median age of 79 years, and sewer mains that are even older. Digging up the streets and front yards to replace mains and the laterals that connect the mains to the residences and buildings is time consuming and disruptive. DC Water has now tested and is deploying trenchless technology that is essentially an inner liner on older pipes—extending the useful life by decades, decreasing construction time, and saving more than $1 million over the last two years. We are expanding the program as we speak. Facing a similar issue with much larger transmission water mains six feet in diameter and larger, we are testing and deploying a carbon fiber wrap that avoids fantastically expensive and time consuming replacement.

Information Technology and Customer Response. DC Water has developed an integrated work and resource management program that integrates every service call, vehicle locations, equipment and inventory staging on the same map. These maps are used by our Command Center to deploy in seconds what had taken 20–30 minutes and will soon be deployed in the cabs for our field crews.

Local Hiring. DC Water Works! is our program to boost local hiring for projects mainly funded and implemented within the District of Columbia. DC Water advertises all open positions on staff and with contractors, collaborates with local job training and apprenticeship programs, and has a financial incentive pilot to encourage contractors to hire local residents. DC Water supplements this effort with three satellite job centers.

Communication. Responding to customers is the highest priority at DC Water—and we deploy a 13-person external affairs office to lead the charge. The team includes in-house designers and videographers, social media experts and a community outreach team. The group tracks our dozens of projects at any given time and interacts with community members and groups throughout the city.

There are dozens of stories to share about innovation at DC Water— and across our industry. We embody the value of water by devoting our time and attention to always improving how we care for and deliver this precious resource. At DC Water, we feel like we have just begun!

GEORGE B. CASSADY, PE
DIRECTOR
HILLSBOROUGH COUNTY PUBLIC
UTILITIES DEPARTMENT

Water - Value, Sustainability, and the Future

A s a water utility, our number one priority is to provide quality water to the customers and community we serve. Nested within that priority are the important everyday components of utility operations, including sourcing the water, treating the water, distributing the water, taking care of the assets, and meeting customer expectations. Our focus is to have an efficient and effective utility operation, and one that delivers products and services at a cost that is understood to be a good value.

I think we can all agree that the business environment for water providers has changed considerably over the past couple of years. The economic downturn taught us that we had to change our fundamental approach to the business itself. The traditional annual rate increases in response to increased operational expenses is no longer the norm. Now more than ever, rate increases of any size are cause for concern in the community. Both elected officials and administration leadership are under great pressure to keep the cost of government down, and especially the cost of what many consider to be essential, basic public services.

Then of course there are the customers themselves, many of which live on limited or fixed budgets where any type of increase, no matter how small, can have a significant impact on their lives. For these reasons, it is important for utility leadership to actively explore every reasonable opportunity to minimize future rate impacts. We consider establishing a utility culture that instinctively strives to maximize efficiency while minimizing costs the hallmark of a viable and sustainable operation.

We have all recently witnessed how the lack of sound fiscal management by a utility can lead to catastrophic impacts to an entire community. One of the aftermaths of the economic downtown for a major metropolitan utility in the United States was the accrual of billions of dollars in debt. This unnamed utility then took actions to shut off water to thousands of residents and businesses in an effort to collect delinquent payments from its customers. The public outcry was swift and far-reaching, including being viewed by the United Nations and the World Health Organization as a violation of public health and safety, with significant negative impacts to children, seniors and low-income residents. This incident was a sobering reminder that there are more than just business objectives to be considered in the operation of a utility—that even in our own country, we cannot underestimate the impact of delivering water to our customers.

Because of the sensitivities to cost increases, utilities have to become more efficient and look for ways to reduce operational costs. Protecting the customer and minimizing the expense of providing water has become a central theme and management focus for most water utilities. As the utility community, there are two questions that we must ask when making decisions about our future. First, what can we do to sustain the utility? And second, what is the ultimate value of the services provided to our customers? More specifically to the second point, what is the acceptable cost threshold that the customer is willing to consider for the water and services provided to them?

Gone are the days of cheap abundant source waters. Water scarcity is occurring throughout the country as a result of population increases, weather pattern changes, source water quality concerns, renewed industrialization, and other causes. The concept of operational sustainability was introduced to the utility industry in about the same time frame as the turndown in the economy. Protecting the resource, ensuring availability, and keeping costs down have become topics of great interest and discussion. We use the word *sustainability* to cover a wide range of issues, from water conservation to financial decision making. All in all, we understand that a sustainable operation is one that minimizes the demands on resources, maximizes efficiencies, and leverages the business opportunities to reduce its environmental footprint going forward.

So how do we get there? Taking advantage of technology enhancements is a good start. Making use of modern, efficient equipment can help drive down the demand for power use and the associated cost of electricity. Advanced instrumentation and control systems help monitor system operations for problems and often times can help resolve small issues before they become costly or directly impact customers.

Gaining economies of scale by outsourcing support services that are not an integral part of the core business can also help reduce costs. Combined, these efforts support an ultimate goal to keep the long-term costs flat, which in our business means the cost to produce a gallon of water is the same or less next year and the following year.

However, there is more to the sustainability discussion than just operational efficiency. There is an element that can often be overlooked but is critical to the sustained success of the utility; that element is the customer. How does all of this sustainability talk and effort translate to our customers? It is simple; our customers can and should expect high-quality, good-tasting water at a cost that is reasonably priced and a good value. Moreover, they should be part of the dialogue, part of the effort and decision-making process. The customer is not just the end user of water that is delivered to their house or business but rather an integral community stakeholder that should be involved and engaged in decisions about the resource that everyone needs and uses.

This brings us to the discussion of the value of water. What is the value of the services we as a utility provide our customers? What are the actual costs versus the perceived values? These are questions we ask ourselves all the time. The concept of value can be quite complex. Beyond the philosophical and emotional value of water, there is the actual dollars and cents component that we must deal with. Often, it is difficult to have the cost discussion without overlapping some aspect of the personal attachment customers have to the water they need and use every day. We have to balance the ultimate expense of delivering water with the perception of our customers as to the value of the services we provide.

The value of water can be measured in several ways. Of course, there is the life-sustaining value that we could say is priceless. There are also cultural values of water that provide an identity for whole populations. Recreational value, business/industrial value and, of course, agricultural value all have a part of the discussion and must be considered in the overall process. I like to think about the value of water as an equation. The value equation suggests that the there is really more than just one factor or aspect to consider when we place a value on the product. It is the combined value of all the potential uses that get us to a place that we can relate a value, or cost. We can segregate the uses, recreation versus safety, life sustaining versus agricultural, but the fact is the water all comes from the same place. For the utility, once we treat and prepare the water for distribution, there is one delivered cost for all purposes.

Interestingly, the end use that carries the most critical need is delivered at the same cost as all the other uses. For example, filling an average size backyard pool (approximately 15,000 gallons) uses enough water to sustain life for the average person for over 75 years! I wonder if you asked someone what he or she would be willing to pay to fill his or her pool compared to a lifetime of water what the answer would be.

The value of water and the value of the services a utility provide its customers are ultimately determined by the partnership developed between the two. The relationship that our utility has with its customers has changed and will continue to change. Twenty years ago, we took the on-ramp to the information superhighway. Today, we are savvy commuters using high speed Internet and mobile devices to communicate, transfer information, and socially engage with the world around us. The utility of old was happy being the best kept secret in town, quietly going about its business of providing water to the community and largely going unnoticed. Today, it is impossible to go unnoticed. Beyond having running water when they turn on the tap, customers want information and access. Customers want an experience that includes immediate feedback on questions and concerns. The utility of today has to engage the customer base, creating that customer experience, and do more than it ever has before to construct a true utility/customer partnership.

The ideal result of such a partnership is that a customer base is so engaged and so connected that the value of water and the value of the utility services is redefined. We need to create a customer base that understands the concept of using the lowest quality water needed for a purpose and water conservation. The customer base would actively implements and pursues those opportunities and consider expanding the use of rain barrels for garden watering, or encouraging the use of low volume fixtures inside and outside the home, or taking advantage of recycled water to help drive down the use of drinking water. We envision a utility working collaboratively with the community to build an understanding of the importance and prioritization of infrastructure upgrades or system improvements.

Our goal is to have a customer-centric culture where employees put themselves in the citizens' shoes to anticipate and provide answers before there are questions and position the community to learn about *their* water utility. Ultimately, it is about showing the residents and our customers that we are an active and caring part of the community we all share, and are investing a sense of ownership and shared responsibility.

This is the utility we need to create; this is our dream for the sustainable utility.

Back to hard reality, let's talk a little more about the cost part of value. As with any consumer-based product, value follows quality and benefit. Anyone involved with market research will tell you that a consumer is generally willing to pay more for a product that is of high quality or of perceived high benefit. It then follows that we need to get the water customer engaged and show them that the water we provide is of the highest quality available; show the customer that from any perspective of the value equation (life sustaining, recreation, business, and agriculture) the cost is clearly a great value. If we compare the cost of water to other services we enjoy, like cell phones, electricity, or cable television, the cost of water is most often many times less.

At the end of the day, the challenge remains to closely link the quality and value of our product with the cost of the service. A partnership with customers can help get us there by building a shared responsibility that reinforces the concept of value for the water and service we provide. Although we inherently understand the importance of water and the essential role the utility fulfills in our community, our future depends on effectively creating customer advocates who recognize the true value we provide to their everyday lives.

BILL GAFFI
GENERAL MANGER
CLEAN WATER SERVICES

It Takes a Village to Restore Mother Nature

Something very special is happening in the Tualatin River Watershed of Washington County, Oregon. Mother Nature is making a comeback and sending her best spokespersons to let us know we must be doing something right. People, water, and nature are experiencing a renaissance. It is amazing to watch the fish and wildlife return to the Tualatin River and its tributaries.

There Is Something in the Water

Walking down the pedestrian path along Fanno Creek, an urban tributary to the Tualatin, one now sees a shaded stream that provides enriching habitat for birds, fish, and humans alike. In the backwater of a recently constructed beaver dam, ducks, and fish are finding the kind of habitat needed to raise their families and, at the same time, support the recreational opportunities that are provided by a pedestrian trail running next to Mother Nature's playground. What is really inspiring is this same story is being played out along 65 river miles of the Tualatin River Watershed.

A half century ago a notable farmer straddled the Tualatin River 40 miles downstream from its headwaters. Something happened along those 40 miles that had reduced river water flows to a trickle. Where there had once been a vast expanse of beaver dams and wetlands blanketed along the valley floor, rural and urban needs began to challenge Mother Nature. Beaver were trapped out and wetlands drained or filled. Streams were straightened, wells dug, water diverted, and thriving farms and cities created. The urban soil/waterscape had been transformed into a Swiss cheese of road cuts, foundation drains, and utility trenches. Water was hurried across and from under rural and urban areas, robbing streams of summer flow. The water that did make it to creeks was pumped out to satisfy the thirst of the watershed's new inhabitants. Dozens of small inadequate sewage treatment plants struggled to serve cities scattered across the basin.

Communities had turned their backs on the once vibrant Tualatin River. Farmers in need of more water convinced Congress to build a reservoir. The state of Oregon placed a building moratorium across the urban portion of the watershed to force a cleanup of the river. A nascent environmental movement joined forces with the business community, the League of Women Voters, every editorial board in the region, and citizens across the basin and in calling for a regional solution to rescue the river. In 1970, citizens overwhelmingly voted to form Clean Water Services (CWS), one of the nation's first regional utilities, to tackle the job.

Within a decade, the Tualatin River began showing signs of life as CWS consolidated and improved treatment facilities and acquired nearly one quarter of this new stored water to bring life-giving flow back to the Tualatin. In 1990, the region again called on CWS to establish a comprehensive stormwater utility to protect streams, to control erosion, and to manage the public drainage system.

Subsequent local, state, and federal regulatory initiatives focused on nutrient reduction and protection of near stream areas. Much effort followed, but as recently as 10 years ago, one could still witness a very different Fanno Creek than exists today. One saw fields emptied of their original tree cover and blanketed with invasive reed canary grass and blackberry bushes. There was little shade, no beavers, no ducklings, and a few juvenile fish struggling for life in water that was too hot. So what has changed? Extensive investments in clean water facilities and stormwater management set the stage for further restoration of riparian and wetland habitats, but streams continued to suffer from a siloed, fragmented statutory, regulatory, and institutional framework.

Hard-won gains had been made in water quality. Challenges remained that demanded that the entire watershed community play a role in welcoming Mother Nature back to the Tualatin River Watershed. The river and its tributaries are still too hot and need more flow. Unprecedented collaboration among disparate local, state, federal and private water resource and land management interests were still needed to address remaining issues. That collaboration has begun and is growing across the Tualatin Basin.

In 2004, CWS asked local governments, farmers, and nonprofit organizations to hurry the return of Mother Nature to the Watershed through broad-based and active restoration of near stream areas. CWS needed to address the impact of nearly 60 million gallons of warm cleaned water it discharged to the Tualatin each day. Rather than investing over $150,000,000 in construction and operation of energy-guzzling chillers that would produce only minor localized cooling, CWS turned to both agricultural and urban partners for help in restoring cooling canopy over streams and transporting stored water into tributaries to restore flow.

The current restoration movement within the watershed builds upon a growing conservation ethic within all parts of the watershed. All hands are helping to bring meaningful scale to the effort. Solid partnerships have been forged with farmers and others were positioned to help. Although such potential partners recognized the need for greater conservation, they lacked the support needed to make it happen.

Clean Water Services, farmers, cities, parks districts, nonprofit organizations, and others to came together to design and begin implementing an array of restoration programs on farms and in urban areas.

Farmers Are Really Smart and Good Business People

Washington County, Oregon, and its Tualatin River Watershed, are home to some of the nation's most productive farmland. Helping farmers succeed, while helping bring Mother Nature back to local streams, required a novel approach. Farmers seem to speak more clearly and more convincingly to other farmers than we do in government. CWS needed their help, and they gave it.

A partnership was formed that was in everyone's economic interest and in the interest of the entire watershed. Agricultural interests and CWS got together and found ways to support a strong agricultural community, to keep sewer rates low, and to bring Mother Nature back to local streams. Together, we enhanced existing federal programs, built new local programs, and helped create community capacity for large-scale, meaningful restoration.

Oregon's Economic Engine Nurtured By Mother Nature

Water and environmental quality have fueled Oregon's economy, the heart of which beats most strongly in the Tualatin Basin. Home to a giant Intel presence and Nike's world headquarters, the Tualatin Basin is Oregon's economic engine.

As the agricultural community helped shape new strategies to assist Mother Nature, other partners worked on similar restoration goals in urban Washington County. Cities, community groups, and civic organizations responded to a "Tree For All Challenge" to restore miles of streamside vegetation and shade. Public open space and parks along urban streams provided a ripe opportunity to bring the needs of nature and the community together by leveraging previously unrelated programs.

The regional government and an area parks district had passed measures to fund green spaces and parks. They partnered with CWS to make their properties available for stream restoration.

Growing Stronger Watersheds and Communities

Together, these partnerships have brought 15,000 acres under conservation and restored over 65 miles of stream within the first 10 years of collaboration. Over four million trees have been planted, and the combined capacity created will plant over 1,000,000 in 2015 alone. The ecological response has been remarkable—it has taken Mother Nature's breath away—it has astonished even the most skeptical. The civic response has been equally impressive.

A local restoration economy was born and long-term stewardship of the Tualatin's natural resources strengthened. It also helped align and magnify the effects of disparate conservation efforts. It allowed Mother Nature and our citizenry to embrace a new and richer water environment.

The principles of "collective impact" have brought great power and speed to the restoration of the Tualatin Basin. Working together, varied interests have accomplished far more than anyone could have alone, but much work remains. Enduring partnerships should make that work something Mother Nature will smile upon. However, there are clouds on the horizon.

A Square Peg In A Round Hole

This describes the challenge of regulating the flow-deprived segments of Tualatin River tributaries and wetlands using Oregon's water quality standards, which were designed for regulating free-flowing rivers. Many have no discernable flow in late summer. Climate change promises to aggravate that situation. Oregon's water quality standards will not be achievable in such stream segments even if all human-caused pollution is abated. Slow, stagnant waters just cannot be expected to have the same water quality as a river with healthy flows. Flow really matters!

Efforts to decrease impervious areas at the same time development is being greatly densified (with resultant shortening of subsurface flow pathways) offer limited promise of restoring summer flows but could reduce flashiness of tributaries. In the Tualatin Basin's claying soil, green streets delay runoff for minutes, not for months as was historically provided by a vast system of wetlands, floodplains, and beaver ponds.

Green streets are serving to reduce overflow frequency and magnitude in communities outside the basin served by sewers carrying both sewage and stormwater. They could play an ever-increasing role as climate change puts more pressure on combined systems. Tualatin Basin communities do not have combined systems, so the focus of drainage management here is the protection of streams from pollution and erosion and property from flooding.

As more is learned about the water quality in tributaries during low flows, more and more of them become slated for new regulatory controls. Neither the state nor the EPA has the resources to promulgate regulations and amend permits to address the many varied circumstances that characterize these tributaries and wetlands. No one is interested in abandoning efforts to restore tributaries to health. To what extent will this dilemma threaten Oregon's economy if not addressed?

So What's To Be Done?

Local interests, in collaboration with state and federal partners, need to fashion a path forward or suffer the consequence of failing to do so. Hopefully, it will offer a vehicle to better understand the needs of the watershed and create the tools, processes, and partnerships critical to finishing the restoration of watershed health. An ecologically and economically sustainable strategy must be created to avoid exhausting public support long before producing the benefits the public expects. Efforts must continue to overcome barriers to Mother Nature's permanent return to the Tualatin Basin.

How Are We Going To Get There?

Together! Our watershed is rather like a patient being treated by dozens of specialists with limited communication and no generalized plan of care. We need a generalized plan of care. Partnerships are critical to delivery of that care. Both engineering and natural systems are needed. More cool, flowing water (nature's lifeblood) must once again nourish the watershed. Restored wetlands (the original kidneys of our streams) will complement engineered means of cleansing runoff.

Floodplains need to be managed for their flood abatement and the ecological services they can provide. Reactivated floodplains and beaver ponds will calm raging currents and create needed habitat. The one ingredient nature cannot compel is the collaboration needed to make this happen. That is our responsibility. The collective WE must emerge to combine and expand our individual capabilities and extend our reach. The alternative path will misdirect scarce resources and squander public confidence and trust that is so precious in today's world.

Great progress has been made, but more effort is required to build the collective we in the Tualatin Watershed and in watersheds across the globe. It will demand talking to and working with strangers and those that challenge us.

It is not likely to be the product of decree or rule, but it is necessary and hard work. Our current trajectory is not sustainable. Mother Nature and our citizenry are depending upon us to engage them and each other in this vital pursuit. Join us!

JAMES A. "TONY" PARROTT
EXECUTIVE DIRECTOR
GCWW/MSDGC

Investment in Infrastructure: Extending the Value of Water for Urban Communities

For many urban communities, the value of water extends well beyond the obvious public health benefits. Aging infrastructure in our urban core areas is currently requiring billions of dollars in investment. That is investment in communities hit hardest by the economic downturn and years of neglect. The critical discussion that must take place today is how to maximize the value of water and wastewater investments by identifying intersections between those investments and the community's challenges and by taking bold steps to address both.

A recent discussion among a group of general managers of water and wastewater agencies across the country revealed that the 20 systems represented plan to spend an estimated $12 billion in operating and capital budgets per year. Economic predictions for our industry also estimate 700,000 jobs will be created across the country, while increasing the nation's gross domestic product by $416 billion over the next two decades through investments in aging water, sewer, and stormwater infrastructure. Figures like these put into perspective the significant outlay that water systems make annually in their local communities, and also elevate the water industry to a status generally reserved for "big business" in terms of dollars invested, jobs created, and overall significance to a community's economic engine.

Harnessing the power of these investments to bring benefits beyond public health can be achieved on several fronts, including building the community of the future through revitalization, adopting integrated solutions, and supporting workforce development.

Building a community of the future means making investments that our children and grandchildren will look back on and agree that the right investments were made at the right time to benefit a generation down the road. That is the true definition of sustainability.

In Cincinnati, we have made a conscious decision to do more than bury water and sewer assets underground where they address only one dimension of our community's challenges. The Metropolitan Sewer District of Greater Cincinnati (MSD) is implementing its vision of solutions that not only meet regulatory requirements but also bring sustainable aboveground investment to the community. The concept is to increase the value of water for our urban area by serving as a catalyst for economic revitalization through the restoration of natural systems and the creation of livable areas that improve quality of life for neighborhoods that for years have been struggling with urban decline. The magnitude of challenges to this approach has been daunting, but MSD leadership stands by the belief that momentous problems require robust solutions.

Like many older urban areas, MSD is focusing a great deal on combined sewer overflows (CSOs). Every year, about 11.5 billion gallons of raw sewage mixed with stormwater overflows from area sewers into local streams and rivers and also backs up into basements across Hamilton County. This is not an accident or oversight but the result of a sewer system designed to meet the needs of an earlier generation. According to the USEPA, Hamilton County is just one of the estimated 772 communities across the United States with aging combined sewer systems. MSD has been working for more than a decade to resolve this problem, and like other urban areas, it was issued a formal Consent Decree by USEPA mandating that MSD capture, treat, or remove a significant volume of CSOs and eliminate all sanitary sewer overflows (SSOs).

MSD expects to spend an estimated $3 billion over the next 30 years to meet the Consent Decree and to improve water quality, one of the largest public works projects in Hamilton County's more than 200-year history. Although the initial solution proposed by the regulatory community was to build a deep tunnel, MSD believed that so substantial an investment should do more for the citizens of Cincinnati and Hamilton County than a tunnel offered. An alternative plan was pursued that would invest the dollars primarily in green infrastructure to spark revitalization, an approach proven in other communities.

The cornerstone of the first phase of what was dubbed Project Groundwork is the Lick Run project that will directly benefit a community that over the past two decades has experienced a 55% decline in property values and an unemployment rate of nearly 40% just within a one-mile stretch of the area. Foreclosures, shuttered businesses, and crime unfortunately defined a community that once had a proud history of working class families. Much of the investment MSD needed to make in addressing the CSO challenge was centered in this community, so an unconventional approach was devised for a more sustainable investment that would not only achieve the objectives of the Consent Decree but also bring forth a tangible community asset. The Lick Run project will bring the historical wealth of water to the surface by creating a natural conveyance system that will offload stormwater from the existing combined sewer system while also creating a scenic community amenity.

The valley conveyance system will include a naturalized waterway with an aboveground meandering stream channel with natural stone, pools and riffles, and a riparian edge planted with native plants and trees. An underground stormwater conveyance box will be constructed beneath the system to handle flows from large rain events. Along the stream channel, members of the community can take advantage of amenities including a multiuse path, an improved civic recreation space, parking, and bridges. Ultimately, when MSD's work is done as a public utility, this amenity will influence private-side investments that will create growth opportunities for local businesses, stimulate the economic job engine, and reestablish this historic community as a place where families can prosper.

Water investments of this type may be easily communicated to the community, because the value is evident aboveground. The greater challenge, not only in Cincinnati, but also across the country, is communicating the value of water investments when the proof is less visible.

Water and sewer agencies make enormous investments every day that protect public health, but go largely unnoticed. A recent example for us in Cincinnati came when a spill in the Elk River upstream in West Virginia threatened the Ohio River, the primary source water supply for our community of more than 1.1 million. Because of investments we had made over the years in our water system, we were able to close our intakes for more than 30 hours while the spill flowed past. Although we have a treatment system that could have handled the spill, the fact that we were able to eliminate any impact to our drinking water underscores the significant value of having an infrastructure in place to save the public from a potentially dangerous spill.

Adopting integrated solutions is another key element of harnessing the power of investment to increase the value of water. Water and wastewater treatment and delivery are among the greatest gifts that we have within our communities. Over the coming decade we need to sharpen our focus on leveraging the investments, we make across these services. One of the most important ways to do that is to break down the silos between water, wastewater, and stormwater and move toward the concept of "one water."

In Cincinnati, we have done that by integrating our water and our wastewater utilities under one administration and one management. This unified approach not only saves money for ratepayers by offering increased service delivery efficiencies, but also allows us to think with one mind when exploring opportunities for added value through infrastructure investments. There are currently about a dozen metropolitan cities that have moved in this direction, and it is important that we continue to explore this trend, particularly for our urban core areas.

The next logical step is to look beyond "one water" at how we can we be more collaborative with other investments that are going on within our urban core communities to further maximize the benefit. Collaboration with agencies such as the U.S. Department of Housing and Urban Development (HUD) should be happening now. To leverage the infrastructure investments that we are making, we must first understand the current conditions of the urban communities that we are serving. Partnering and working collaboratively with agencies such as HUD that have intimate local knowledge of neighborhoods with blighted properties, unemployment, and other constraints to success allows us to make meaningful decisions about investment.

Understanding the objective HUD has on a national basis to create livable and walkable communities allows us to enter the discussion of how sustainable and green infrastructure can support those objectives. We can begin to set up or change local codes to ensure that neighborhoods are livable and walkable, a key element in bringing back populations to the urban core of our communities. Collaborative vision means a reality where communities are based upon what the community wants to see.

As water utilities look out over the next few decades, we must recognize the opportunity we have to be a voice in the social outcome of the communities that we are serving by supporting workforce development. In the urban core of American cities such as Milwaukee, Cleveland, and

Cincinnati, it is not uncommon to have unemployment of 40%–50%. As water and sewer agencies, we are providing service to that urban core, so the question becomes why not invest in technology and a new class of jobs that offer opportunities for the residents that we serve to find work.

There are examples of programs, such as in San Francisco where more than 36,000 jobs were created in rebuilding the water and wastewater system. According to the Department of Commerce, every dollar we invest creates another $2.62 in the local economy, and for every job we create, an additional 3.6 jobs are created within our economy. Given that, the investments that water and wastewater agencies make must be viewed in terms of the return on investment to the local economy.

Water and wastewater utilities are in a unique position across the country. Recidivism is a major issue in our urban areas, and those areas are the focus of much of the infrastructure investment. As agencies poised to make an impact, we should be at the table taking part in discussions about how to train and employ ex-offenders to take the strain off law enforcement. Actively seeking a role in that social discussion in the communities that we serve will reshape our role as utilities and release even greater value for the water we manage.

Now is the opportunity for water and wastewater agencies to deliver the value of water to our urban core areas with investments that improve not only public health, but also overall quality of life. The time is right for us to do this because we are at such a critical stage with our infrastructure—we recognize that significant investments must be made.

Harnessing the power of these investments for revitalized communities, integrated solutions, and a strong local workforce should be at the heart of our decisions today and well into the future.

DAVID KOHLER

PRESIDENT AND CHIEF OPERATING OFFICER

KOHLER CO.

Water Efficiency: A Business Imperative

I was blessed to be born in a part of the world (East Central Wisconsin, USA) that has always had abundant supplies of freshwater. My great grandfather established Kohler Co. in 1873 near the shore of Lake Michigan, and for most of the company's history, water scarcity was never a concern. Water was clean, plentiful, easily accessible and essentially free. However, as our business expanded globally, water has become a significant factor in deciding where to site plants, what technologies to develop, and how to engage with customers.

Kohler's global manufacturing operations use water in a variety of ways. Most significant of these are cooling water in our foundries, process water in our potteries, and irrigation of our golf courses. As part of our corporate sustainability strategy that was formally launched in 2008, we committed to reduce water use intensity of our business by 50% by

2035. As of 2013, we have achieved a 23% reduction from the 2008 baseline, with other projects still being implemented. I've personally challenged our business leaders to prioritize water efficiency in all regions, particularly where local water supplies are less secure. I believe a "near net zero" manufacturing facility is feasible, and probably a necessity in places like Texas and California in the United States, and in India, China, and Mexico. Water availability is clearly a business risk, but one that we feel can be mitigated through improved process control and treatment technologies. Our success so far gives us confidence that we can reach our goals.

Irrigation of our golf courses poses a different set of challenges. Kohler Co. operates four championship caliber courses in Sheboygan County, Wisconsin, and one in St. Andrews, Scotland. In normal years, rainfall supplies a large portion of the water needed to keep the courses healthy and provide an exceptional golf experience for our guests. But hot, dry years, such as 2012, can be a challenge. Our courses are specially designed and managed to minimize the need for irrigation water and fertilizers. In doing so, we are able to provide our patrons with an aesthetically pleasing course, to improve the playability of the courses, and to minimize runoff into the local watersheds.

Kohler's mission statement drives us to "contribute to a higher level of gracious living for those who are touched by our products and services." The design of our products and the experiences our customers have with them is the essence of our brand. And within our Kitchen and Bath business, those experiences are largely created with water. Whether it is a relaxing shower at the end of a long day, or preparing dinner for family in the kitchen, Kohler products are created to make those tasks easier, more efficient, and more "gracious." Water is also central to providing world-class recreational experiences at our hotels, spas, and championship golf courses. As water resources become scarcer and increasingly more expensive, we are being challenged to provide better experiences that employ less water and energy.

Providing those experiences more efficiently requires cooperation between our company and those who use our products. Most people around the world start and end their day with water, whether for personal hygiene, sanitation, or food preparation. Water is woven into the fabric of all our lives, and because much of that water enters and leaves homes through Kohler plumbing products, we have a unique opportunity and important responsibility to engage and educate our consumers on water issues.

Efficiency of the plumbing fixture or faucet plays an important role, but the actual amount of water used by a product also depends on how it is used. So a fundamental question for our business is: "How can we provide an ever more gracious experience in a world where water supplies are increasingly stressed and water quality is declining?"

It is clear that the first thing that Kohler should do is to design our products to be more efficient. Over the past 10 years, this has been a major focus for our product development teams around the world. Guided by the specifications of the U.S. Environmental Protection Agency's WaterSense product labeling program, Kohler has re-engineered most of its toilets, bathroom faucets, urinals and many of its showerheads to use at least 20% less water than legally allowed.

Although this may sound fairly straightforward, in fact, it has demanded significant breakthroughs in product design, most of which the end user would not notice. For the most part, the products look very similar to what they did 10 years ago, but they use less water and, much to our delight, function a great deal better. This has had a significant impact—from 2007 through 2013—Kohler products sold in the United States have reduced water use by approximately 50 billion gallons and energy that would have been required to pump and heat that water by approximately 3 billion kWh.

Although our plumbing products have become more efficient, we also recognize that how they are used affects overall water consumption. Kohler is using its leadership position to help consumers understand how their choices can make a difference. Through a combination of education and awareness outreach strategies, such as our dedicated website and targeted marketing campaigns to consumers, skilled trades and professional specifiers, we have engaged and inspired others to join us in making responsible decisions to reduce water use. We have had good success in the United States and are developing appropriate messages on water efficiency for other regions where we do business.

For example, in 2011, the Bill and Melinda Gates Foundation began funding projects to address health and sanitation issues. The California Institute of Technology was one of several teams awarded grants to develop a prototype toilet system.

Their system includes a self-contained water purification and disinfection process, which allows water to be reused and does not require wastewater disposal. It made us proud to see Kohler collaborate with CalTech by providing them with all the plumbing products and design support the team required, as well as our full-fledged, on-the-ground technical support for the system's field trial in India in 2014. We were impressed with the CalTech team for its innovative and resourceful thinking, and we were only too pleased to help rally around this concept and offer our technical and product support. There are no guarantees of success, but transforming this plan into action will help us better understand the technical, social, and economic challenges of new models of dealing with human waste.

Reducing water use is a necessary first step that buys time for society to implement more wide-ranging solutions. Our longer-term concern is about water availability and water quality, especially in places like China and India. How can a Kohler customer have a gracious experience with our products if he or she does not trust the purity of the water? It is clear that the rapid growth of demands for water for agriculture, industry, power generation and direct human use such as sanitation and hygiene are unsustainable over the coming decades.

A new model is needed. Perhaps technologies such as decentralized water and wastewater treatment that can be built quickly and do not require large amounts of capital funding up front will soon become mainstream. New treatment technologies that remove not only pathogens but also emerging contaminants, such as pharmaceuticals and endocrine disruptors, will augment existing water treatment systems. And automation and communication technologies will give consumers real-time access to information about their water supply. They will expect to know that the water entering their homes for everyday use is safe and will not put their families in harm's way.

Society as a whole ultimately needs a new ethic for how we value and manage our water supplies. Water is essential for economic and environmental prosperity. It is also essential for human health and rejuvenation of the spirit. Kohler Co. plans to continue to help lead this transformation with new products, technologies, education, and advocacy. We accept the responsibility and are ready to take action.

DEAN AMHAUS
PRESIDENT AND CHIEF EXECUTIVE OFFICER
THE WATER COUNCIL

Emerging Water Crisis Creates Economic Opportunities for an American Water Technology Cluster

While "water, water, everywhere, nor any drop to drink" was certainly the tale of many a sailor centuries ago, I cannot help but also think about the current residents of California, or more recently, Toledo, Ohio, as they see massive amounts of water close to where they live but their refrain would still be "nor any drop to drink."

In many ways, water is all around us whether in our oceans or glaciers, buried deep underground, or in the lakes and rivers that weave through most of our planet. Unfortunately, salt water comprises 97.5% of all of the water on Earth's surface with less than one percent of the world's freshwater available for direct human consumption.

It is a precious resource for all of us today, but what is more alarming is the outlook for the future with population growth that seems to have a trajectory that is only straight up. We are also seeing an important shift in where these growing populations live with more and more people moving to cities as they seek economic opportunities—cities that are likely already under huge strain to provide water for its citizens.

Energy gets a lot of attention from governments to the media, but there was a time when we as humans actually did live without oil. That cannot be said for water. Other than breathing air, water is essential to life for humans as well as plants and animals.

Although water has been shortchanged for a very long time, I do believe that a dramatic shift is underway, and there is a realization that the "value of water" is great.

The World Faces a Water Challenge

The world is undergoing a catastrophic water crisis. As populations continue to surge around the world, developing countries like India and China are increasingly feeling the crunch to address the poor water qualities that plague their lands, which is also the cause of water-borne illness and, in many instances when speaking of children, death. It is estimated that every 20 seconds, a child dies due to poor water quality or lack of a clean, reliable water source.

The water crisis that was once thought of as a tragedy of the third world and undeveloped countries has now made its way to many parts of the United States. Although the challenges we face are slightly different than those faced overseas, the sense of urgency is very real, and just as immediate.

"According to the U.S. Drought Monitor, over 48% of the United States was in drought status as of May 2014. 77% of California is now considered to be in 'extreme or exceptional' drought conditions. Parts of the Plains states are experiencing drought circumstances comparable to the 1930s Dust Bowl. In 2012, drought conditions cost a record $30 billion in damage.

Water shortages aren't likely to slow down, since population growth in drought-prone states including CA, TX, AZ, NV, and CO is booming. Although businesses are prospering in many of these water-stressed states, the effects of growing populations, limited resources, and increasing consumption are a triple threat to companies of any size."

You might guess that the above quote came from a federal agency, an environmental organization or a large, water-dependent business. It did not. It is from a message by AT&T's Director of Sustainability Operations on June 8, 2014. Why should a telecommunications company like AT&T care? Although it is important to them to wisely use this precious resource, the bottom line for AT&T and many other global companies is to save money.

Global water issues will take center stage in the coming years as economically devastated countries search for answers and solutions; tragically, the human toll will unmercifully ravage thousands of innocent lives before the situation gets better. Pressure will undoubtedly be felt in the global water clusters of the world, including Singapore, the Netherlands, and now Milwaukee, as we are appointed with the monumental task of solving the world's water issues.

Emergence of the Water Council and Milwaukee's Water Technology Cluster

Back in 2007, private sector leaders saw the potential of water emerging as a global issue, and also recognized that Milwaukee was uniquely positioned to become a solution provider for global challenges because of its established and extensive history engaged in the study, treatment, storage, and movement of water within the full water cycle. Milwaukee's broad-based water technology leadership has evolved over more than 100 years of finding innovative solutions for the most important water issues facing the world.

With companies that can trace their history back many generations and whose names are synonymous with the world's leading water businesses are the births of new water-technology companies that are helping to shape the region into a world water hub.

The Milwaukee region already had the assets needed to accomplish this fete, but it lacked a central unit to guide the development of this future water technology cluster, that is until the creation of The Water Council.

The Water Council is the nonprofit, economic development organization founded to be the convener of Milwaukee's water technology cluster based on three broad goals: Economic development, technology development, and education. We have spent the last seven years building upon Milwaukee's established, historic and extensive water technology industry; investing in the development of the cluster that now has widespread recognition as a global water hub of excellence and innovation.

On the cusp of elevating Milwaukee and our water technology cluster to the next level, The Water Council has adopted a new Leadership Strategic Vision, which positions us as an international organization focused on improving the human condition around the world through focused research, collaboration, innovation, standards setting, and entrepreneurship.

The Water Council has established itself as a global leader in the water industry and one of America's premier economic development clusters. Driving this success has been the spirit of collaboration between the public and the private sectors and a shared commitment to finding innovative solutions to critical global water issues. The Water Council has convened industry professionals, government, nongovernmental organizations, academia, and innovative entrepreneurs to develop solutions and address these pressing global water issues.

Economic Development Around Water Technology

One of the main goals of The Water Council has been economic development in the Milwaukee region as it applies to water technology. Here is a sample of achievements Milwaukee can now boast:

- Being home to more than 160 water technology companies employing well over 20,000 workers
- Capturing $10.5 billion or four percent of the world's water industry market
- Opening the Global Water Center, a 98,000 square foot remodeled warehouse that now serves as a business accelerator and research center focused on advancing water technology commercialization
- Serving as the home to the UW–Milwaukee School of Freshwater Sciences and its $54 million recent renovation and expansion into a state-of-the-art research facility
- Being the home to numerous small and mid-sized businesses providing niche solutions, large global corporations providing key products and services, countless skilled engineers, renowned scientists, and higher education programs including Center for Water Policy, Institute for Water Business, Great Lakes Genomics Center, Water Quality Center and Center for Limnology

In order to successfully establish the region as a global water hub, The Water Council had to gain support from key stakeholders and build an environment of collaboration not just among the public and private sectors, but also between the various universities and various water companies. Floating the idea that each stakeholder would mutually benefit from a shared vision of coalescing these strengths and creating this center of excellence in innovation was very attractive to all involved. It would give the region a competitive advantage and, in turn, trickle down to each of the respective organizations.

The opening of the Global Water Center in September 2013 was a huge milestone as The Water Council transformed the shuttered warehouse into a state-of-the-art water innovation facility. It became the physical hub of Milwaukee's water technology cluster, and a world-class model of collaboration for research and technology development. The center houses office and research space for industry giants, academic institutes, small and medium sized water businesses, and energetic water entrepreneurs.

The building also houses The BREW (Business. Research. Entrepreneurship. In Wisconsin.) Accelerator, the only mentor-driven seed accelerator program in the country that is strictly focused on solving global freshwater issues. The idea is that these young startup companies and small- and medium-sized businesses will provide innovative, disruptive technologies that will challenge the status quo of current practices and offer new perspectives to addressing the global water crisis. Many of our entrepreneurs have already formed partnerships with the larger corporate entities within the building, and we hope this environment of collaboration and synergy spills over, outside the walls of the Global Water Center to our entire water network, driving further economic and technology development.

Water has truly become an economic driver in Milwaukee, as the city has invested millions of dollars over the past few years to develop Reed Street Yards into a global water technology business park. The site, a former brownfield that is across the street from the Global Water Center, has been transformed into a showcase of smart water and energy management systems. It is meant to be a haven where delegations, government officials, and other international visitors can come to learn from our best practices and innovative technologies that are being produced in Southeastern Wisconsin.

The 17-acre site, which has the potential of accommodating one million square feet of office buildings, includes rain gardens, bio-swales, pervious pavement, a purple-pipe system, and a water plaza that will pull water from the adjoining canal, treat it on-site, and release it back into the natural environment. Reed Street Yards will further establish the Milwaukee region as the "go-to" place for water innovation and excellence.

More importantly, the energy behind the Global Water Center and Reed Street Yards has been the trigger that transformed a formerly blighted region of the city into the water mecca of the world, which in turn has caused a positive ripple-effect for the entire neighborhood known as Walker's Point.

Block after block, a change is under way in the form of public improvements, private investment, and the adaptive reuse of buildings that were once used by the manufacturers that helped brand the city as the "machine shop of the world," more than 100 years ago, into what *Forbes* magazine called in 2013 "The Capital of Water." The impact that the work of The Water Council has had on our surrounding community is beyond words and will continue to grow as we continue to command attention from a global audience.

There is no question that Milwaukee is undergoing an economic renaissance as it embraces and unites itself around the development of water technology solutions that will impact the world. One question is: "Where does our nation stand when it comes to addressing this water crisis and economic opportunity?"

Where is the United States When It Comes to Growing a Water Industry?

"As we found in our energy–water nexus and high-risk work, federal agencies often operate in a 'stovepiped' manner and do not take a holistic, collaborative approach to crosscutting issues, such as freshwater availability and use."[1]

This statement from the General Accounting Office (GAO) in a May 2014 report identifies the need for coordination. According to the report, "Key issues related to freshwater availability and use—such as concerns about population growth straining water supplies, lack of information on water availability and use, and trends in types of water use—remain largely unchanged since 2003..." The economic ramifications of a lack of water in the United States are alarming. Even more significant is what is occurring beyond our shores.

The loss of life, economic stagnation, and the risk of societal unrest in numerous countries make tackling the water crisis a priority for those countries, as well as for the United States' global interests. A significant and increasing amount of funds are being spent by federal, provincial, and state governments on finding and delivering solutions. This presents an economic opportunity for some countries to be the solution provider.

Where does the United States fall in this rush for the "new oil" of the future? Will it lead or will it follow Singapore, Israel, the Netherlands, and Germany? The 2014 water crisis in the U.S. and abroad demonstrates that the course must be set now.

As the growing water issues around the world continue to affect quality of life, economic progress, and risk societal unrest, the United States, the global leader that it is, must be diligent in finding and developing innovative solutions to help alleviate the world's water crisis.

Looking forward, water will take center stage as the forces of global economic growth continue to collide with the forces of global resource scarcity; the world's economy will reorganize itself and the availability of water will be a crucial pivot point.

---

[1] U.S. Government Accountability Office. (2014, May). *Report to Congressional requesters, Freshwater—supply concerns continue, and uncertainties complicate planning.* pp. 46-47.

Places that lead in innovating new water technologies and master the complex blend of expertise needed to efficiently clean, store, process, distribute, and use water will have the foundations to gain strong positions in the global economy.

One thing that is certain is that the knowledge and innovations within the Milwaukee region will significantly contribute to solving water issues across the United States and the world—a truly transformative initiative for one American region that believes its future is in "valuing" water technology.

TODD DANIELSON, PE, BCEE
CHIEF UTILITIES EXECUTIVE
AVON LAKE REGIONAL WATER

We're Not Coke® or Pepsi®: Why Should We Brand?

e're the only game in town. Why should we spend money marketing ourselves?" "I have to spend millions on repairs and capital improvements. I'm not going to waste money on new logos and Facebook." "Our customers won't stand for us spending tens of thousands of dollars on developing new logos, especially when we are raising rates to pay for our capital program."

Quotes like these are common in public utilities; unfortunately, it is thinking like this that makes the lives of the staff of those utilities more difficult.

No longer is the average American influenced by only what he or she sees in the newspaper, on the radio, and on TV. People are barraged by messages and advertisements: Billboards, ads on smartphones, banners on almost every web page on the Internet, sponsorship of buildings,

"Adopt a highway" programs...the list goes on—adding up to thousands of messages per day. Most go unnoticed, but subliminally, some bury into the psyche.

Most of these messages are advertisements or "marketing"—a push to "buy my product." To respond to those that think the utility is the only game in town, they are correct in that most utilities are not going to lose appreciable market share to the bottled water industry. Therefore, marketing, per se, is not specifically necessary.

However, branding is a much broader term and is more encompassing than marketing. In a 2011 Forbes article, Jerry McLaughlin stated that a brand is what a person thinks when he or she hears your name. It is both factual and emotional.

When you watch a Coke commercial, what are the things you see, feel, or remember? You open the bottle, smile, and "light up." You have friends around you. You feel refreshed. All of those feelings relate to the brand that Coke has established.

When a customer hears your name, what feelings does that customer have of you?

Many utilities are dealing with aging infrastructure. Water main breaks and rate increases are headlines. Neither of which evokes a positive response and reassurance. Branding works to fight against the natural negative response that customers have when they hear the bad news that how much they have to pay for water service is increasing or that they cannot use their water due to a water main break.

Branding should be done in advance of an issue or, possibly, parallel to it. Some utilities receive phone calls from newspapers or politicians asking opinions about or for background on a certain topic. This is because those utilities have established that they are the experts and a source of information. The same goes for customers. If customers view the utility as the expert and one that cares about their best interests, customers will be more likely to support rate increases and/or not express outrage when their service is affected.

I started with my utility in 2010, when it was called Avon Lake Municipal Utilities. Although always overseen by a board, rather than a city council, customers view the organization as a department of the city and under the purview of the mayor and city council. Being inappropriately tied to the city means that our reputation is also tied to the city. No matter how much good we do, if the city suffers from roads that need repair, is slow to respond to customer inquiries, or is raising taxes, it affects how customers view us. It was hard enough to maintain our own reputation; I did not want to be responsible for the city's reputation as well. This was one reason why I pushed to rebrand the organization.

In addition to not wanting to be tied to another's reputation, there were other reasons to develop a stronger understanding and support by our customers and those around us. Like other utilities, our infrastructure was aging and, with our long-term control plan, customers are experiencing more disruptions and rate increases. Also, one of the ways we have kept rates among the lowest in the state is through regionalization. Distancing our organization from the city helps to remove political rivalries and competing interests from the decision by other jurisdictions whether or not to consider purchasing water and services from us.

Our organization was blessed and cursed. We were a well-run organization, with relatively few service interruptions and a customer service staff that responded well to situations that arose. Therefore, most customers had no real reason to know us. Those that did liked us.

Like many utilities, we grew organically over time. By growing this way, our letterhead looked different than our business cards, which looked different than our vehicles.

Experts state that to have the most impact, one look and feel must be maintained across all communications and media seen by customers. We had no consistency. Therefore, we did not have a strong impact. Add on top of that a name that was confusing. The word "Municipal" made customers think of city government and tied us to the city. The word "Utilities" was too broad. Many thought about electricity, gas, and trash service. A name is a company's/organization's best statement regarding who it is and what it does. Our statement was a misstatement.

Many utilities find themselves in similar situations. Their names were established 50 or more years ago when words had different meanings, and their logos evoke feelings of lethargic, bureaucratic government entities. Some utilities are even further cursed by having staff that do not realize they are in the service sector. Rather, they feel they are entitled to their paycheck and are bothered by either the aspect of coming to work or of having to respond to customers' inquiries while at work. Although this latter issue greatly affects brand, it has been well-discussed elsewhere and will not be further mentioned here.

For several years before undertaking the name and logo change that we eventually implemented, we had been working to become better known by our customers. In 2011, I began a bimonthly piece in a local paper and used that as the basis for a blog on a community website. Also in 2011, we started our social media presence, focusing primarily of Twitter and eventually tying Facebook to our Twitter account. (We later determined that Facebook was a more effective medium than Twitter to interact with our customer base.) In 2012, we modified our annual water quality report to include information about ongoing projects and serve more like an annual report.[1]

It is usually hard to determine the impact of those efforts. Anecdotally, people tell us they like our water quality report and like reading the bimonthly piece. However, sometimes it takes a major event to see the value of something. In January 2014, with a 50-degree drop in temperature and slight turbulence on Lake Erie, our organization experienced a partial ice blockage of the intake screens for our water filtration plant. Shards of ice, known as frazil, were entrained in the water column and allowed ice to accumulate on the intake screens approximately 20-feet below the water surface. As the intakes were blinding over and the staff

---

[1] Retrieved from http://avonlakewater.org/services/test/water-quality-report/

was unable to clear it, the primary water supply for approximately 200,000 people in Northern Ohio was in jeopardy.

Obviously, this became a big story for the local media, so we decided to keep our customers informed on our Facebook page (www.facebook.com/AvonLakeWater). This was a huge success. In a period of 24 hours, our Facebook followers grew by a factor of seven (from 250 to 1750), and through "Likes" and "Shares," our updates reached 63,000 people that week. Hundreds thanked us for informing them and the work we did.

Although no one would want an event such as that to happen, by pulling back "the green curtain" a little bit and spending some time to keep our customers informed, we went immeasurable distances in creating/reinforcing our brand with our customers. The Facebook posts and pictures showed our customers we are caring and dedicated and helped them get a much better appreciation for what we do and for what we are willing to do for them.

Completely unrelated to the icing event, during the fall of 2013 and winter/spring of 2014, we were undertaking our rebranding. With the assistance of a print, brand, and web design firm, we decided to change the name our organization from "Avon Lake Municipal Utilities" to "Avon Lake Regional Water" and change our logo from a classic, governmental look to a more modern, warm, and green/environmental look.

We were conscious of the cost of rebranding and worked to keep costs at a minimum by doing some of the work in-house and implementing the switch when we needed new vehicles, stationery, and so on. We specifically did not want a "flashy" look because that could lead customers to thinking we were wasting their money. We wanted a warm, caring, environmentally conscious look that was consistent across all media. We believe we have accomplished this and are especially proud of the new tag line, "Serving the region, protecting our resource." This unified look and feel will much better help customers remember us.

Just as it is important to have the same look and feel across the various forms of media customers see (e.g., vehicles, stationery, and websites), it is important to try through several different channels to reinforce the same ideals about an organization. To this end, we organized the Lake Erie WaterFest in 2014. The underlying goal of the WaterFest was to help sensitize people to the benefits and plight of Lake Erie, our water supply and receiving body. Living beside 20% of the world's fresh surface water supply can allow people to take water for granted. Lake Erie contains about 130 trillion gallons of water—a sizeable amount by any standard and one that people would think would be hard to pollute.

However, when about 13 million to 26 million pounds of phosphorus, along with a host of other pollutants, enter the lake each year, even 130 trillion gallons can be affected. This was the case that made national headlines the weekend before WaterFest, when the city of Toledo announced that their drinking water was unfit to drink because microcystin levels exceeded World Health Organization standards due to a toxic algae bloom and weather that caused the bloom to be drawn into their intakes at unanticipated levels.

The Lake Erie WaterFest brought together organizations with missions to protect the lake with organizations who promote recreation on the lake. Artisans who are inspired by the lake also took part in the WaterFest. The WaterFest started off with a sprint triathlon and kids' splash-and-dash with the lake as the venue and a backdrop, and the event took place on its shore. All told, about 1,000 attendees had the opportunity to learn more about how to protect and enjoy the lake. We think it was a huge success for a first-time event and a great way to positively impact our brand with our customers and stakeholders.

Going back to Jerry McLaughlin's statements about branding in his 2011 Forbes article, a brand is what a person thinks when he or she hears your name. It is both factual and emotional. If an organization does not specifically set out to create and maintain its own brand, then it is subject to the whims of the media and the customers to formulate their own opinions based upon whatever they see.

Importantly, most people usually remember the negative much easier than they remember the positive. We want our fate and our reputation to be in our own hands. Therefore, we have specifically set out to brand ourselves as "a smart, caring, reliable neighbor working tirelessly to ensure our customers' wellbeing." This works well for our suburban midwestern town.

How do you want to be branded by your customers?

HARLAN L. KELLY, JR.
GENERAL MANAGER
SAN FRANCISCO PUBLIC UTILITIES COMMISSION

Being a Good Neighbor: The Role of Public Utilities in Building Inclusive Communities

Hidden in Yosemite National Park's peaceful northwest corner, the Hetch Hetchy Valley is a treasure worth visiting in all seasons. In addition to majestic waterfalls, granite cliffs and wildlife, the Hetch Hetchy Valley is also home to one of San Francisco's most valuable treasures—the Hetch Hetchy Reservoir, which delivers clean, efficient water to 2.6 million residents and businesses in San Francisco, San Mateo and parts of Santa Clara and Alameda counties.

Following the devastating 1906 San Francisco earthquake, the city faced a dire need for reliable water supplies. Congress passed the 1913 Raker Act, granting the city and county of San Francisco access to land within Yosemite National Park and Stanislaus National Forest to build the Hetch Hetchy Regional Water System.

Since its earliest days, water has been vital to the growth and prosperity of the Bay Area. During California's Gold Rush, the construction of San Francisco's sewer system further allowed the city to safely support a burgeoning population and boom into an economic hub of the West Coast. From Silicon Valley to San Francisco, the Bay Area's rich regional history and thriving economy were made possible by building reliable water and wastewater infrastructure.

Today, the Hetch Hetchy Reservoir can store up to 117 billion gallons of pristine drinking water for the water system, while the sewer system treats more than 80 million gallons of wastewater every day. Both systems are operated and maintained by the San Francisco Public Utilities Commission (SFPUC).[1]

Investing in Water Infrastructure Strengthens the Economy and Creates Jobs

The primary responsibility of the SFPUC is to provide essential 24/7 water, wastewater and municipal power services that are reliable and efficient. In doing so, the agency serves as an economic engine in the region, through the employment of thousands of people. The SFPUC's network of pipes and tunnels is literally the scaffolding upon which San Francisco is built.

Like many utilities nationwide, the SFPUC is grappling with aging water and wastewater infrastructure. The SFPUC's capital program is an

---

[1] The SFPUC is a department of the city and county of San Francisco that provides retail drinking water and wastewater services to San Francisco, wholesale water to three Bay Area counties, and green hydroelectric and solar power to San Francisco's municipal departments. The SFPUC's mission is to provide customers with high-quality, efficient, and reliable water, power, and sewer services in a manner that is inclusive of environmental and community interests and that sustains the resources entrusted to the department's care.

excellent opportunity to expand employment and small business opportunities across our service territory.

For example, in 2004, the SFPUC launched a capital program to improve the water system's reliability and seismic safety. This $4.6 billion program is one of the largest infrastructure programs in the country, consisting of more than 80 projects across seven counties. To date, this water system rebuild has generated over 6 million construction craft hours and almost 11,000 jobs. De-bundling contracts for the program allowed contracting opportunities to reach a broader group of local contractors in our service territory. In addition, the program is guided by one of the largest project labor agreements in the nation, which binds construction projects over $5 million to California prevailing wages and local workforce and apprenticeship goals.

Building on the success of the water system improvement program, the SFPUC is now embarking on a 20-year, multibillion-dollar citywide investment to bring our sewer infrastructure to a state of good repair. The first phase of the sewer system project consists of $2.7 billion in repairs, including the rebuilding of the city's largest wastewater treatment plant, which is located in one of San Francisco's most disadvantaged neighborhoods—Bayview Hunters Point. The current operation of the treatment plant negatively impacts the residents of the neighborhood, and the sewer system improvement program presents a historic, once-in-a-generation opportunity to utilize a large-scale infrastructure program to reinvest in the community. Like the water system rebuild, this program will expand contracting and procurement opportunities for local businesses and also generate employment for local workers.

The 21st Century Utility Can Be a Positive Force in the Community

As the SFPUC works to address operational challenges, it also has the ability to positively contribute to the neighborhoods it serves. This is especially important for a city like San Francisco, where prosperity and poverty coexist. In many ways, San Francisco is experiencing a period of incredible growth and prosperity as vast numbers of people and businesses are moving to the city. The city has a low 4.3% unemployment rate,[2] and median home prices have increased 15.5% year to year.[3] At the same time, the gap between the average household income of wealthy residents and that of poor ones has grown wider and faster in San Francisco than in any other city in the country.[4] Between 2007 and 2012, income for San Francisco's typical 20th percentile household dropped $4,000, while income for its typical 95th percentile household soared by $28,000.[5]

As one of the largest city agencies (in terms of revenues, contracts awarded, and land owned), the SFPUC has a major economic impact on San Francisco and recognizes the imperative to engender benefits for *all* communities across its service territory.

The SFPUC is proud to be the first public utility in the nation to adopt an Environmental Justice Policy (2009) and a Community Benefits Policy (2011) that guide the agency's efforts to be a "good neighbor" in every community directly affected by the operation of its water, wastewater, and power services. The implementation of these policies has enabled the SFPUC to support numerous local community improvements.

---

[2] San Francisco–San Mateo–Redwood City Metropolitan Division. Labor Market Information Division. State of California (Employment Development Department) (2014, July).

[3] *County market update.* (2014, June). California Association of Realtors (CAR). CAR Research & Economics.

[4] *San Francisco's widening income inequality and economic trends.* (2014, May). San Francisco Human Services Agency (City & County of San Francisco).

[5] *All cities are not created unequal.* (2014, February). Metropolitan Opportunity Series. Brookings Institution.

Implementing the SFPUC Environmental Justice and Community Benefits Policies

In the interest of achieving mutually beneficial outcomes for the utility and the broader community, the SFPUC seeks to be a good neighbor to all communities across its service territory.

Environmental Justice. By implementing its environmental justice policy, the SFPUC is doing its part to support a healthy, safe, and sustainable environment for communities. The policy guides the integration of environmental justice principles[6] into all business decisions that affect the agency's core operations, programs, and policies.

For example, the SFPUC recently conducted a citywide urban watershed assessment to inform our sewer system planning. As part of that work, we identified particular environmental justice areas of concern in the city and incorporated metrics that allowed us to assess if our public outreach efforts were adequately engaging residents in neighborhoods that were of concern. Furthermore, the process also highlighted considerations for SFPUC project managers at each relevant step of the assessment to help analyze potential social, health, and economic impacts of various project options, with special focus on more beneficial alternatives or redesigns.

Place-Based Revitalization. The SFPUC recognizes the importance of the places its operations impact. Located in the heart of the Bayview Hunters Point neighborhood and adjacent to the SFPUC's largest wastewater treatment plant, the Southeast Community Facility (SECF) and greenhouses were originally built as a mitigation measure in the 1980s. The SECF and greenhouses are owned and operated by the SFPUC, with guidance from a community advisory board appointed by the mayor. Today, the SFPUC is reinvesting in the SECF and green-

---

[6] Environmental justice is defined by the U.S. Environmental Protection Agency as "the fair treatment and meaningful involvement of all people regardless of race, color, national origin, or income with respect to the development, implementation, and enforcement of environmental laws, regulations, and policies."

houses to make significant physical and programmatic improvements and is dedicated to creating a thriving community center for Bayview Hunters Point residents. Over the next five years, the SFPUC will carry out structural upgrades to the facility. By actively partnering with local nonprofit organizations, educational institutions, and foundations, the SFPUC will also ensure that the SECF and greenhouses deliver high-quality workforce development programming that matches the needs of local residents and maximizes the use of both facilities.

Education. The SFPUC prioritizes teaching children about environmental stewardship and how to take care of precious resources at home, school, and work, so that future generations will continue to have access to high-quality drinking water. In partnership with local nonprofit organizations, philanthropists, and other city agencies, SFPUC-led initiatives like Our Water, Tap the Sky, and Conservation Connection expose and educate school-aged children to eco literacy objectives focused on water and energy conservation, pollution prevention, and sustainability.

For example, in 2010, legislation was passed at both state and federal levels requiring schools to provide access to clean drinking water when meals are served. The following year, the SFPUC approached the San Francisco School District to propose a partnership that would help meet this unfunded mandate, through the Drink Tap in Schools program. The Drink Tap program has been launched at 26 schools to date and the SFPUC has worked with other city agencies to implement drinking fountains and bottle refill stations, to give out reusable water bottles, and to evaluate student behavior and decision-making. As part of the program, SFPUC staff also leads school assemblies designed to educate teachers and students about the program and making freshwater part of a healthy lifestyle. According to results from initial school surveys, the Drink Tap project has resulted in twice as many students drinking tap water, three times as many students identifying the sources of water, and increased use of reusable bottles at school and at home.[7]

Workforce Development. Many local agencies are faced with a considerable percentage of workers who are preparing to retire in the next 5 years, making succession planning of critical concern. The SFPUC understands the importance of building a strong and skilled 21st century workforce that reflects the diverse communities we serve, especially for the utility's mission critical[8] positions. As part of a holistic approach, successful workforce investment strategies that include on-the-job training and internships also take into account participants' barriers to employment and the need to include job opportunities in communities historically and disproportionately burdened by pollution.

The SFPUC supports these tenets through both adult and youth workforce programs, such as *CityBUILD*, a pre-apprenticeship and construction training program where participants earn college credits while learning foundational skills to successfully enter the construction trades, and *Project PULL*, a professional mentorship program that exposes high school students to careers in architecture, business, engineering and science by interning with city employees from various departments.

Contracting and Business Opportunities. The SFPUC has embedded community benefits requirements in its entire professional services contracts over $5 million. Through these requirements, both multinational and local engineering, construction, and architecture firms have made commitments to local nonprofit organizations, small businesses and schools in the form of direct financial contributions, volunteer hours, and in-kind donations over the life of their SFPUC contracts. The SFPUC has leveraged more than $5 million of private sector investments into communities through programs such as education scholarships, commitments to local vendor sourcing, installation of solar

---

[7] The SFPUC is in the process of expanding the program to 50 public schools by 2016.

[8] Mission critical refers to occupations that pose a serious risk to operations if they are not filled (e.g., plant operators, maintenance and repair workers, construction laborers, etc.).

panels on low-income households, and greater promotion of corporate social responsibility.

Simultaneously, the SFPUC recognizes that while leveraging contracts with large firms is important, small local businesses must be equipped with the tools and resources to adequately get access to, compete for, and perform on large contracts. The SFPUC Contractors Assistance Center offers a range of services to local small businesses—from technical assistance and classroom training to networking events—to increase their competitiveness for SFPUC and city contracting opportunities. In the center, small firms, construction companies, vendors, and suppliers have a unique and free resource that supports the city's economic vitality and strengthens its commercial corridors.

Lessons Learned

As the SFPUC reflects on its efforts to contribute toward building more inclusive communities, several key lessons have emerged:

1. **Being a good neighbor makes good business sense.** Being a good neighbor not only promotes community benefits, but there is a nexus with the utility's core operations and services. For instance, the SFPUC partners with the Sheriff's Department and "The Garden Project," a local nonprofit, to employ at-risk youth and ex-offenders for watershed maintenance on SFPUC lands. This creates a win–win situation: The SFPUC fulfills maintenance and landscaping needs, and participants receive wages as well as important work experience. Business strategies like these can increase a utility's visibility and demonstrate the value of its services to the public, elected officials, and important stakeholder—all while taking care of day-to-day business.

2. **Institutionalizing environmental justice and community benefits guidelines helps support long-term implementation.**

The ability of the SFPUC to proactively implement community benefits and prioritize addressing environmental justice concerns was strengthened by institutionalizing these tenets. In formally passing and adopting the agency's Environmental Justice and Community Benefits policies, and then hiring subject-matter expert staff, the SFPUC Commission demonstrated its commitment to these concepts and established them as regular components of SFPUC decision-making processes. Internally, the institutionalization of the two policies results in more consistent implementation and integration into the bottom line, while also creating a baseline for evaluation and accountability. Externally, it reflects the SFPUC's values and promotes stakeholder support.

3. **Utilizing innovative engagement tools can maximize community participation.** The SFPUC strives to foster meaningful and sustained engagement with community stakeholders. When a community feels included in the planning and development, it creates momentum for implementation and generates trust and support for the final project. As part of the outreach for the sewer system rebuild, the SFPUC hosted numerous engagement activities—both traditional and innovative. For example, our Urban Watershed Assessment planning game allowed attendees a hands-on opportunity to work together to plan for green and grey infrastructure projects for 20-years of sewer system improvements. This initiative led to more informed and engaged ratepayers, enhanced community involvement, and allowed for valuable discussion on neighborhood-specific tradeoffs.

Clearly, the SFPUC's impact enhances its duty to deliver high-quality water, power, and sewer services to its customers. The agency also generates significant economic impact throughout the region, strives to integrate environmental, social, and economic components into its work, and makes an effort to cultivate meaningful partnerships with community stakeholders. To the extent these efforts might be replicable, we hope that the experiences of the SFPUC can serve as a useful example for other utilities that face similar challenges and opportunities.

NICHOLAS DEBENEDICTIS
CHAIRMAN AND CHIEF EXECUTIVE OFFICER
AQUA AMERICA, INC.

Maintaining Municipal Water Systems: How to Keep It Flowing

In the United States, it is easy to take water for granted. After all, this natural resource is readily available at the turn of the tap. It arrives in our homes clean and safe to drink, cook with, and bathe in—all at a cost of about a penny per gallon. But the truth is, our nation's water infrastructure is in dire straits.

The United States has approximately 700,000 miles of aging underground water pipes, some of which are more than a century old. Aging pipes can cause inefficiencies and eventually lead to structural damages due to ruptured water mains and interrupted water service to customers. The Environmental Protection Agency (EPA) has estimated that $384 billion of necessary infrastructure improvements are needed through the year 2030 for our nation's water systems to continue providing safe drinking water to 297 million Americans.

An added challenge is the fact that the water industry is our nation's most fragmented utility industry, with a majority of our nation's 54,000 water systems serving relatively small populations. In fact, the EPA reports that 83% of the nation's water systems serve fewer than 3,300 people and less than one percent of systems serve more than 100,000 people. This fragmentation makes enforcing regulations and imposing large-scale upgrades exceedingly challenging.

Today, municipalities own most water systems with the balance—less than 15%—being privately held. However, both the private or municipal owners of small systems find it increasingly difficult to maintain their systems. With tight budgets and limited resources, some are being forced to delay or forego much-needed investments to upgrade aging water infrastructure. Others are struggling to keep up with increasingly stringent environmental and health regulations. In addition to the typically significant capital investment necessary to maintain compliance, there is the issue of accessing the engineering and technical expertise that accompanies that responsibility.

For municipalities facing these challenges, public–private partnerships (PPPs) or operations and maintenance (O&M) contracts can be an ideal solution. In the PPP model, a public entity, such as a federal, state or local government agency, contracts with a private water company to manage and invest in water and wastewater systems. Private companies have the capital resources required to update infrastructure and are in the financial position to invest resources into improvements and renovations to update aging systems, which ultimately benefits customers by providing clean, safe water at an affordable cost. With the more traditional O&M relationship, the private entity will take on the day-to-day responsibilities of the utility in exchange for a service fee.

One example of a successful O&M contract is with the Horsham Water Authority in Pennsylvania, which began in 1997. The contract has been renewed continually since then and has broadened in scope to include water treatment, meter operations, laboratory service and compliance monitoring, and system maintenance and repairs including main breaks. Horsham continues to own their assets, while employing private sector professionals to operate and maintain it.

A similar wastewater O&M agreement with Greenwich Township in Warren County, New Jersey, which began in 2002, has been renewed continually since then. It has provided O&M services for the sewer collection system and pumping station that serves about 1,000 residential customers. Also provided in the O&M agreement are emergency services for sewer backups and pipe breaks.

In addition to the benefits a private water company can bring to water systems and customers, the funds generated by a PPP can also be hugely beneficial to a municipality. Take, for example, the Pennsylvania borough of West Chester, which in 1996 was faced with the prospect of having to sharply increase its water rates in order to afford $15 million of required upgrades to keep its water system in accordance with health and safety regulations. Instead, West Chester opted to sell its system for $25 million. The town put half of the revenue generated from the sale toward debt retirement and invested the remaining capital to fund the construction of a much-needed parking garage for the growing borough.

It is undeniable that reliable water service is a necessity of life, and as such, the pipes, treatment plants, wells, tanks, and fire hydrants that deliver these services must be properly maintained. However, we cannot rely on state and local governments to bear all of the costs. Private water companies can play a critical role in rebuilding our nation's water systems. After all, private companies can bring the technical expertise and financial resources needed to repair and operate aging systems, which are a win–win for all parties involved.

CHARLES V. FIRLOTTE
PRESIDENT AND CEO
AQUARION WATER COMPANY AND SUBSIDIARIES

Harnessing Your Power Through Transformational Change

The utility industry once had a well-deserved reputation for being conservative and slow moving. Today, utilities are unbundling their traditional business models and developing new service delivery capabilities. Although IT systems are now used to operate the product life cycle, continuous changes in our operating environment demand a constant response. In the past decade, the industry has undergone a series of dramatic changes as new technology capabilities have been applied to core business processes, and companies need to continuously adapt to changes in our business and technology environment.

Effective change management demands a holistic approach. The people, processes and technological aspects must be actively managed as events occur that change baseline points of reference. The result of a well-planned and well-executed systematic change to our business' systems represents nothing less than the water industry transforming itself and expanding the delivery of benefits to not only water service providers, but also to customers, investors, and other stakeholders.

Aquarion Water Company is one of the largest investor-owned public water supply companies in the Northeast, serving Connecticut, Massachusetts and New Hampshire. Based in Bridgeport, Connecticut, Aquarion has been in the public water supply business since 1857.

Steeped in history, the story of Aquarion is one of growth and innovation. From the company's early days, when entrepreneur and showman P.T. Barnum served as its president, Aquarion has worked steadfastly to leverage resources and strategies that enabled it to serve its customers needs. From discovering and establishing new water sources to building out infrastructure across cities and towns, Aquarion's legacy has long been one of adaptation, innovation and looking to the future to find solutions to current challenges.

Sourcing quality water, meeting stringent treatment standards and delivering reliable service remain core challenges for Aquarion. Nonetheless, new opportunities are ever present, and we endeavor to leverage these opportunities for the benefit of our customers, investors, and other stakeholders.

In the face of a changing market, a central challenge—and opportunity—lies in balancing the business influencers. As with many others in the water industry, three key business influencers for Aquarion are regulators, investors and customers. In terms of regulators, water companies need to operate effectively in a fixed revenue/ROE framework, while achieving important conservation, energy efficiency, public safety, and environmental goals. For investors, it is critical to reduce operational costs and upgrade aging assets while creating capital efficiencies.

Most importantly, the changing market we operate in presents opportunities to upgrade the customer experience. From mobile-enabled account management to e-billing, we have the opportunity for unprecedented improvement to the customer experience, enhancing the ways in which customers connect with us and manage their water services.

In the midst of these challenges and opportunities, we are witnessing a revolution in digital technology. Now more than ever, tangible benefits to business outcomes can result from the application of technology solutions. The water industry is one where digitization is becoming more and more widely adopted. From customer engagement and operational processes to data-driven systems and employee engagement, leveraging digital resources is creating a more efficient workforce and a more effective industry.

Every company is unique and may choose to leverage digital resources for a variety of reasons. Aquarion developed its business case for making use of these resources to address a series of challenges, including the following:

- Silos of independent and antiquated legacy systems
- IT products at the end of useful life
- Limited data exchanges between systems
- Limited data-reporting capabilities
- Early retirement program and 20% reduction of workforce resulting in the loss of institutional knowledge
- Need for centralized data (assets, customers, etc.)
- Transparency of business activities
- Standard and integrated business processes
- Need for operational efficiencies
- Centralized resource planning

In 2007, we undertook a program that would serve as a business systems solution. We evaluated current systems, and in addition to retiring multiple legacy systems, we deployed SAP for core functions, centralized enterprise data, and enabled mobile for field work force. We also implemented GIS capabilities to improve field responsiveness. From procurement and asset management to customer service and engineering, these new resources proved to be transformational. As a result of leveraging emerging digital technologies to solve challenges in a changing market, Aquarion has been able to realize a host of positive outcomes such as the following:

- Improved customer service capabilities
  - Call center time to answer inquiries better by 50%
  - Time to resolve billing issues reduced by 25%
  - Time to complete final customer bills cut by 80%
- Improved asset management
  - Reduced inventories
- Improved staff efficiencies
  - Finance staff productivity up 20%
  - Improved field workforce scheduling
  - Recovery from impact of early retirement
- Reduced costs
- Enhanced reporting

We are particularly proud of what we achieved in regard to customer service. While improving our employee/customer ratio, we have also reduced customer complaints and increased satisfaction.

Imperative to Aquarion's transformational success was the crafting of a vision and clearly articulating the central role for IT systems. Our vision is to be customer-centric and environmentally sound, while delivering solid shareholder value. Our goals include integrated business systems; rich, customer-enabled capabilities; robust data for reporting; intelligent metering for field operations; and an innovative workforce.

We have also worked hard to develop an engaged workforce and enhance our processes. To achieve an engaged workforce, we began by assessing organization aptitude and identifying organization structural barriers. Then, leveraging best practices, we retooled and reskilled our staff, beginning with company leadership, whose commitment to improvement provided a role model for the new the organization-wide mindset.

Lastly, we enhanced company processes by creating a governance framework, aligning IT and business goals, and integrating cross-functional objectives. Finally, abiding by the adage "you can't improve what you don't measure," we incorporated frequent baselining to provide adjustments as needed, enabling us to drive continuous improvement.

Using these practices has helped us to get out ahead and proactively manage our business in a rapidly changing utility industry and technology marketplace. To successfully engage in these opportunities, and eliminate ineffective legacy models and systems, it is important to keep a number of factors in mind.

1. Know your aptitude for change
2. Inspire a shared vision
3. Enable others to act
4. Promote innovation and exploratory evaluations
5. Re-tool, educate, and equip the workforce
6. Develop an organizational commitment at all levels of the company

Achieving transformational success comes about through a sustained commitment by leadership, an engaged workforce, and a customer-centered vision. The journey never ends. Companies need to continuously adapt to changes in their business and technology environments. Our employees, investors, and, most importantly, our customers stand to derive significant benefits as we continue the journey.

LARRY BINGAMAN
PRESIDENT AND CHIEF EXECUTIVE OFFICER
SOUTH CENTRAL CONNECTICUT REGIONAL WATER
AUTHORITY

Navigating Through Financial Challenges: Strategies, Solutions, and Leading Practices

After working at another water utility for almost 20 years, including running its operations in two states, I was recruited to join the South Central Connecticut Regional Water Authority (Authority) in January 2009 as its fifth president and CEO.

The Authority is a regional, nonprofit, public corporation and a political subdivision of the state of Connecticut. As an organization focused on the value of water, the Authority's mission is to provide customers with high-quality water and services at a reasonable cost while promoting the preservation of watershed land and aquifers. The Authority is fully self-funded and derives its revenues primarily through its water supply services.

At the time I joined the organization, the Authority faced the perfect storm with unprecedented challenges. The summers of 2008 and 2009 were the wettest on record causing a sharp decline in water usage (no one waters their lawn when it is raining!). This led to tapping the Authority's Rate Stabilization Fund (RSF) to close out those two fiscal years. Had the rainy pattern continued for another year, there were barely adequate dollars in the RSF to support expenses. The financial crash in 2008 created the longest recession in history causing many customers hardship; they were unable to pay their quarterly water bills. The adequacy of the Authority's Debt Reserve Fund, partially guaranteed by surety policies, was facing reassessment from the rating agencies due to the downgrade of the underlying financial guarantors. The Authority faced an ongoing decline in water demand of one percent per year due to conservation and the plumbing regulations passed in the mid-1990s mandating low-flow appliances and toilets. Its capital program, wholly funded through bonds, was scheduled to add $40 million in infrastructure work in each subsequent year. The Authority was highly leveraged with no way to generate extra money to fund its capital program. With its operations being stable prior to 2008, the Authority was also an organization that was not used to change.

It was also notable that in the 2006 perception survey conducted with customers, only 6.4 out of 10 survey respondents said that the Authority's water was "fairly priced." Given that the majority of our infrastructure is underground, we knew we had perception issues to address concerning the value of our water.

Development of FY2010-FY2014 Strategic Plan

With significant issues facing the Authority, the leadership team, comprised seven individuals, drove the development of the organization's first formal Strategic Plan in 2009. We were in a state just short of a crisis, and an immediate turnaround was necessary. Changes had to be made quickly in order to right the ship, reduce costs, and target inefficiencies to offset rate increases and stabilize the organization. In addition to these challenges, we needed employees to recognize the urgent need to change the way the Authority conducted business.

As a starting point, the leadership team performed a strengths, weaknesses, opportunities and threats (SWOT) analysis of the organization in February 2009, with the results used as the basis for developing the first Strategic Plan that was organized around the Four Perspectives of the Balanced Scorecard—Customer and Constituent; Employee Learning and Growth; Financial Viability; and Internal Business Process. The Balanced Scorecard was originated by Drs. Robert Kaplan (Harvard Business School) and David Norton (founder and director of the Palladium Group) and is a great vehicle to define, communicate, and drive needed change in an organization by aligning the business activities to the mission, vision, and strategies. The Balanced Scorecard also improves internal and external communication by using a common language about business performance measured against strategic goals.

During the next four-and-half months, the leadership team developed 10 strategies and 15 goals to position the Authority as a water industry leader and community resource while addressing the many issues we faced. The plan was presented to the Authority Board (similar to a Board of Directors) for input and approval. Subsequently, it was presented to the Representative Policy Board (RPB), the organization's economic regulator, for their input. Since the RPB has one representative from each of the 20 towns in our district, plus one appointed by the Governor of the State, we were able to receive input from a wide spectrum of stakeholders.

The goals of the first Strategic Plan served as the Authority's roadmap for the first five years of my tenure and identified imperatives for improving operational efficiency to reduce costs, to control rate increases, to improve service, and to communicate the value of water. A leadership team member (i.e., "goal owner") led the teams and championed a goal. The goal teams comprised a cross section of the organization, providing opportunities for management and bargaining unit employees to work together to achieve the goals of the Strategic Plan. The goal teams developed the initiatives and action plans to achieve the strategic goals and met approximately monthly with assignments to be performed outside of the meetings.

As an organization not used to change, and despite presenting the facts of the situation to employees, some actively resisted the initiatives in the Strategic Plan; they did not believe the crisis was real. They did not understand the financial situation we were in and mistrusted upper management, because historically, the Authority had been a top-down-driven organization. It took multiple communication strategies over the last five years for most employees to understand the realities facing the Authority and to build trust in senior management. Eventually, about 30% of the employees served on one or more goal teams.

The plan included metrics that allowed us to track our progress in finance, customer service, operations, and organization capacity. However, the Strategic Plan was much more than a metric or performance measurement system. With the underlying Balanced Scorecard, the plan became a system of strategic management that drove decisions including those related to capital and operating budgets, annual goals, and initiatives. As a result, we continuously improved the Authority's performance and long-term management of the organization.

Progress on the goals was reported to the Authority Board and to the RPB. Progress was also reported to all employees in periodic financial and organizational presentations given by our Chief Financial Officer, other leadership team members, and me.

The 2009 Strategic Plan focused us on the key actions required to regain our fiscal footing, become more efficient, and improve customer service so they better understand the value of water. Much has been accomplished through the work of many employees. Despite the external factors that are still pressing on the Authority, we have gotten better and stronger. For example, we:

- Established a robust 10-year Financial Planning Model to help us understand the impact of changes in interest rates, as well as the capital and O&M budgets on customers' water rates
- Created a depreciation mechanism in rate applications to generate funds internally for the annual capital investment program, thereby reducing our reliance on debt financing
- Increased the debt coverage ratio to generate additional cash to replenish our operating reserves
- Developed a Capital Budget Prioritization Matrix to prioritize one-year capital expenditures and a multi-year matrix for our 10-year capital budgets to ensure wise and prudent investment of capital funds and understand the implications of reducing our capital spending
- Reduced our capital budget by some $10 to $13 million annually, saving customers $5 million in debt service costs every year going forward
- Reduced our operating expenses by over $7 million, or 18%, and improved efficiency in many areas
- Used historical consumption modelling to understand the long-term trend in water consumption, so we are better able to plan our operating profile
- Pursued lower cost alternative financing by participating in the Connecticut Drinking Water State Revolving Fund
- Amended our enabling legislation to expand the Authority's non-core revenue initiatives to include both non-utility water and

environmental-related activities both within and outside its District

- Reduced our net accounts receivable greater than 60 days past due, from a high of $4.39 million to $2.49 million, the lowest level since the fall of 2010
- Understand that for every increase in our non-core net revenues by $1.0 million, water rate increases are offset by about one percent
- Developed a program of customer outreach and communication that included regular stories in the media about water-related issues, periodic surveys of customers and their views about the service we provide and greater community engagement

Through these actions, we were able to replenish and increase the Rate Stabilization Fund from a low of $3 million to $10 million and the General Fund from $158,000 to more than $9 million. We have also deposited over $7 million in internally generated funds to the Authority's Construction Fund. Being financially prudent and sound gives us more options. We can now begin to talk about making investments to expand our noncore business. We also have better data on which to make plans and decisions and have fewer surprises.

Although demand continues to decline at a rate of about one percent per year, and our service area is mature with little growth, the cost reductions, capital investment reductions, and refinancing of debt at lower rates have provided enough funding in the RSF to support three consecutive wet summers, if necessary. All of these improvements have offset rate increases by approximately eight percent.

Development of FY2015–FY2020 Strategic Plan

Now that the ship is upright again, the Authority is "tapping the possibilities" with a new Strategic Plan for FY2015-FY2020. The process we used to develop this plan was significantly different than the one used for the 2009 plan and involved employees at every level in the organization.

Recognizing that there will always be challenges ahead, and to help employees cope with the many changes that were necessary to "right the ship," the leadership team scheduled training in change management for all employees and training in leadership principles and communication for managers and team leads. The training helped employees to better understand the reasons behind the changes that have been made since my arrival in 2009 and to deal with challenges yet to come. The response to the training also provided the structure for development of the new plan.

The strategic planning process for the new plan began in the fall of 2013 with the leadership team, a broader team of managers, and team leads performing a new SWOT analysis. This information was shared with all employees through the employee newsletter, handouts with paychecks, my weekly messages, and on posters hung around the building. Facilitated workshops were then conducted in February 2014 with 92 employees who volunteered to attend the sessions. They each brought a list of five ways to move the Authority forward along with feedback on the top SWOTs identified by the management team.

The energy at the workshops was palpable. Employees were excited and engaged, and each of the 133 ideas generated at the workshops was included in the final edition of the Strategic Plan. Even those who did not participate in the workshops became engaged, because their peers had a hand in shaping the Authority's future. The majority of employees feel they have a stake in this Strategic Plan and now understand its role in their work lives.

Armed with input from the Strategic Plan workshops, four teams were formed. Each was composed of a member of the leadership team and management employees. Their task was to develop and refine the strategic initiatives and action plans associated with each goal in their assigned Balanced Scorecard perspective. The teams also prioritized the action plans and start dates, so we are able to focus on the most critical challenges first.

In early June 2014, employees were once again invited to meetings to review the draft strategic plan and offer input. In total, 135 bargaining unit, hourly and salaried employees—52% of the organization—were involved in formulating the strategic plan.

As we finalized the structure of the plan according to the four perspectives, we also aligned it with the Ten Attributes of Effectively Managed Water Utilities developed in 2007 by the U.S. Environmental Protection Agency and six national water and wastewater associations. The attributes align with each of the Balanced Scorecard Perspectives.

Once their ideas had been incorporated into the final plan, the leadership team with a group of employees from every level of the organization participated in presenting the plan to the Authority Board at its June meeting. This was the first time many of them had interacted with the Board. The leadership team subsequently presented the plan to members of the RPB at their July 2014 meeting.

Conclusion

Every task performed by every employee in the organization can be connected in some way to the Strategic Plan. Employees now see themselves as an integral part of the organization, not just of their department or division. Goal ownership will change with the new plan. While the leadership team members will still be accountable for goal achievement, they will become "goal sponsors" rather than "goal owners" as was the case in the first plan. The goal owners and leads will be management employees who will set direction and develop the plans needed to achieve results. This type of goal management furthers the desired achievement of employee engagement in the plan. In addition, the strategic goals and action plans are thoroughly threaded throughout many employees' annual goals and objectives upon which they receive their annual reviews and compensation adjustments.

The FY2015–FY2020 Strategic Plan is our road map to take the organization from our mission to our vision of being best in class as a provider of water and related services. It guides everything we do—from improving the Authority's reputation, to serving its customers, to growing and maintaining its highly qualified and flexible workforce, to financial decisions, to management of our assets.

The plan is designed to be a living, breathing document, guiding us to providing better customer service, being a better place to work for employees, becoming financially stronger, and operating more efficiently. The new plan will allow the Authority to "tap the possibilities" of our bright future through the collective involvement of all its employees to enhance customers' perceptions of the value of water.

About the South Central Regional Water Authority: The Authority is a regional nonprofit public corporation and a political subdivision of the state of Connecticut. Its mission is to provide customers with high-quality water and service at a reasonable cost while promoting the preservation of watershed land and aquifers. It is fully self-funded and derives its revenues primarily through its water supply services.

The Authority supplies an average of 46 million gallons per day to 428,000 people in a 20-town region centered in New Haven, Connecticut. The utility maintains 1,700 miles of distribution mains and more than 118,000 service connections across 260 contiguous square miles in its district.

Two boards govern the Authority. The Authority Board is a five-person board that oversees the adoption of annual operating and capital budgets and provides strategic direction to management. The Representative Policy Board serves as the economic regulator and comprises one representative from each of the 15 towns where the Authority supplies water as well as five additional municipalities where the Authority owns land, plus one member appointed by the governor of Connecticut. The chief elected official of each municipality appoints an individual to the Policy Board, who is confirmed by the municipality's legis-

lative body. The Representative Policy Board operates through three permanent committees: Finance, Land Use, and Consumer Affairs.

As of June 1, 2014, the Authority employed 261 people, of which 52% are represented by the United Steelworkers labor union. The Authority utilizes its own employees for the majority of its operations.

DAVID B. LAFRANCE
CHIEF EXECUTIVE OFFICER
AMERICAN WATER WORKS ASSOCIATION

Water's Price Paradox

Even monopolistic power has its limitations. That is certainly the case for water and wastewater utilities when they price their services. Economic theoretical models refer to monopolies as "price makers." This means, all other things being equal, an entity with a monopoly can set whatever price it wants, because for it, there are no competitors. The absence of competitors means there are no market pressures forcing prices downward.

Water and wastewater utilities are considered "natural monopolies," which are a special form of monopoly. In this case, a single provider is the most efficient way to produce a service or product. Natural monopolies, like water and wastewater utilities, often exist because of the large upfront capital costs of entering a market.

When it comes to water and wastewater service, the general public is protected from the risks of a "price maker" through the establishment of municipal governing boards, city councils, and regulators. All of these oversight groups have a duty to protect the public's interest, including protecting it from price gouging.

The price of water and wastewater services, however, continues to increase, and that pattern will continue—for good reasons—for the foreseeable future. The pattern of price increases is not related to a utility's monopolistic power—real or perceived—but rather it is related to other market forces and how those forces impact laws of economics for water.

If unchecked, these forces ultimately lead to a paradox in which, in order to increase a utility's revenue, the utility will reduce, not raise, the price of water. I refer to this as water's price paradox. Water's price paradox, potentially, has some significant financial, social, and environmental impacts—all of which are explained by economic theory.

Water Demand and an Economist's Perspective

In the field of economics, a demand curve is a schedule of prices and quantities for a product or service that describes all the combinations that customers are willing to pay. Most often this schedule is displayed in a graph such as in Figure 1. Water professionals don't often think of

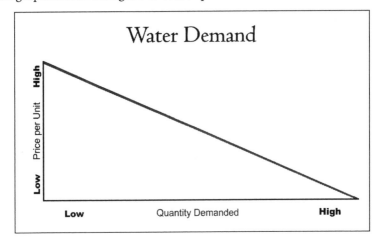

Figure 1. Demand Curve.

water demand the same way economists do, but studying water through this lens can reveal a lot and help guide future pricing risks.

The basic characteristics of a demand curve are that as the price of a product decreases, a purchaser will want a greater quantity of the product and vice versa. All demand curves also have two important zones. The first zone is at the higher prices of the curve and is referred to as the elastic portion of the demand curve. In this zone, customers are very price sensitive. It might help to think of this portion of the demand curve as the portion used to price luxury items—like high-end luxury cars. The second zone includes the lower prices and is referred to as the inelastic portion of the demand curve. In this zone, customers are much less price sensitive. Again using the analogy of cars, think of this portion of the demand curve as the portion used to price affordable cars. The point where the demand curve transitions from being inelastic to elastic is called the point of perfect elasticity—and while in theory this point is well understood, in practice it is largely unknown.

The important thing to understand about the different zones of the demand curve is their relationship to a producer's total revenue. This relationship is shown in Figure 2. Essentially, there are two points at which a producer will not produce any revenue. Those points include when the price is so high that no product is purchased (identified as "A" in Figure 2) or when the product is free (identified as "C" in Figure 2). In between these two points, total revenue is represented by an inverted U-shaped curve where total revenue increases through the elastic portion of the demand curve, reaches its peak at the point of perfect elasticity (identified as "B" in Figure 2) and then decreases through the inelastic portion of the demand curve.

For a variety of reasons, the price for water service has resided in the inelastic portion of the demand curve—the affordable zone. This means that as price goes up, customers are not overly price sensitive. And while customers will use less, the price increase overcompensates for the reduction in quantity demanded and total revenue increases.

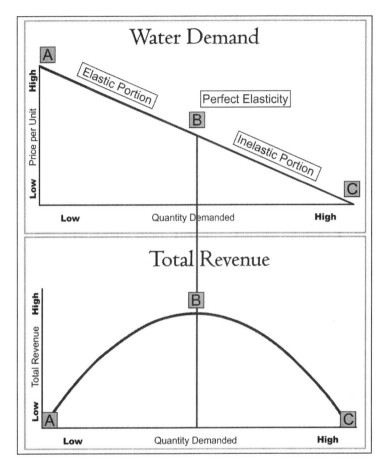

Figure 2. Relationship of Demand Curve to Total Revenue.

Water Price Objectives

There are multiple objectives that a utility balances when setting the price of water service for its customers. Three critical objectives are:

- **Revenue sufficiency.** It is essential that utilities generate sufficient funds to operate, maintain, grow, and reinvest in the water system so that it continues to provide the community with sustainable service, protects public health, extinguishes fires, and remains a critical asset for all business and economic activity.

- **Wise usage.** From an economic standpoint, water utilities rely on the natural environment as their primary raw material (i.e., water supplies). Promoting wise usage of water and avoiding water waste is critical to a water utility's sustainability and operations.

- **Affordability.** As a supplier of a community service and a social good, a water utility has a responsibility to assure affordable access to water for the community it serves.

From a traditional utility financial planning standpoint, the dynamics of prices in the inelastic price zone (i.e., the affordable zone) provide a great advantage when trying to achieve all three of these objectives. Because the price of water is generally in the inelastic portion of the demand curve, price increases and their impact on revenue sufficiency are relatively predictable—price increases lead to more revenue. Also, as price increases, customers are incentivized to use less and to invest in low water using faucets, sprinklers, washers, etc., all of which promote wise usage. Finally, while price increases create affordability concerns, the value of water is uniformly perceived as far exceeding its cost. This is in part because water is priced at the lower end of the demand curve and not at the "luxury" end of the demand curve.

Traditional Pricing Approach at Risk

Traditional Cost of Service Rates. Water rates, like other utility rates, are established based on an analysis of utility costs, customer demands, and engineering and operational requirements needed to meet those demands. This analysis is known as a Cost-of-Service Rate Setting Methodology and is often simply referred to as "cost-based rates."

Cost-based rates are a tried and true approach. They are well recognized by the legal system as a fair, equitable and defendable way of setting water rates. One of the greatest benefits of this approach is that, when done properly, this methodology supports the objective of revenue sufficiency, and the revenue will also be paid by customers and customer groups in proportion to the cost of serving them.

Changes to Traditional Water Demands. Earlier in this essay, I presented demand curves that helped to describe how the quantity of water demanded by a customer changes with price. Traditionally, this dynamic has been reasonably well understood by those who set water rates. Largely, however, because water is priced in the inelastic portion of the demand curve, these changes in the quantity demand have only presented minor challenges in establishing cost-based rates.

But what if the entire curve moved? In economic terms, this would represent a change in demand, not a change in the quantity demanded, as previously described. A change in demand means that something, other than price, has impacted how much of a product or service customers need, and as a result, at each of the existing price points, the customer needs less or more. Thus, an entire new schedule of price and quantities is established.

This is exactly what has happened in the water sector. The market place has introduced low-using water devices like faucets, showerheads, clothes washer and lawn sprinklers, all of which allow customers to use less water. In these cases, the customer uses less not because of a price change but because of technology changes. This change in demand is displayed in Figure 3 where the new demand line (B) is closer to the origin than the original demand line (A).

This phenomenon provides great support for a utility's objective of promoting wise usage. Throughout North America, utilities are seeing the demand for water decrease because of these technological advancements. Couple this with strong public awareness campaigns, and utilities and their customers are taking gigantic steps toward more responsible stewardship of the world's most important resource.

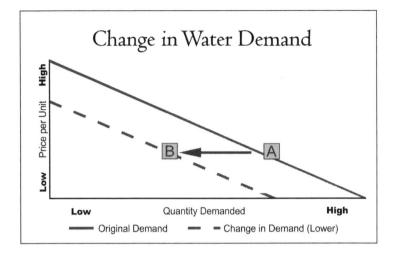

Figure 3. Change in Demand Curve (Lower Demand Curve).

However, reductions in demand—a shift of the demand curve toward the origin—without corresponding changes in water prices result in reduced revenue to the utility. Because utilities are natural monopolies, they have high fixed costs. And while the reduction in demand lowers the utility's variable costs, the fixed costs remain. Thus, in order to meet the objective of revenue sufficiency, a utility has no other option than to raise the price.

Utility Costs are Rising. One modern day challenge in setting water rates is that costs—both operational and capital—are rising rapidly. For example, as the infrastructure used to deliver drinking water ages, it needs to be replaced. Much of this infrastructure—pipes, valves, and fittings—is buried and was put in place 70 to 100 years ago. In its 2012 report, *Buried No Longer: Confronting America's Water Infrastructure Challenge*, the American Water Works Association estimated that $1 trillion will be needed to repair and expand buried water pipes over the next 25 years.

As infrastructure is replaced—as it must be to protect public health and safety—the cost of running a utility will increase. As the cost of running the utility increases, water managers will need additional revenue.

And traditionally, raising revenue has meant raising rates using a cost-based rate setting approach.

However, continually raising the price of water, no matter how justified for revenue sufficiency reasons, has affordability consequences. Even with technologies that reduce customers' demand for water and thus lower their water bills, the rising costs often outpace demand reductions. Furthermore, the rising costs—and higher bills—most impact those who can least afford water efficient devices, making these customers most vulnerable.

Water's Price Paradox

Water utilities have a difficult challenge in balancing revenue, water use and affordability objectives. The traditional approach of achieving revenue sufficiency through cost-of-service rate setting has generally been considered as fair and equitable. Water efficient devices and rate structures that support wise water use have done their job to reduce customer demand. But faced with rising costs and massive re-investment needs in buried infrastructure, utilities face increasing difficulty in supporting their affordability objectives.

One thing seems certain, however. The production of water requires utilities to have a high fixed and low variable cost structure. And in order to continue to be financially sustainable in a rising cost, lower demand economic environment, utilities must continue to raise water rates.

Or do they? The question remains, how long will this approach last?

Water's price paradox is that at some point, as utilities continue to raise the price of water, they will move from the inelastic, less price sensitive, more affordable portion of the demand curve, and into the elastic, high price sensitive, luxury portion of the demand curve. Some would argue that this may already be occurring for certain water uses such as lawn watering. But if in aggregate the price of water should rise to a level above perfect elasticity, traditional approaches to pricing will have to change.

The traditional economic demand curve model would tell us that once the price of water is in the elastic luxury portion of the demand curve, a water utility only has to lower the price in order to raise total revenue (and restore revenue sufficiency). In this case, the lower price will result in a proportionally larger increase in quantity demanded and total revenue will increase—exactly the opposite of today's situation.

At first blush, lowering prices would seem like a poor choice from a wise usage standpoint because it would increase water use—perhaps even encouraging water waste. But one also needs to consider that once the price reaches the elastic portion of the demand curve, most if not all waste that can be controlled by price is likely eliminated.

From an affordability standpoint, at first blush, a drop in price seems likely to support affordability goals, and in fact to some extent it would. But one needs to consider that once the price of water has reached these upper tier prices, affordability challenges will have already impacted many customers at various income levels, not just the lowest levels.

So are we approaching a new paradox in pricing water? Are we reaching a point at which lowering rates—rather than raising them—is the smarter approach to increase revenue? It certainly seems that we are on this trajectory. If we reach this point, traditional rate setting approaches will likely have abandoned affordability goals, and the elimination of water waste as influenced by price will nearly be fully achieved.

The paradox, however, is not that simple. The basic economic assumption of a demand curve is that a change in price results in changes in quantity demanded. Simply put, economic theory says that upward price changes result in reductions of the quantity demanded and downward price changes result in increases in the quantity demanded. As it relates to water pricing, that simple assumption will likely not hold, especially in the elastic portion of the demand curve.

The risk is that once water is priced in the elastic, luxury, portion of the demand curve, downward price change will not result in an increase in the quantity demanded. If that occurs, then total revenue will not increase; in fact it would further decrease. While simple economic models don't lead to this conclusion, it seems plausible that this could be the case for water, because once the price of water enters the elastic portion of the demand curve, customers will form new ultra low water using habits. As a result, their demand will become sticky or hardened at the new high price level. And while lowering the price may result in some increases in the quantity demanded, it seems highly plausible that a price decrease will not change the new learned water using habits in predictable ways.

As a result, this water price paradox will create the water rate setter's dilemma: How do utilities increase revenue in an environment where both raising and lowering the price does not increase revenue?

Concluding Thoughts

As a society we should not confuse the value of water with its price. The value of water and its contributions to public health, community and economic benefits, and our way of life far exceeds the price of water. Still, the way we price water has immense implications for the sustainability of both our invaluable water resources and our communities.

Utilities and professional rate setters face immense challenges. Many of the economic, social, environmental, regulatory, and technological realities of today pressure utilities to raise water rates. At the same time, raising rates can jeopardize a utility's obligation to keep its critical services affordable.

While water utilities are natural monopolies, their power as price makers is kept in check by municipal boards, city councils and regulators. And while it seems inevitable that prices must increase, even a price maker cannot assure revenue when the quantity of demand does not behave in a predictable manner as prices change—as may be the case when water is priced in the elastic portion of the demand curve.

One thing seems clear, we all will benefit if water is not priced as a luxury item. If water remains in the inelastic, affordable portion of the demand curve, revenue sufficiency objectives can be met, the price-demand response is more predictable, wise use objectives are achievable, and affordability objectives are less at risk. For a plethora of reasons, avoiding water's price paradox is in everyone's best interest.

Afterword

DONNA VINCENT ROA, PHD, ABC
MANAGING PARTNER AND CEO
VINCENT ROA GROUP, LLC

"One Water" Communication Can Change Value of Water Perceptions

The provocative and hard-hitting narratives from top thought leaders in the industry offer insights and perspectives that can inform and change our understanding of the value of water. These CEOs, who are at the forefront of shaping water's future, advocate for the implementation of a "one water" sustainability and resource management paradigm. They reiterate the fact that water is everyone's business.

If we are to advance stakeholder understanding and support of the value of water, I would propose that we develop a complementary "one water" communication effort that shapes the thinking of the current generation, stimulates ownership, and enhances awareness about the sustainable use and economic importance of water.

We need to teach people through clear communication how to value our water resources. Technical terminology oftentimes does not facilitate the level of understanding that we seek. And, when it does not, it is easy for the media to "sloganize" the messaging (e.g., toilet-to-tap, the "yuck factor," or the innocuous "showers to flowers")—terms that do not give justice to important and sustainable water processes and the water stories that we all need to hear. Buzzwords create confusion. We need to disconnect water from media-driven clichés and outdated technical buzzwords. We need to eliminate stigmatizing language.

In addition, it is hard to bring the genie back into the bottle when processes have been labeled with negative terminology or language with inherently negative connotations—words working against the value of water. I hesitate even including other negative terms here because of the damage it does to our effort to educate the public on water and its value. Repeating the negative terminology just perpetuates the problem and hampers our ability to tell water's story.

Language directs and influences our thoughts and helps us to understand concepts of time and space. Language affects how we conceptualize the world. Although I am no expert in linguistic relativity, I do know that we are often at the mercy of the language, icons, signs, symbols, and colors we use. Language plays an important role in shaping our realities, perceptions, and understanding, but I would also argue that icons, signs, symbols and colors influence cognitive processes (e.g., thought and experience). This puts pressure on those who communicate about water to take extra care and consider the positive and negative impacts of these elements.

Recently, at a high profile, global international conference whose theme was to enable societies to get more value from their water systems, attendees were asked to fill out a survey on the language of water. This survey stimulated my interest in more precisely examining how we communicate about water—the language that we use to describe and talk about water.

However, I did not stop there. I looked beyond language. I've been evaluating visual representations (e.g., graphic, color and iconic) of the water cycle, treatment cycle, virtual water flows, water scarcity, infographics on the global water footprint, and presentations by senior leaders from water associations and water organizations. I've also been looking at projects involving public outreach and public perceptions regarding recycled water, reclaimed water, resource recovery, water language rebranding, and utility branding.

I found that communication about water is muddled by inconsistent use of colors and icons representing the water cycle, water processes, equipment, and so on. My favorite example is the use (or mixed use) of "Irvine Purple" (a.k.a. Pantone 512; RGB: 131,49,119; CMYK: 53,99,3,18; Hexadecimal: #833177) as a national standard to designate the color of pipes that carry recycled or reclaimed water.

The use of purple for pipes has an interesting story. According to the Irvine Ranch Water District, one of the first water districts involved in recycling water: "The head of the IRWD Planning Department asked one of the engineers to come up with a color palette, thinking that using a different color pipe for recycled water would be effective. A challenge came with this request—the department head was severely color blind and only saw shades of gray."

According to the story, purple looked different to the engineer, who could only see shades of gray, so it was chosen. The team worked with the American Water Works Association to designate purple as the national standard for the pipes that carried recycled water.

Purple pipes, as a concept, do have the potential to help with public education about reclaimed water. However, creating and using dark pink pipes, maroon colored pipes, or pipes in other variations of the color purple can be confusing. If we are to educate and communicate more about reclaimed water (i.e., reused water or recycled water that is not intended as a drinking water source), manufacturers need to follow the industry color standard. Is this issue about a lack of awareness that a standard exists or something else?

I recently reviewed a well-designed infographic published by an international organization with major investments in the water sector. The "education" product showed purple pipes mapped to the house kitchen sink, bathtub, washroom tub, and bathroom lavatory. As we should know, purple pipes carry a lower grade of semi-treated water for use in gardens, washing cars and flushing toilets, but certainly not for drinking, cooking, or personal use.

This is an example of a missed opportunity to educate the public about water. There were many more examples. The research brought home the fact that at a minimum, we need to establish a visual, conceptual framework to communicate about water beyond just the hydrological cycle. When asked, as already mentioned by many of the essayists in this book, most people do not know where their drinking water comes from—a critical piece of information for the value of water dialogue.

Charles Fishman, author of *The Big Thirst,* says, "Water expressions infuse our language...(b)ut we do not really have much of a language or a framework for talking about water itself" and "(o)ur everyday attitude about water is filled with contradictions."

He says that our very success with water has allowed us to become water illiterate. "We are on the verge of a second modern water revolution—and it is likely to change our attitudes at least as much as the one a hundred years ago. The new water scarcity will reshape how we live, how we work and how we relax. It will reshape how we value water and how we understand it."

In my opinion, this effort should include more than developing a common language. We need a visual conceptual framework that facilitates more exact and consistent communication about water. We need to create awareness about water issues, develop a universal water ethic, and change behavior at the citizen level toward our most precious resource on earth. Standardized visual communication can aid the process.

I believe that we also need to acknowledge the impact of language and make a concerted effort to provide a linguistic and visually accurate conceptual window into the world of water. In an effort to move us in that direction, I created The Roa Conceptual Model for Water Communication™ and accompanying water icons and color palette to provide a framework for standardized visual communication about water and aid us in expressing the spirit and nature of water.

Tested and reviewed by industry colleagues, water engineers and school children under the age of 16 years, this figure drives home the messages that water is water, water is treated to different classes or levels of water quality, the cycle is closed looped, and there are many resources to be extracted from water that has been used or what I call **asset water**—used water that is full of assets that can be recovered.

Language coupled with standardized visual cues can create sensory representation to support linguistic representations. By using all three— language, icons, and colors—we can shift our understanding of water and its value to society.

The water icons and color palette components of the model include carefully selected colors and iconic designations to represent the various types of water and to define water quality levels as well. The logic behind the choices can be defined as follows:

1. A universal "texture" symbol was chosen to symbolize water treatment (utilization and application)
2. A color was chosen to most closely represent the specific kind or type of water (lighter colors represent cleaner water and the darker colors represent water not as clean)
3. Icons, which include the color chip and matching icon object were created to compliment the color representation

4. The A, B, C, C*, D, E letter icons represent or designate the classes of water or water quality level

5. The CMYK, RGB, and Hexadecimal coordinates are provided to ensure color use accuracy and consistency in the development of water communication materials (e.g., educational materials, infographics, technical white papers, marketing materials, videos, PowerPoint, etc.)

We value what we understand. We use scales, models, and frameworks to help us understand complex matters and materials. Review the conceptual models and categorization efforts of Daniel Defoe, Charles Darwin, Anders Celsius, John Smith Elgin Marbles, Seamus Heaney, Tycho Brahe, Captain Bligh, and, my favorite, Rear Admiral Francis Beaufort, author and developer of the Beaufort Wind Scale.

Study the naming of wind, and you'll find that getting to a standard was not easy. At the time that Rear Admiral Beaufort, hydrographer to the British Admiralty and an Irish Royal Navy officer, developed the Beaufort Wind Scale, there were many wind scales in use. The profusion of scales led to much confusion and inaccurate measurement and communication about wind.

If you've never seen the Beaufort Wind Scale, it is one of simplicity and clarity with only four categories in the table: The Beaufort number (0–12), name, wind speed, and description. Midshipmen in the Navy learn about the Beaufort scale. Sailing courses include instruction on it.

Beaufort succeeded in standardizing the way those who made weather observations could provide objective and concise descriptions about what they saw. The modern scale uses colors (e.g., spanning from a light teal to orange and red), concise labels and descriptions, sea conditions, numbers, and photos to indicate the level or force of the wind. Some versions include a variety of pictures illustrating the wind's force.

Beaufort's intentions were to shape the views of the world on wind. I believe that we have a similar opportunity to shape the views of the world on water, to provide opportunities for learning about water and its value, and to drive a standardization effort that will breed familiarity of water concepts.

Throughout history, we have had an affinity for categorizations, including using color to categorize. All societies have social codes and systems based on color—from the Roman period through the Middle Ages to the church's use of color for symbolic and practical purposes to the use of color categorization in present day graphic design and communication.

For example, what company do you associate with the color brown or the color orange? I would suspect you thought about UPS and Home Depot. Color categorization is a familial concept and a universally understood framework that has the potential, when used correctly and consistently, to enhance understanding and carry messages. A simple taxonomy and clear framework can help to standardize visual communication for water and could be used by water associations, water utilities, engineers, scientists, water leaders, water communicators, and others worldwide to communicate visually about water. The impact of consistent visual communication about water would be tremendous.

For example, in the model, there's an icon and color chip for resource recovery. We badly need an icon for resource recovery. Shouldn't resource recovery have the same awareness, prominence, and authority as the ubiquitous three-arrow recycling logo? We can get there. Standardized visual communication can help us to introduce new ideas and principles embedded in the water story.

It is been said by water utility leaders that the single greatest benefit to water infrastructure asset management is our ability to explain water. We can and need to improve the way we communicate about water and the value of water to society. Informed and educated stakeholders will think about, value, and manage water in a different way, and that is a very good thing.

We need partners and champions if we are to shift the value of water thinking. A standardized communication effort can achieve this goal and change mindsets about the value of water and the value of water utilities. From the American public's perspective—if I may speak from that perspective—I believe that we appreciate and value water, the product. This is confirmed by recent research from the Value of Water Coalition, which suggests that Americans in general understand water and water infrastructure as a local issue with local solutions. Connecting these ideas with tangible changes (e.g., more jobs and a strengthened local economy), we can affect favorable opinions, attitudes and actions, which can ultimately affect our investments. The report emphatically states, "One of the most important messages in all of this discussion is that increased investment will bring economic benefits to local economies."

The missing link here, in my opinion, is that most Americans do not know much about, understand, appreciate, or value the water utilities that manage the processes and infrastructure that deliver the product. I think that people, in general, understand and appreciate that water—the product—is fundamental to life. In essence, they value the product without really much thought about it, almost instinctively. They know the serious consequences when there is a lack of water or when there is too much of it. I do not think we need to convince people of the value of water from a personal standpoint. What may need to be addressed is how we can connect this instinctive valuing of water to specific actions and behaviors.

As detailed in nearly every essay in this book, water and wastewater utilities face unprecedented fiscal, aging infrastructure, affordability of service, management, operator training, regulatory, treatment, and weather-related challenges. More often than not, the voice of the utility amid these challenges is not heard. I've written at length that water and wastewater utilities no longer have the luxury of being the "silent utility" that no one talks about until a water main breaks, or there is sensational coverage of a security-related issue or water disaster.

Utilities are vital business enterprises (public and private), and are essential to thriving, sustainable, and healthy communities. We need to position them as such. Integrated management plans for the utility of the future must have a stronger emphasis on strategic business communication that directly supports the mission, vision, and operational and planning goals of a utility. With leadership support and the right level of funding, strategic communication has the power improve the public perceptions of the value of water and our water utilities.

Water utilities make so much possible—contributing directly to the economy, business continuity, our health, and our existence. They are entrusted with moving, cleaning, and delivering the most important product on our planet. In my opinion—which has been further informed by this project—water utilities carry the greatest embedded value in whole value of water equation. We need to unveil that value.

The real story of water is inside the fence of our public and private water utilities that consistently perform—delivering a high quality, life-giving product—despite the myriad challenges they face. My most important message is that if we can uncover and consistently communicate the value of water utilities, we will surely raise the profile of the value of water.

Access and download The Roa Conceptual Model for Water Communication™ *files, the color palette, industry icons and infographic at http://bit.ly/watercomm*

⌘

I am pleased to have had the opportunity to work with the Value of Water Coalition Book Project Committee, including Linda Kelly, Water Environment Federation; Lorraine L. Koss, U.S. Water Alliance; and Marybeth Leongini, National Association of Water Companies. With their cooperation and willingness to respond to my emails any day of the week and nearly any time of the day, we were able to meet the very tight deadlines for this book.

Further, I am especially grateful for and honored by the participation of our CEO essayists—thought leaders who are raising the profile of the value of water and are driving some of the nation's most important achievements for and in our water systems, infrastructure, and industry.

Contributor Bios

DEAN AMHAUS

President and CEO
The Water Council
Milwaukee, Wisconsin

Dean Amhaus has served as served as the first President and CEO of The Water Council since March 2010. The Council was formed with the express purpose of growing the Milwaukee region into the world hub for water research, education, and economic development. The only organization of its kind in the United States, the Water Council is successfully coalescing these attributes into a powerful force that is garnering international recognition.

The Council's most significant achievement occurred in September 2013 with the opening of the Global Water Center, a one of a kind water technology research and business accelerator located in a 98,000 square feet/30,000 square meter seven-story, refurbished Silver LEED warehouse in Milwaukee's downtown. One of the programs within the Center is The BREW, which assists water technology entrepreneurs in developing their companies and expanding their commercialization opportunities.

Prior to leading the Water Council, Dean served as the President of the Spirit of Milwaukee, which is dedicated to enhancing Milwaukee's image. Dean has served as the president of Forward Wisconsin, the state's economic development organization, and executive director of the Wisconsin Sesquicentennial Commission.

For six years, Dean was with the Wisconsin Arts Board; first as Deputy Director and later as Executive Director. During the 1980s, Dean worked in government relations in Washington, D.C.

Schooled in Wisconsin, Dean received his master of business administration degree from the University of Wisconsin–Whitewater and his bachelor's degree in business from the University of Wisconsin–Platteville.

LARRY BINGAMAN

President and Chief Executive Officer
South Central Connecticut Regional Water Authority
New Haven, Connecticut

Larry Bingaman, an executive with 24 years of experience in the water industry, was named president and chief executive officer of the South Central Connecticut Regional Water Authority in January 2009. He is the fifth president to lead the organization.

Bingaman gained his utility experience at the Aquarion Company, one of the 10 largest investor-owned water companies in the United States with operations in Connecticut, Massachusetts and New Hampshire. Most recently, Bingaman was senior vice president in charge of operations for the Massachusetts—New Hampshire division of Aquarion. Previously, he spent 15 years at Aquarion's headquarters in Bridgeport, Connecticut, where, in addition to serving as senior vice president and corporate secretary, he was a director of the company, oversaw corporate communication, government, legislative, and legal affairs. Prior to joining Aquarion, Bingaman held leadership positions at Sikorsky Aircraft, United Technologies, and Texaco.

Active in community affairs, he currently serves as Vice Chairman of the Greater New Haven Chamber of Commerce Board of Directors and its Executive Committee and serves on the Board of Directors for the United Way of Greater New Haven. Larry also serves on the Griffin Hospital Board of Directors, its Development Fund Board, strategic affairs committee, and is cochair of the Griffin Gala committee.

Bingaman graduated from California State University at Long Beach with a bachelor's degree in business administration, and received an executive master's degree in business administration from the University of New Haven.

BERTRAND CAMUS

Chief Executive Officer
United Water and
SUEZ ENVIRONNEMENT NORTH AMERICA
Harrington Park, New Jersey

Bertrand Camus serves as CEO of United Water's nationwide water and wastewater operations. These encompass both regulated and non-regulated businesses. In addition, he is the CEO of SUEZ ENVIRONNEMENT NORTH AMERICA.

Prior to joining United Water, Camus served as director of internal audit for SUEZ ENVIRONNEMENT, United Water's parent company. In that capacity, he was responsible for overseeing compliance within the group's operations in 30 countries around the world.

In addition to expertise in finance, long-term investment and sustainable development, Camus has a wealth of experience in international water operations. He served as chief operating officer of Aguas Argentinas, an affiliate of SUEZ ENVIRONNEMENT. In that capacity, he was responsible for overseeing water and wastewater operations, which served eight million people living in Greater Buenos Aires.

Before joining Aguas Argentinas, Camus held various business development positions with SUEZ ENVIRONNEMENT. As business development director of Southeast Asia he was based in Kuala Lumpur, where he was involved with the development of new contracts and acquisition of companies in Malaysia, Indonesia, Philippines, Thailand, Vietnam and Korea. Prior to that Camus was based in Paris where he served as director of international projects. His accomplishments included public–private partnerships in Budapest and Casablanca.

Camus began his career in project financing at Banque Nationale de Paris, where he structured and implemented funding for large infrastructure projects throughout the world.

He is a graduate of Ecole Nationale des Ponts et Chaussées, where he received a degree in civil engineering. He is also a certified internal auditor.

GEORGE B. CASSADY, PE

Director
Public Utilities Department
Hillsborough County, Florida

George Cassady is an environmental engineer with over 30 years of experience. He is the Director of Public Utilities for Hillsborough County Florida, providing water and wastewater service to over 600,000 residents. George is focused on the long-term sustainability of the utility and ensuring that the financial integrity is maintained at the highest level.

He has a bachelor's degree in chemical engineering from Auburn University and a master's degree in environmental engineering from the University of South Florida. A registered professional engineer in the state of Florida since 1989, he has a strong background in project planning, design, construction, and startup.

George's work experience includes private industry, consulting, and municipal government.

CHUCK CLARKE

Chief Executive Officer
Cascade Water Alliance
Bellevue, Washington

Chuck Clarke is CEO of Cascade Water Alliance, a municipal corporation of five cities and two water and sewer districts that provides water to almost 400,000 residents and more than 22,000 businesses. Under
his leadership, Cascade embarked on an extensive, inclusive public process to determine how best to deliver water supply to its members over
the next 50 years and beyond. In December 2009, Cascade acquired Lake
Tapps, the last major water resource in the region.

He was most recently the director of Seattle Public Utilities (SPU).
SPU is responsible for managing four utilities: Water, wastewater, solid
waste and drainage. SPU provides water to 1.4 million customers with a
budget of $500 million/year and a staff of 1,500.

Prior to joining SPU, Chuck served as one of former Seattle Mayor
Paul Schell's deputy mayors; he is the former Regional Administrator for
the USEPA managing its operations in Alaska, Washington, Oregon and
Idaho.

Chuck has served as director for the Washington State Departments
of Community Development and Ecology. In Vermont, he served as
agency director of the Vermont Agency of Natural Resources under
Governor Howard Dean.

He currently serves as chair of the Water Supply Forum serving
Snohomish, King, and Pierce Counties, is a board member of the
Association of Metropolitan Water Agencies and a founding member of
the Water Utility Climate Alliance.

Chuck is a Washington native and grew up in Bremerton. In 1971,
he earned a Bachelor of Arts with a major in biology, and in 1982, he

earned a master's degree in business administration, both from Pacific Lutheran University in Tacoma.

In 1995, Chuck received the Outstanding Alumnus Award from Pacific Lutheran University's Division of Natural Sciences.

GLEN DAIGGER, PHD, PE, BCEE, NAE

President
International Water Association
Senior Vice President and Chief Technology Officer
CH2M HILL
Englewood, Colorado

Dr. Daigger is currently a senior vice president and chief technology officer for CH2M HILL, where he has been employed for 35 years. He also served as professor and chair of environmental systems engineering at Clemson University. Actively engaged in the water profession through major projects, and as author or coauthor of more than 100 technical papers, four books, and several technical manuals, he contributes to significantly advancing practice within the water profession.

Deeply involved in professional activities, he is currently president of the International Water Association (IWA) and a member of the Board of Directors of the Water Environment Research Federation (WERF) and the Environmental Engineering and Science Education Foundation.

He is the recipient of numerous awards, including the Kappe, Freese, and Feng lectures and the Harrison Prescott Eddy, Morgan, and the Gascoigne Awards. He is a distinguished member of ASCE. A member of a number of professional societies, Dr. Daigger is also a member of the U.S. National Academy of Engineering.

TODD DANIELSON, PE, BCEE

Chief Utilities Executive
Avon Lake Regional Water
Avon Lake, Ohio

Appointed as the chief utilities executive in 2010, Todd Danielson ensures that the staff of Avon Lake Regional Water has the resources necessary to provide progressive and proactive, high-quality service to its 8,000 direct water and wastewater customers and its bulk users that provide service to another 58,000 customers.

Both a professional engineer and a board certified environmental engineer, Danielson spent 15 years in Virginia working with Loudoun Water as the manager of community systems.

He has master's degrees in public administration from George Mason University and civil engineering degree from the University of Texas at Austin and a bachelor's degree in civil engineering from the University of Maine.

Danielson is active with committees both for the Water Environment Federation and American Water Works Association.

MICHAEL DEANE

Executive Director
National Association of Water Companies (NAWC)
Washington, DC

Michael Deane is the executive director of the National Association of Water Companies (NAWC). Before joining NAWC in 2009, he was associate assistant administrator for water at the EPA, where he played a key role in developing and implementing national water policy. He has also served in executive roles at several water management companies, including United Water—and its parent company, Suez—and the U.S. operations of Vivendi (now Veolia), where he focused on innovative financing and infrastructure policy.

Under his leadership, the association has increased outreach efforts on the regulatory and legislative fronts. Michael has also made educating Americans about the value of water and the challenges facing our nation's water infrastructure a key priority for NAWC. With a focus on raising awareness of the benefits offered by NAWC member companies, he is frequently quoted in trade publications, as well as national outlets including *Bloomberg*, the *New York Times* and the *Wall Street Journal*. Michael is a sought-after speaker for conferences and events across the country and abroad.

In addition to his role with NAWC, Michael serves on the Pictet Water Fund Advisory Board, the Board of Directors of the National Council for Public–Private Partnerships, the Executive Committee of AquaFed, the International Federation of Private Water Operators, and he is chair of the Association for the Improvement of American Infrastructure's water subcommittee.

Originally from Minnesota, Michael holds a master's degree in environmental management from Duke University and a bachelor's degree in biology and geography from Gustavus Adolphus College.

NICHOLAS DEBENEDICTIS

Chairman and Chief Executive Officer
Aqua America, Inc.
Bryn Mawr, Pennsylvania

Nicholas DeBenedictis was elected chairman of Aqua America, Inc. (formerly Philadelphia Suburban Corporation) in May 1993, and 10 months after joining the corporation as its president and chief executive officer and chairman. The company has grown from a market capitalization of $100 million in 1993 to $4.5 billion today.

Aqua America, Inc. is a publicly traded water and wastewater utility holding company with operating subsidiaries serving approximately three million people in Pennsylvania, Ohio, North Carolina, Illinois, Texas, New Jersey, Indiana, Florida, Virginia, and Georgia. Aqua America is listed on the New York Stock Exchange under the ticker symbol WTR.

Prior to joining Aqua America, DeBenedictis spent three years (1989–1992) as senior vice president of corporate and public affairs for PECO Energy, a $4 billion publicly traded nuclear utility. He was responsible for government relations, economic development and environmental policies, plus implementation of the utility's public policy positions. He now serves on the Board of Exelon, of which PECO is now a subsidiary.

From 1986 to 1989, DeBenedictis was president of the Greater Philadelphia Chamber of Commerce. He successfully designed and implemented various economic and business development programs to service the Chamber's growing membership, which dramatically increased to more than 5,500 businesses, putting it among the five largest in the nation.

DeBenedictis served in two cabinet positions in Pennsylvania government: Secretary of the Department of Environmental Resources (1983–1986) and director of the Office of Economic Development (1981–1983). Before joining the cabinet, he spent eight years (1973–1981) with the U.S. Environmental Protection Agency, first as the assistant regional administrator for Region 3, based in Philadelphia, before being transferred to serve in Washington, D.C. from 1980 to 1981.

DeBenedictis received a bachelor's degree in business administration from Drexel University in 1968 and a master's degree in environmental engineering and science from Drexel in 1969. He served in the Army Corps of Engineers between 1970 and 1973 reaching the rank of captain. DeBenedictis has received an honorary doctorate of science degree from Widener University, an honorary doctorate of letters degree from Drexel University, and an honorary doctor of humane letters from Misericordia University.

DeBenedictis was elected Chairman of the Philadelphia Convention & Visitors Bureau's (PCVB) Board of Directors in July 2004 and is president of the Pennsylvania Society in 2014. He currently serves on the policy committee of the Pennsylvania Business Council and is a former chairman of the Council (formerly the Pennsylvania Business Roundtable). DeBenedictis is a member of the Executive Committee of the Greater Philadelphia Chamber of Commerce. He also serves on the Board of Directors for many regional businesses, economic, and environmental organizations. These include the following: Drexel University, Exelon Corporation, PNC Bank—Southeast Pennsylvania Advisory, P.H. Glatfelter Company, and Independence Blue Cross. He is a past president of the National Association of Water Companies. DeBenedictis has also received numerous awards for public service and civic leadership.

PATRICK DECKER

President and Chief Executive Officer
Xylem Inc.
Rye Brook, New York

Patrick Decker was named president and chief executive officer of Xylem in March 2014. He also serves on the Xylem Board of Directors.

He joined Xylem from Harsco Corporation, a global industrial services company, where he was president and chief executive officer since 2012. At Harsco, he was successful in establishing company-wide programs focused on business simplification, Lean Six Sigma continuous improvement, talent development, innovation, and safety.

Prior to that, he served in a number of leadership roles at Tyco International, ultimately serving as president of Tyco Flow Control, a $4 billion leader in industrial flow control solutions, where he was able to grow revenue significantly in emerging markets, execute the company's largest acquisitions in Brazil and the Middle East, and champion a three-year philanthropic commitment to clean water access. In addition, he led the effort that resulted in the separation of the Flow Control business from the parent company.

Earlier in his career, Decker held a number of progressively responsible financial leadership positions at Bristol-Myers Squibb Company, including nine years of international assignments in Latin America and Asia. He started his career with Price Waterhouse LLP, now PricewaterhouseCoopers LLP.

He currently serves on the energy and environment committee for the Business Roundtable, as well as on the advisory council for the Dean of the Kelley School of Business at Indiana University. He holds a bachelor of science degree in accounting and finance from Indiana University in Bloomington, Indiana.

DENNIS DOLL

Chairman, President and Chief Executive Officer
Middlesex Water Company
Iselin, New Jersey

Dennis Doll serves as chairman, president and CEO of Middlesex Water Company (NASDAQ:MSEX), a publicly traded, investor-owned water and wastewater utility company primarily serving in New Jersey and Delaware. The company also provides contract utility services to governmental and industrial clients.

Prior to joining Middlesex, Mr. Doll served as vice president and controller of E'town Corporation, a publicly traded company engaged in regulated and non-regulated water utility operations. Mr. Doll has a diverse management background related to water and wastewater utilities, contract operations and capital management.

He received a bachelor's degree in accounting and economics from Upsala College and is a Certified Public Accountant.

Mr. Doll is treasurer and a member of the Board of Trustees of the Water Research Foundation, the research arm of the drinking water industry with more than 1,000 subscribers across the United States, Canada, Europe and Australia, and also serves on the Foundation's Executive Committee.

He is a director and past chairman of the Board of the New Jersey Utilities Association, representing the state's electric, gas, water, and telecommunications industries.

Mr. Doll also serves as a director of the National Association of Water Companies, currently serving as the Association's president and chair of its Board.

He is a member of the Advisory Committee of the New Jersey Climate Adaptation Alliance and also serves on the Board of Directors of

Raritan Bay Medical Center in New Jersey, further serving as treasurer and a member of the Executive Committee of this nonprofit institution.

CHARLES V. FIRLOTTE
President and Chief Executive Officer
Aquarion Water Company and Subsidiaries
Bridgeport, Connecticut

Charles ("Chuck") V. Firlotte was appointed president and chief executive officer of Aquarion Company in September 2003. Aquarion Company's principal business is public water supply, and through its Aquarion Water Company subsidiaries, it is one of the 10 largest investor-owned water utilities in the United States serving the North Eastern States of Connecticut, New Hampshire and Massachusetts. Aquarion is a subsidiary of Macquarie Utilities Inc. of NYC, a division of Macquarie Bank of Sydney, Australia.

Firlotte joined Aquarion Water Company's predecessor, Bridgeport Hydraulic Company (BHC) in 1987, as director of human resources, and was elected an officer of the Company within a one-year period. He served in a number of assignments, and was appointed senior vice president and chief operating officer in 1995. From 2000 to late 2003, Chuck resided in the UK and served as Director of Yorkshire Water, Aquarion's former parent, providing water service to some five million inhabitants of the north of England.

Firlotte has lived in three countries, on two continents, and began his career in his native Canada. With a background in human resources management, he developed a reputation as an agent of change and turnaround specialist, with a focus on enhancement to operating efficiencies and service delivery.

Some of the awards and acknowledgments that Aquarion has earned under his leadership include the Connecticut Improvement Quality Award, the state equivalent of the prestigious national Baldrige Award, and the Connecticut Energy Efficiency Award for reduction of carbon footprint. For five consecutive years, Aquarion surpassed all other utilities in the state in customer service, as measured by the Public Utilities Regulatory Authority, and most recently, *Hearst Newspapers* identified Aquarion in the Top 10 Places to work in the state.

Involved in the promotion of Connecticut economic development and commerce, Chuck is past chairman of the board for the Bridgeport Regional Business Council, an organization of 1,000 business members, and presently serves on the board of the Connecticut Business and Industry Association (CBIA). He also serves on the board of his alma mater, St. Thomas University in Eastern Canada.

Chuck holds an undergraduate degree from St. Thomas University in New Brunswick, Canada, a master's degree in social sciences from the University of Ottawa, and is a graduate of Harvard Business School's Advanced Management Program. He resides in Stratford, Connecticut.

PAUL FREEDMAN
President and Chief Executive Officer
LimnoTech
Ann Arbor, Michigan

Mr. Freedman is co-founder, president and CEO of LimnoTech, a firm specializing in water sciences and engineering services since 1975. He has been involved with thousands of water-related projects throughout the United States and around the globe. His clients include major corporations, municipalities, government agencies, research institutes, and various nonprofit organizations.

Mr. Freedman's research and consulting have focused on water quality and watershed management, stream and lake restoration, pollution remediation, sustainability, and regulatory issues.

In the area of water sustainability, he and LimnoTech have been playing a leadership role in the development, application, and critical review of a wide range of sustainability and risk assessment tools, including developing strategies for risk reduction and replenishing watersheds to achieve sustainable water uses.

Mr. Freedman has written, presented, and lectured widely involving over 250 presentations and papers. He has chaired numerous conferences, task forces, committees, expert panels and work groups affecting national policy issues.

He has participated in two National Academy of Sciences and National Research Council panels and submitted testimony and prepared reports to Congress. He is a professional and board-certified environmental engineer, and an ASCE and WEF Fellow.

Mr. Freedman is a past president of the Water Environment Federation, the largest association of water professionals worldwide.

Mr. Freedman is also the founding president of Equarius Risk Analytics, providing companies and investors with metrics on the financial significance of water issues to company profits, share value, and operational risks.

BILL GAFFI

General Manager
Clean Water Services
Washington County
Hillsboro, Oregon

Bill has served as the general manager of Clean Water Services since 1994. Clean Water Services is the water resource management utility serving more than 550,000 residents of Washington County, Oregon.

Bill holds a degree in civil engineering from the University of Washington, is a past president of the Oregon Association of Clean Water Agencies, a past board member of the National Association of Clean Water Agencies, and the past chair of the Willamette Partnership, a nonprofit focused on increasing the pace, scope and effectiveness of conservation investments.

Bill is perhaps best known nationally for his leadership in transforming CWS into a recognized leader in competitive business practices, while retaining a long-held reputation for technical excellence. In 2003, Bill was chosen by Fortune Small Business as a finalist as the country's most innovative leader in building an employee-friendly and productive workplace.

Bill has spent more than 40 years working in service to Oregon's environment as a practitioner and a leader of efforts to understand and address issues affecting Oregon's rivers. Bill's love for rivers is best reflected in his year-round devotion to canoeing and sea kayaking.

BEN GRUMBLES

President
U.S. Water Alliance
Washington, DC

Ben Grumbles is president of the U.S. Water Alliance, an environmental nonprofit, 501©(3), based in Washington, DC, that educates the public on the value of water and the need for "One Water" solutions as part of a national water strategy. Mr. Grumbles has served as assistant administrator for water at U.S. Environmental Protection Agency, director of Arizona's Department of Environmental Quality, and environmental counsel and senior staff member on the Transportation and Infrastructure Committee and the Science Committee in the U.S. House of Representatives. He is a member of the Virginia Water Control Board and the National Academy of Sciences' Water Science and Technology Board.

Mr. Grumbles has a master's degree in environmental law from George Washington University, a juris doctor degree from Emory University Law School, and a bachelor of arts degree from Wake Forest University. Ben lives with his wife and kids in the Spout Run watershed of the Potomac River, Arlington, Virginia and grew up in the Beargrass Creek watershed of the Ohio River, Louisville, Kentucky.

GEORGE S. HAWKINS

General Manager
DC Water
Washington, DC

George Hawkins serves as general manager of the District of Columbia Water and Sewer Authority (DC Water). On his arrival in 2009, Mr. Hawkins launched an ambitious agenda to improve aging infrastructure and comply with stringent regulatory requirements. DC Water is implementing the $2.6 billion Clean Rivers Project to significantly reduce overflows of sewage and stormwater to local waterways.

To achieve the next level of nutrient reductions to meet the 2015 permit levels and help restore the Chesapeake Bay, DC Water invested $950 million in Enhanced Nutrient Removal facilities. In addition, DC Water is nearing completion of a $470 million waste-to-energy program to help manage solids being removed from reclaimed water. Finally, Mr. Hawkins tripled the rate of DC Water's program to replace water and sewer infrastructure.

Prior to joining DC Water, Mr. Hawkins served as director of the District Department of the Environment (DDOE). Previously, Mr. Hawkins was executive director of New Jersey Future, a nonprofit organization, which, under his leadership, came to be recognized as the state's foremost advocacy group promoting smart growth.

Mr. Hawkins held senior positions with the U.S. Environmental Protection Agency (EPA), and he served Vice President Gore on the National Performance Review, playing an integral role in strengthening environmental protection programs at EPA and OSHA.

Mr. Hawkins began his career practicing law for the Boston firm Ropes & Gray and is a member of the Bar in Massachusetts and the District of Columbia.

He graduated summa cum laude from Princeton University and cum laude from Harvard Law School. Since 1999, Mr. Hawkins has taught Environmental Law and Policy for the Princeton Environment Institute at Princeton University.

RAY HOFFMAN

Director
Seattle Public Utilities
Seattle, Washington

Ray Hoffman is the director of Seattle Public Utilities, which has four distinct business lines that provide efficient and forward-looking utility services that keep Seattle the best place to live.

These services include solid waste, sewage and drainage for Seattle residents and businesses, and drinking water for the 1.3 million regional customers both in Seattle and the 26 municipalities and special water districts also served by SPU. Hoffman's responsibilities involve management of SPU's $925 million annual budget and oversight of its rates and utility funds, as well as conservation of the city's watersheds and compliance with federal and state water quality and environmental laws.

Hoffman takes a pragmatic, yet customer-focused approach to his public service role. He has strengthened the department's asset management program to guide the decision making regarding its large capital improvement and other projects. Examples of recent public projects include the construction of two new transfer stations, totaling approximately $168 million for both projects, and the 15-year, $500 million (CIP) program to address combined sewer overflows and storm runoff from going into local waterways.

As part of this, Hoffman is leading the department through a strategic business plan process. Launched in late 2012, the business plan will guide the utility's investments, services, and rates through the year 2020. The process is involving significant community outreach, including a series of public meetings and focus groups with non-English-speaking communities, as well as the formation of a customer review panel. Included is an emphasis in getting public input representative of the city's demographics and key stakeholders of the utility.

Prior to being named director, Hoffman served as acting director from January of 2009 to May 2010. Before that, Hoffman was director of Corporate Policy and Performance, with responsibilities for external governmental relations, legislative affairs, and risk management at Seattle Public Utilities.

In addition, he previously was an advisor to former Seattle Mayor Paul Schell on utilities and environmental issues, served as the lead for regional affairs and negotiations for Seattle Public Utilities, worked in recycling planning and program development for Seattle Solid Waste, and served as executive director for Washington Citizens for Recycling.

With more than 20 years of increasingly responsible roles in public policy and management, Hoffman is known for negotiating multiparty agreements on complex policy issues. Among these is the Cedar River Watershed Habitat Conservation Plan, a long-term agreement among state and federal agencies with input from tribal biologists and leading regional scientists to protect endangered species and preserve the city's drinking water supply.

Other examples involve the multimillion dollar deal between the city and the Boeing Company to help pay for cleaning up a Superfund site on the Duwamish Waterway and the consent decree with the Environmental Protection Agency and the Department of Justice allowing for a more integrated approach to Seattle's compliance with the Clean Water Act and state regulations.

Hoffman has also played an integral role in some of the city's most significant conservation programs, including its waste reduction and recycling effort, the one percent water conservation initiative, and Seattle City Light's greenhouse gas mitigation program, as well as SPU's goal to become carbon neutral by 2015.

He holds a doctoral degree in business administration from the University of Washington, as well as a bachelor's degree and a master's degree in accounting from the University of Illinois. A native of Illinois, Hoffman moved to Seattle in 1980. He is an avid cyclist and gardener who enjoys outdoor activities with his wife and son.

HARLAN L. KELLY, JR.

General Manager
San Francisco Public Utilities Commission
San Francisco, California

Harlan L. Kelly, Jr. is General Manager of the San Francisco Public Utilities Commission (SFPUC), a department of the city and county of San Francisco that provides retail drinking water, wastewater, and municipal power services to San Francisco, and wholesale water to three Bay Area counties.

He previously served as SFPUC's assistant general manager of infrastructure, and was responsible for implementing over $10 billion in capital programs for water, sewer, and power, including the $4.6 billion Water System Improvement Program, the $6.9 billion Sewer System Improvement Program, and the $191 million SFPUC Headquarters and Administration Building at 525 Golden Gate Avenue.

His civil engineering career spans nearly three decades and includes his tenure as the city engineer of San Francisco. At San Francisco Department of Public Works, he held functional and project management positions, including acting general manager, and deputy director of engineering, during which he managed complex capital improvement programs that included the rebuild and seismic retrofit of city hall, and expansions of convention, hospital, county jail, and public arts facilities.

Mr. Kelly is a licensed professional engineer and a graduate of the University of California at Berkeley.

KEN KIRK

Executive Director
National Association of Clean Water Agencies
Washington, DC

Ken Kirk is the executive director of the National Association of Clean Water Agencies (NACWA), formerly known as the Association of Metropolitan Sewerage Agencies (AMSA). Prior to joining NACWA, he worked with a Washington, DC-based private consulting firm, where he had responsibility for the management of several associations, including AMSA.

Mr. Kirk also worked in the Environmental Protection Agency's Office of Legislation and served as public affairs manager at the Water Environment Federation. He has degrees from New York University, the Georgetown University Law Center, and the George Washington University Law Center, where his specialty was environmental law.

Mr. Kirk serves as cochair of the Water Infrastructure Network, a broad-based coalition dedicated to preserving and protecting the health, environmental and economic gains that America's drinking water and wastewater infrastructure provide.

He helped found—and is a past president and current Board Member of—the U.S. Water Alliance, a 501©(3) nonprofit organization established to explore the complex issue of water sustainability. The U.S. Water Alliance plans for the future by improving public awareness that advances holistic, watershed-based approaches to water quality and quantity challenges.

DAVID KOHLER

President and Chief Operating Officer
Kohler Co.
Kohler, Wisconsin

David Kohler is president and chief operating officer of Kohler Co. and was elected to the position by the Board of Directors in April 2009. He is the eighth individual to serve in the role of president since the company's inception in 1873. A member of the company's Board of Directors and Executive Committee, Kohler oversees three of Kohler Co.'s four worldwide businesses—Kitchen & Bath Group, Global Power Group, and Interiors Group—as well as the Corporate Technical Services organization, including Information Technology, Operations Support, Global Procurement, and Business Travel and Aviation.

Kohler currently serves on the Board of Directors of the following three organizations: Interface Inc., headquartered in Atlanta, Georgia; and Internacional de Cerámica S.A.B. de C.V., headquartered in Chihuahua, Mexico; and the Green Bay Packers. Kohler is a past chairman of the National Kitchen and Bath Association's Board of Governors of Manufacturing and a former member of the board of directors of Menasha Corporation.

Kohler received his bachelor's degree in political science from Duke University and his master's degree in management from the Kellogg School of Management at Northwestern University. David and his wife Nina have four children and live in Kohler, Wisconsin.

Of golf note, Kohler will serve as the general chairman for the 2015 PGA Championship at Whistling Straits—the sixth Major Championship hosted by Kohler Co. Whistling Straits will also be the host site for the 2020 Ryder Cup.

He has previously played in the AT&T Pebble Beach National Pro-Am for the past six years and the Alfred Dunhill Links Championship since 2012.

ALAN J. KRAUSE

Chairman and Chief Executive Officer
MWH Global
Broomfield, Colorado

Building a Better World is both a professional and a personal mission for Alan, chairman and chief executive officer of MWH Global, headquartered in Broomfield, Colorado. Committed to protecting and developing the world's natural resources in a responsible and appropriate way, he embraces the vision that technology offers to provide better solutions. At the same time, he shares a father's hope that the environmental legacy he leaves for his children and for future generations will be of immeasurable benefit.

Closely connected to each project undertaken by MWH, Alan is known to travel to many of the company's projects sites, eager to face the challenges first hand with our clients and our MWH teams. His strong personal interest in client success is matched only by his perspective as a global leader in water and a distinguished geotechnical engineer. It is here that his ability to advance the organization's commitment to providing customized engineering, management, and construction services through world-class projects across the globe is most readily seen.

According to Alan, what challenges him most are goals that some would say are unachievable. "I get no greater satisfaction than moving myself and MWH through great step changes instead of more gradual linear improvements. Our work on the Third Set of Locks Project at the Panama Canal is an example of a project that was a reach for many giants in the engineering industry including MWH. I marveled at how our integrated team took up the challenge of this iconic project, and applied our unique sustainable solutions to a work of such global importance."

Alan's leadership acuity also extends to the successful completion of other major global initiatives, such as the Tekeze Hydropower Project in Ethiopia that increased power stability and provided reliable access to light, heat, and water for 80 million people.

His ability to advance the organization's position as the global leader in the wet infrastructure sector comes from his conviction that to be a sustainable, growing company "is a series of intelligent and successful moves that advance to a specific outcome. Each move forward teaches us how to improve over time, as we gain more knowledge and achieve greater success."

With more than 35 years of industry and market experience, he will readily acknowledge, "I learned very early on in my career working with outstanding engineers the value of quality, diligence and effort. These qualities are paramount to sustainable excellence. I would add integrity, intelligence and energy as the other essential qualities."

Alan's peers agree that he embodies these qualities and that he seeks these same qualities in the employees at MWH. There, winning the most valued, visible, and challenging projects around the globe is a key component in successfully engaging employees at every level. Those who have worked closely with him through the years cite his informal style and innate ability to instill a sense of community and common mission as hallmarks of his leadership. Alan will tell you it is about the MWH promise to its people.

"Our promise is *Building a Better World* through the extraordinary power of human potential. I am honored to lead MWH today largely because of the caliber of our staff and our mission. My responsibility as CEO is simple: To create the conditions in which talented, passionate people thrive."

Since merging his natural resources business TerraMatrix with Montgomery Watson in 1997, Alan has continued to successfully grow the business. He played a significant role in the integration of Harza and

Montgomery Watson in 2001, which led to the formation of MWH. He has held numerous executive positions within the organization, including president of the natural resources, industry, and infrastructure section. He became president and chief operating officer in 2008 and was named president and CEO in November 2011, adding chairman to his title in December 2012.

Alan holds a master's degree in geological engineering from the University of Nevada Mackay School of Mines. He has completed the Owner/President Management Program at Harvard Business School, and is a member and distinguished engineer for the Pan American Academy of Engineering.

MARTIN A. KROPELNICKI

President and Chief Executive Officer
California Water Services Group
San Jose, California

Martin A. Kropelnicki is president and chief executive officer of California Water Service Group, the third largest investor-owned water and wastewater utility in the United States. He brings to the position a strong background in economics, having spent much of his career in executive- and management-level finance positions. But Kropelnicki has demonstrated keen insight far beyond the world of finance, and has earned a reputation for his innovation, creativity, and dynamic management style. One hallmark of his leadership is his commitment to fulfilling the company's purpose, which is to enhance the quality of life for customers, communities, employees, and stockholders.

Kropelnicki holds a bachelor of arts degree and a master of arts in business economics from San Jose State University, which named him Graduate of the Decade in 2002 and Alumni of the Year in 2005 and 2010. The 2009 Bay Area CFO of the Year is also a published author and former faculty member at his alma mater.

He serves on the Bay Area Council and the Silicon Valley Leadership Group and formerly served as director of the National Association of Water Companies. Kropelnicki resides with his wife, Nicole, and their three children in Marin, California.

DAVID B. LAFRANCE

Chief Executive Officer
American Water Works Association
Denver, Colorado

David LaFrance is chief executive officer of the American Water Works Association, the largest association of water professionals in the world. Established in 1881, AWWA has approximately 50,000 members in 43 sections throughout North America and beyond. In his role as CEO, Mr. LaFrance directs a staff of 150 people and writes and speaks nationally and internationally on a broad range of water issues.

Mr. LaFrance was chosen to lead AWWA in 2010 following 16 years with Denver Water, where he served as chief financial officer and manager of rate administration. One of the nation's foremost experts in water rate setting principles and practices, he began his relationship with AWWA as a member of the Rates and Charges Committee in 1995.

LaFrance's entire career has been spent in the water sector. As a Denver water utility executive, he successfully engaged boards, city councils, and customers; worked with the media, and developed and implemented strategic plans. Prior to that, he was project manager and rate consultant for CH2M HILL and a natural resource economist for the Corps of Engineers, where his first assignment involved the evaluation of options to clean the rivers of the Pacific Northwest following the eruption of Mount St. Helens.

Mr. LaFrance holds a bachelor's degree in economics from Lewis & Clark College and a master's degree in business administration in finance from the University of Colorado.

TERRY MAH, PHD

CEO and President
Veolia North America
Chicago, Illinois

As CEO and president of Veolia North America, Terry leads the water, energy, and waste management activities of Veolia's North American zone, which has approximately 8,000 employees and more than $2 billion in revenues.

Terry has a unique global perspective on water and environmental issues. He most recently served as chief operating officer, Veolia Water Solutions and Technologies, International Municipal (which includes the Nordic countries, Baltic countries, Poland, Spain, Portugal, Middle East, China, and Southeast Asia), and from 2007 to 2012, he served as executive vice president of one of Veolia Water Solutions and Technologies' global regions. In both roles, Terry was responsible for the management of the Veolia Water businesses in those countries, as well as for special corporate global assignments. From 1997 to 2007, Terry was managing Veolia businesses in the United States and Scandinavia.

Before joining Veolia, Terry worked in the areas of strategic planning, business development, research and development, engineering, consulting and finance for U.S. and Canadian technology companies. He holds a bachelor's degree and a master's of science degree in microbiology and a doctor of philosophy degree in applied science from the University of British Columbia in Vancouver, Canada.

HEINER MARKHOFF

President and Chief Executive Officer
GE Power & Water, Water & Process Technologies
Trevose, Pennsylvania

Heiner Markhoff is president and chief executive officer of GE Power & Water's Water & Process Technologies, a global business that focuses on the world's most complex water-related challenges. Employing approximately 8,000 people and operating in over 100 countries, Water & Process Technologies provides innovative solutions that address the growing demand for increased water availability and quality, while improving customers' productivity and meeting more stringent environmental regulations.

Before assuming his current role in October 2008, Heiner led GE Plastics Europe, Middle East, and Africa for two years. Throughout his tenure at GE, he has held several leadership positions, including general manager–automotive for GE Plastics Americas and CEO of GE Bayer Silicones. Heiner began his GE career as a member of the Corporate Business Development team in Fairfield, Connecticut, in 1994. Prior to joining GE, Heiner served as an associate with Booz Allen & Hamilton, a strategy and technology consulting firm.

Heiner graduated from the University of Cologne, Germany, with a degree in business administration and economics. He and his wife have three children and live in the greater Philadelphia area.

LINDA MCCREA

Superintendent
Tacoma Water
Tacoma, Washington

Linda McCrea was named Tacoma water superintendent in 2010. She started her career with Tacoma Public Utilities in 1980 after graduating from the University of Washington with a bachelor of science in civil engineering. Over the next 13 years, she advanced through engineering positions in Tacoma Water's distribution section, and in 1993, she was appointed water distribution manager.

Her accomplishments include establishing preventive maintenance programs and renewal and replacement programs for the distribution system, along with successful acquisition of multiple small water systems into the Tacoma system. She was an early proponent of addressing aging infrastructure issues through asset management, benchmarking, and coordination of infrastructure projects to minimize costs and community disruptions.

She is active in several regional water supply organizations, including chairing the Washington Water Utility Council.

GREG MCINTYRE

Global Water Market President
CH2M HILL
Englewood, Colorado

Greg McIntyre serves as CH2M HILL's Global Water Market president. In this role, Mr. McIntyre has full profit and loss responsibility for the global water business and is responsible for all water activities within CH2M HILL, including overseeing consulting, program management, design, design-build, construction, and operations solutions for government, civil, industrial, and energy clients. He previously served as the global operations director for CH2M HILL's water market.

Mr. McIntyre has more than 30 years of professional experience in the construction and engineering industry and has held key management, operations and technical roles in the infrastructure, water, environmental, and telecommunications sectors. He has been with the firm his entire career and is a member of the CH2M HILL Board of Directors.

Mr. McIntyre is a member of the American Society of Civil Engineers, American Water Works Association and the Water Environment Federation. He holds a master of science degree in environmental and water resources engineering from Vanderbilt University and a bachelor of science degree in environmental engineering from the University of Florida. Additionally, McIntyre is a graduate of the Advanced Management Program for International Senior Managers at the Harvard University Graduate School of Business Administration.

DAVID V. MODEER

General Manager
Central Arizona Project (CAP)
Central Arizona Water Conservation District
Phoenix, Arizona

David V. Modeer joined the Central Arizona Water Conservation District (CAWCD) as a general manager overseeing all Central Arizona Project (CAP) operations in January 2009. Mr. Modeer has been a leader in water resource management for 40 years and has significant experience in all areas of water system operations, financing, customer service, and planning. He has a thorough understanding of political and operational water issues impacting the western United States.

Prior to his arrival at CAP, Mr. Modeer was the director of Water Services for the city of Phoenix and spent 10 years as the director of Water in Tucson, Arizona. Mr. Modeer also has more than 26 years of management experience with American Water Works, Inc. as vice president of operations for both the Pennsylvania-American and Western Region divisions. He also held various managerial positions in the Midwest.

Mr. Modeer served six years on the publicly elected Board of Directors of the CAWCD prior to his selection as general manager. Mr. Modeer is currently a member of the Board of Directors of the Association of Metropolitan Water Agencies, an organization of the major metropolitan water utilities throughout the United States; a chairperson of the Western Urban Water Coalition, an organization of the major western water agencies; and President of the Colorado River Water Users Association.

Mr. Modeer is a graduate of the Creighton University in Omaha, Nebraska with a Bachelor of Science in Biology and a minor in chemistry and philosophy.

In addition to managing and delivering the state's largest allocation of Colorado River water to 80% of Arizona's population, CAP operates the Central Arizona Groundwater Replenishment District and is the operating arm of the Arizona Water Bank. In addition, CAP owns and operates six groundwater recharge facilities, helps shape public and political water policy, and plays an active role in addressing local, regional, and national water management and environmental issues.

SUE MURPHY

Chief Executive Officer
Water Corporation
Leederville WA, Australia

Sue Murphy is CEO of the Water Corporation which is one of Western Australia's largest state-owned businesses managing assets valued at more than $15 billion to supply drinking water to two million customers and provide wastewater services to homes, farms and businesses across the state's one million square miles (2.6 million square kilometers).

She has a key role in shaping the state's future with responsibility for ensuring that sustainable water and wastewater services are maintained at a demanding and complex time of declining rainfall yet strong resources-led growth and increasing competition for scarce water supplies.

Since 2009, she has been regularly included among Australia's 100 most influential engineers and was named as the nation's Civil Engineer of the Year for 2013.

An earlier long involvement in the private sector with major mining and energy engineering contractors, Clough Ltd., saw her influence the company's development and become its first female board member. For these achievements, she was announced as the 2000 Telstra national businesswoman of the year in the private sector.

She is a Board Member of the University of Western Australia Business School and the Water Services Association of Australia, Chairman of the Navy Clearance Diver Trust, Member of the General Council Chamber of Commerce and Industry, and Fellow of the Australian Academy of Technological Sciences and Engineering.

Sue has three daughters and lives in Perth.

PAUL O'CALLAGHAN

Chief Executive Officer
O₂ Environmental and BlueTech Research

Paul O'Callaghan is the founding CEO of O_2 Environmental, a leading consultancy providing expert analysis on global water technology market opportunities. Paul also founded BlueTech® Research, a subsidiary of O_2 Environmental that provides intelligence services to clients to identify key opportunities and emerging trends in the global water industry.

With more than 19 years of experience in the water sector, Paul is widely recognized for his expertise in market analysis and success in providing business development support to venture-backed water companies, including Ostara, SCFI, UV Sciences (now NeoTech Aqua), and Microdynamics UV. Paul also worked with companies, such as The Body Shop, Atkins, and Noram Engineering, before founding O_2 Environmental.

In addition, Paul has assisted a number of funds, such as Leaf Clean Energy, XPV Capital, and Emerald Ventures, providing market analysis and helping identify water sector investment opportunities. He worked with Fortune 500 companies on developing their overall water strategy, determining acquisition opportunities, and assisting with the launch of new water business divisions.

Paul holds a bachelor of science degree in biochemistry and a master's degree in water resource management. He has authored and presented numerous papers on emerging water and wastewater treatment technologies, guest lectured at Harvard Business School, provided commentary on the Discovery Channel, and delivered keynotes at numerous international events including the Singapore International Water Week TechXchange Workshop.

In 2010, Paul completed a cutting-edge analysis of BlueTech investment opportunities for a leading international water industry publication, titled "Water Technology Markets—Key Opportunities and Emerging Trends."

Among Paul's more recent accomplishments is the establishment of the annual Innovation Showcase at WEFTEC in collaboration with the Water Environment Federation (WEF) and Imagine H$_2$O. In addition, his firm BlueTech Research hosts a yearly conference, the BlueTech Forum, to further promote the identification of innovative and disruptive technologies within the water sector.

EILEEN O'NEILL

Executive Director
Water Environment Federation
Alexandria, Virginia

Eileen O'Neill is the Executive Director of the Water Environment Federation (WEF), an international organization of water quality professionals headquartered in Alexandria, Virginia.

Most recently, WEF's interim executive director, Dr. O'Neill has worked with the Federation for more than 20 years in a variety of positions, including with responsibility for oversight of WEF's technical, international and communications programs, and served as the organization's chief technical officer before becoming deputy executive director in late 2011.

Before joining WEF, Dr. O'Neill worked as an academic in environmental consulting in the United States and in Europe. She has a bachelor of science in soil science from the University of Newcastle-upon-Tyne (U.K.) and a doctorate degree in soil science from the University of Aberdeen (U.K.). Dr. O'Neill also undertook a postdoctoral traineeship in Environmental Toxicology at the University of Wisconsin at Madison.

About WEF

Founded in 1928, the Water Environment Federation (WEF) is a not-for-profit technical and educational organization of 36,000 individual members and 75 affiliated member associations representing water quality professionals around the world.

WEF members, member associations, and staff proudly work to achieve our mission to provide bold leadership, champion innovation, connect water professionals and leverage knowledge to support clean and safe water worldwide. To learn more, visit www.wef.org.

KAREN PALLANSCH

Chief Executive Officer
Alexandria Renew Enterprises (AlexRenew)
Alexandria, Virginia

Ms. Pallansch currently serves as CEO for Alexandria Renew Enterprises (previously the Alexandria Sanitation Authority). She has served as CEO since October 2005. In that time, she led a rebranding effort that incorporated a successful public—developer partnership, creating a neighborhood from an industrial area that once served as the city landfill.

This site will use AlexRenew's blurenew reclaimed water product. Prior to leading AlexRenew as CEO, she worked in various roles at the agency, starting as the Staff Engineer. Ms. Pallansch also worked for the Virginia Department of Environmental Quality as a Senior Engineer and as an Engineer with the Department of the Army, managing rehabilitation of army ammunition bases and associated research.

Ms. Pallansch holds a bachelor's degree in chemical engineering from the University of Pittsburgh and a master's degree in business management from Texas A&M University, Texarkana.

She is a registered engineer in Virginia, has a Class I wastewater license and is board certified in environmental engineering by the American Academy of Environmental Engineers.

She volunteers with several organizations, including the National Association of Clean Water Agencies (NACWA) where she serves as a Board member and President (2014–2015). She is currently chair of the Virginia Municipal League Insurance Pool.

She was previously chair of the Water Environment Research Foundation (WERF) Research Council and served as an ex officio member of the WERF Board.

She enjoys downtime with her husband and two adult sons.

JAMES A. "TONY" PARROTT

Executive Director
GCWW/MSDGC
Cincinnati, Ohio

Tony Parrott has been in the public utility business for nearly 30 years. After completing his degree in business and communications at Georgetown, Tony joined the front-line ranks at the Butler County Department of Environmental Services, a water and wastewater utility serving a population of 120,000 in Southwest Ohio.

During his first 10 years, Tony moved through the department, working in almost every area before serving as executive director from 1995 through 2004.

In 2005, Tony moved to the Metropolitan District of Greater Cincinnati, where he is now the executive director of both the water and sewer utilities—serving more than 1,200,000 residents of Cincinnati, Hamilton County, Southwest Ohio, and Northern Kentucky. The two utilities have a combined operating budget of over $400 million. Tony and his team successfully negotiated a Federal Consent Decree with the Department of Justice and U.S. EPA, which was approved by the Federal Court in August 2010.

The decree mandated a multibillion-dollar capital program to remove combined sewer overflow from the Ohio River and the tributaries. Challenged with a multimillion dollar capital program and managing a $350M annual operating budget, Tony keeps a visionary outlook and charges his staff with raising the bar every day.

Tony also sits on the National Board of Directors for NACWA, representing Region 5 and the National Board of Directors for WERF.

In 2011, Tony was named a WEF Fellow by the Water Environment Federation and was recently recognized by NACWA with a National Environment Achievement Award in February 2014. Under Parrott's leadership, MSDGC won the 2014 U.S. Water Prize in April in Washington DC.

KEVIN L. SHAFER, PE

Executive Director
Milwaukee Metropolitan Sewerage District (MMSD)
Milwaukee, Wisconsin

Kevin L. Shafer is the executive director of the Milwaukee Metropolitan Sewerage District (MMSD) and is responsible for the overall management, administration, leadership, and direction for MMSD in meeting short- and long-term goals and objectives; coordinates the establishment of strategic goals and objectives and their approval by the Commission; oversees the development of policies and operating plans; and represents MMSD to its customers, bond rating agencies, and the public.

Prior to joining the District, Shafer spent 10 years in private industry with an international engineering firm in Chicago and Milwaukee, and six years with the U.S. Army Corps of Engineers in Fort Worth, Texas.

He holds a bachelor's degree in science and civil engineering with a specialty in water resources from the University of Illinois and a master's degree in science and civil engineering from the University of Texas. He is a past president of the National Association of Clean Water Agencies and the Chair of the U.S. Water Alliance's Urban Water Sustainability Leadership Council.

He currently serves on the EPA's Local Government Advisory Committee and is the vice chair of the Water Environment Research Foundation (WERF) Board of Directors.

THOMAS W. SIGMUND, PE

Executive Director
NEW Water
Green Bay, Wisconsin

Tom Sigmund is the executive director of NEW Water, the brand of the Green Bay Metropolitan Sewerage District in Green Bay, Wisconsin, where he has been since 2007. NEW Water is a regional wastewater conveyance and treatment utility serving Northeast Wisconsin with 92 employees and an annual budget of $35 million.

NEW Water expresses its attitude of viewing what is sent to its facilities as a resource to be recovered and a commitment to continued improvement of the watershed. Before coming to Green Bay, Mr. Sigmund was a vice president with CH2M HILL, where he was responsible for projects and clients in the upper Midwest.

Mr. Sigmund is a professional engineer in Wisconsin, Illinois, and Ohio. He is the chair of the National Association of Clean Water Agency's (NACWA) Utility and Resource Management Committee. He was the chair of the Water Resources Utility of the Future Task Force and serves as one of NACWA's representatives to the Steering Committee.

He was the lead of Volume III (Solids) of the *5th Edition of WEF Manual of Practice 8, Design of Municipal Wastewater Treatment Plants*. He was also a member of the Utility Advisory Group for the development of *Effective Utility Management, a Primer for Water and Wastewater Utilities* developed by NACWA, Water Environment Federation (WEF), Environmental Protection Agency (EPA), et al.

In 2013, he was the recipient of NACWA's *President's Award*. In 2007, he was the recipient of the WEF *Schroepfer Innovative Facility Design Medal*. Mr. Sigmund has a master's degree and a bachelor's degree in civil and environmental engineering from the University of Wisconsin.

352 | DONNA VINCENT ROA AND THE VALUE OF WATER COALITION

LISA SPARROW

President and Chief Executive Officer
Utilities, Inc.
Northbrook, Illinois

Lisa Sparrow has over 25 years of experience in manufacturing, energy, and infrastructure companies, including General Motors, BP and Utilities, Inc. Her responsibilities have ranged from the design and construction of operating assets to policy development and executive management. She joined Utilities, Inc., a leading national water and wastewater utility company, in 2002 as director of operations and is currently president and CEO.

She is an active member of the professional water community. She was appointed to a three-year term on the National Drinking Water Advisory Council in 2009 and the EPA Climate Ready Utilities Working Group later that year and elected to the Water Research Foundation Board of Directors in 2014. She continues to be a board member of the National Association of Water Companies, having served as vice president and president, in addition to serving on the Government Relations, Communications, and Executive Committees for a number of years.

She has a bachelor of science degree in mechanical engineering from Michigan State University and a master's degree in management from Northwestern University.

ROBERT J. SPROWLS

President and Chief Executive Officer
American States Water Company
San Dimas, California

Bob Sprowls has more than 30 years of experience working for public utilities, utility holding companies and diversified affiliates of utility holding companies. He was appointed to his present position as president and CEO of American States Water Company (AWR) and each of its subsidiaries effective January 1, 2009.

AWR provides water service to 257,000 customers throughout 10 counties in California and electric service to 24,000 customers in one county in California, both through subsidiary Golden State Water Company. It also provides water and wastewater services at nine military bases in six states through subsidiary American States Utility Services, Inc. Mr. Sprowls joined AWR in 2004 as senior vice president of finance, chief financial officer, treasurer and corporate secretary. He serves on the board of directors of AWR and each of its subsidiaries. American States Water Company is listed on the New York Stock Exchange under the ticker AWR.

Prior to joining AWR, Mr. Sprowls spent 21 years at CILCORP Inc. (CILCORP), a public utility holding company whose largest subsidiary, Central Illinois Light Company (CILCO), served approximately 250,000 gas and electric utility customers. During his tenure with CILCORP, Mr. Sprowls held positions as president, business unit leader—energy delivery, chief financial officer (CFO), and treasurer of CILCO; CFO of a non-regulated subsidiary of CILCORP, QST Enterprises Inc.; and vice president and treasurer of CILCORP.

He also served on the boards of directors of CILCORP and CILCO. Mr. Sprowls left CILCORP and CILCO following the sale of the company to Ameren Corporation in 2003.

Mr. Sprowls is currently a member of the board of directors and executive committee of the National Association of Water Companies and has served as its president. He is also a member of the Southern California Leadership Council. He has been a past chairman and member of the board of directors of the Illinois Energy Association, a past chairman and member of the board of directors of Goodwill Industries of Central Illinois, and a committee chairman for the Heart of Illinois United Way Campaign.

He holds a bachelor of arts in economics and business administration from Knox College in Illinois and a master of business administration from Bradley University, also in Illinois. He is a certified public accountant (inactive) and a certified management accountant.

SUSAN N. STORY

President and Chief Executive Officer
American Water
Voorhees, New Jersey

Susan N. Story is president and chief executive officer of American Water, the largest publicly traded U.S. water and wastewater utility company providing water, wastewater, and other related services to an estimated 14 million people in more than 40 states and parts of Canada. A veteran utility executive with more than 30 years of experience, Ms. Story leads a team of 6,600 employees who deliver safe, clean, affordable, and reliable water services to its customers.

Before joining American Water, Story served as executive vice president of Southern Company, one of America's largest generators of electricity serving regulated and competitive markets across the Southeastern United States. In that role, she was also president and CEO of Southern Company Services. She began her career at Southern Company as a nuclear power plant engineer and had increasing leadership responsibilities in power plant and T&D operations, customer service, human resources, corporate real estate, and supply chain.

Story currently serves on the Bipartisan Policy Center Board of Directors and the Moffitt Cancer Center Board of Advisors. She was recently the national chairman for the Center for Energy Workforce Development and served on the boards of the National Renewable Energy Laboratory and the Alliance to Save Energy.

DAVID ST. PIERRE

Executive Director
Metropolitan Water Reclamation District of Greater Chicago
Chicago, Illinois

David St. Pierre is the executive director of the Metropolitan Water Reclamation District of Greater Chicago where he manages a staff of nearly 2,000. The District covers 883 square miles and provides wholesale wastewater treatment for over five million residents in Cook County, Illinois. The District operates seven wastewater treatment plants, which treat one billion gallons per day. The District also provides regional stormwater services.

The District has been a leader in the industry since its creation in 1889, and David is committed to ensuring this rich tradition of leadership continues under his tenure. Among other tasks, the District is leading efforts among utilities in adopting a resource recovery model.

David has been committed to excellent service and fiscal responsibility throughout his 30-year career in the water industry.

ERIC W. THORNBURG

Chairman, President, and Chief Executive Officer
Connecticut Water Service, Inc.
Clinton, Connecticut

Eric W. Thornburg is chairman, president and chief executive officer of Connecticut Water Service, Inc. (CTWS). His entire career of more than 30 years has been in the investor-owned public water utility industry. He started as a management trainee at one the nation's largest water utilities and achieved positions of increasing responsibility. In 2006, he was named president of Connecticut Water Service, Inc.

CTWS, through its regulated public water utility subsidiaries, serves 400,000 people in 77 towns across Connecticut and Maine. Under his leadership, CTWS has undergone significant growth and change:

- CTWS has grown its customer base by more than 33% through acquisitions completed since 2012
- CTWS is consistently ranked in the top tier among all publicly traded water utilities for its total return to shareholders
- Customer satisfaction surveys conducted by an independent research firm show that the company routinely provides world-class service to its customers
- Employee satisfaction and engagement is measured regularly and is a metric used to measure executive performance

Eric also serves on the board of directors for Middlesex Hospital and is chairman of the Madison, Connecticut Board of Police Commissioners. He is a past president of the National Association of Water Companies.

He has a bachelor of arts degree from Cornell University and a master of business administration degree from Indiana Wesleyan University. He resides with his wife in Madison, Connecticut, and has two adult children.

Notes

Visit www.valueofwaterbook.com to sign up for book updates or publication news about the forthcoming global and country editions.

Made in the USA
Lexington, KY
24 June 2015